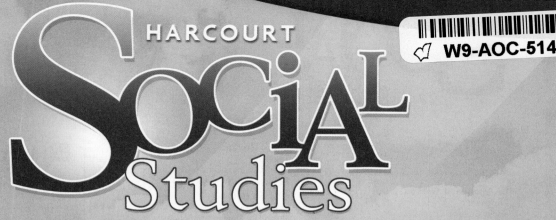

HARCOURT SOCIAL Studies

W9-AOC-514

The United States, Canada, Mexico, and Central America

Harcourt
SCHOOL PUBLISHERS

www.harcourtschool.com

HARCOURT SOCIAL Studies

The United States, Canada, Mexico, and Central America

Series Authors

Dr. Michael J. Berson
Professor
Social Science Education
University of South Florida
Tampa, Florida

Dr. Tyrone C. Howard
Associate Professor
UCLA Graduate School of Education &
    Information Studies
University of California Los Angeles
Los Angeles, California

Dr. Cinthia Salinas
Assistant Professor
Department of Curriculum and Instruction
College of Education
The University of Texas at Austin
Austin, Texas

North Carolina Consultants and Reviewers

Jenny Bajorek
Teacher
Northwoods Elementary School
Cary, North Carolina

Dan Barber
Teacher
Idlewild Elementary School
Charlotte, North Carolina

Brianne Beck
Teacher
Allen Jay Elementary School
High Point, North Carolina

Melissa Blush
Teacher
Allen Jay Elementary School
High Point, North Carolina

Ardelia Brown
Teacher
Pearsontown Elementary School
Durham, North Carolina

Alice M. Cook
Teacher
Paw Creek Elementary School
Charlotte, North Carolina

Lori D. Davis
Teacher
C. Wayne Collier Elementary School
Hope Mills, North Carolina

John D. Ellington
Former Director
Division of Social Studies
North Carolina Department of Public
    Instruction
Raleigh, North Carolina

Laura Griffin
Teacher
Sherwood Park Elementary School
Fayetteville, North Carolina

Sharon Hale
Teacher
Hillandale Elementary School
Durham, North Carolina

Dr. Ted Scott Henson
Educational Consultant
Burlington, North Carolina

Charlotte Heyliger
Teacher
C. Wayne Collier Elementary School
Hope Mills, North Carolina

Tony Iannone
Teacher
Nathaniel Alexander Elementary School
Charlotte, North Carolina

Judith McCray Jones
Educational Consultant
Former Elementary School Administrator
Greensboro, North Carolina

Gwendolyn C. Manning
Teacher
Gibsonville Elementary School
Gibsonville, North Carolina

Courtney McFaull
Teacher
Sherwood Park Elementary School
Fayetteville, North Carolina

Lydia Ogletree O'Rear
Teacher
Elmhurst Elementary School
Greenville, North Carolina

Marsha Rumley
Teacher
Brooks Global Studies
Greensboro, North Carolina

Dean P. Sauls
Teacher
Wayne County Public Schools
Goldsboro, North Carolina

Melissa Turnage
Teacher
Meadow Lane Elementary School
Goldsboro, North Carolina

Joseph E. Webb
Educational Consultant
Adjunct Professor
East Carolina University
Greenville, North Carolina

Harcourt
SCHOOL PUBLISHERS

Printed in the United States of America

ISBN-13: 978-0-15-356640-0
ISBN-10: 0-15-356640-X

3 4 5 6 7 8 9 10 11 030 17 16 15 14 13 12 11 10 09

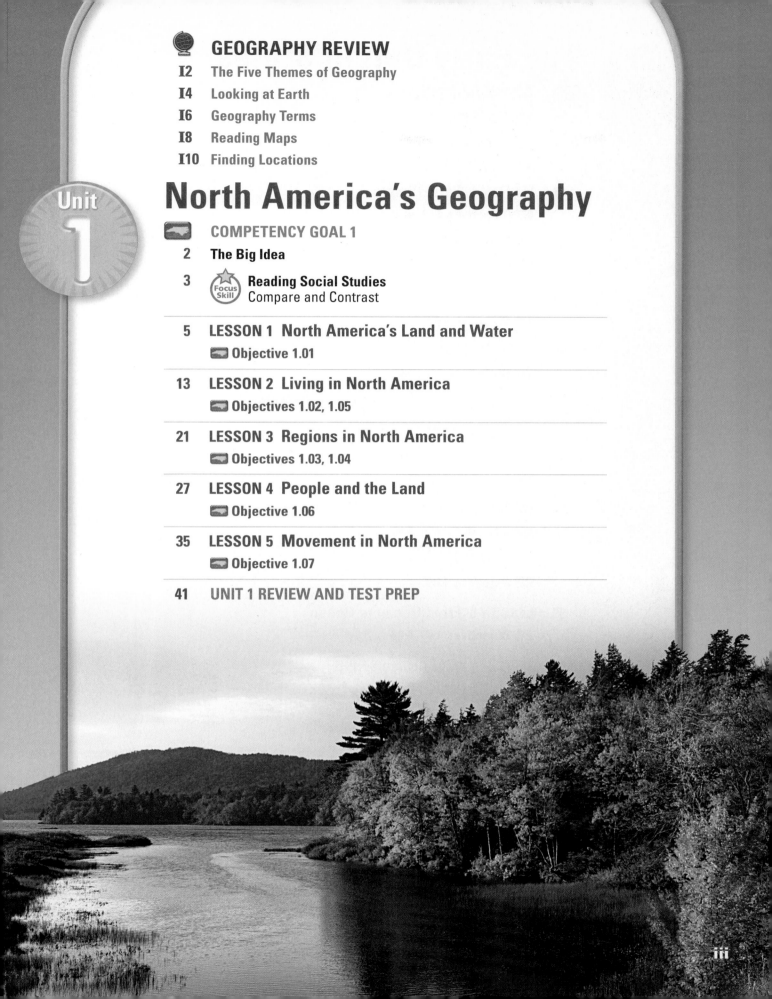

Unit 1

North America's Geography

Unit

2

The Early United States

COMPETENCY GOAL 4

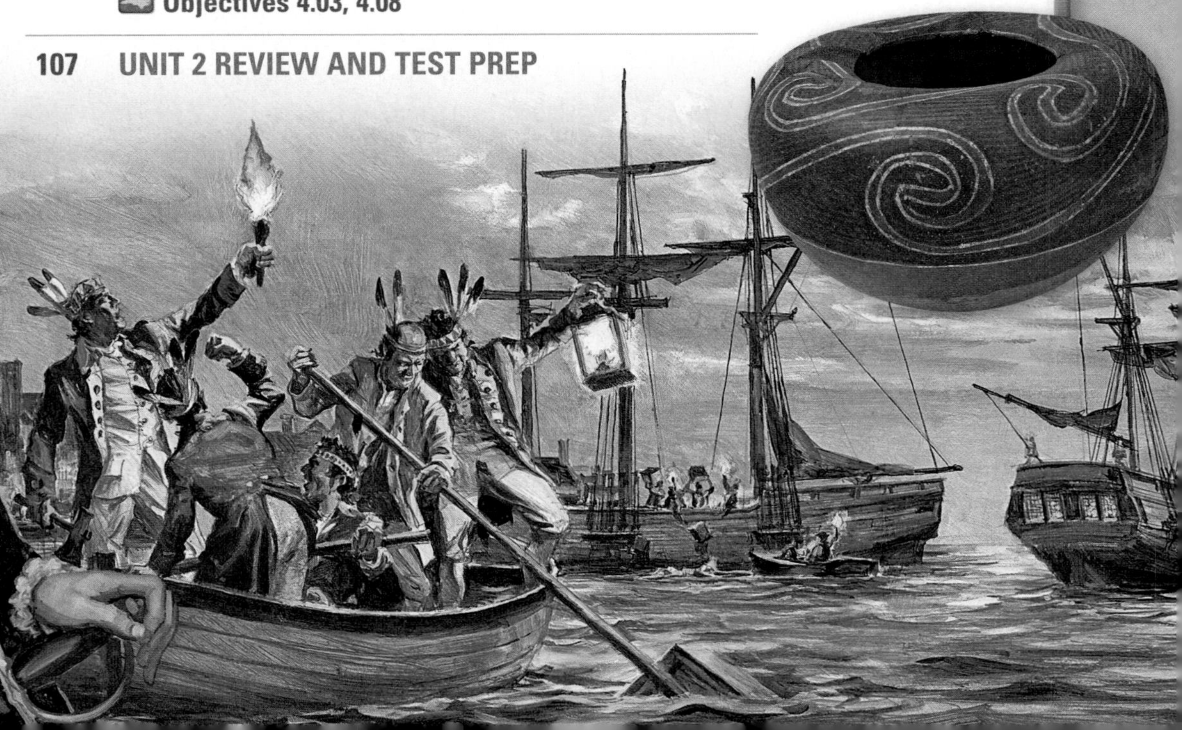

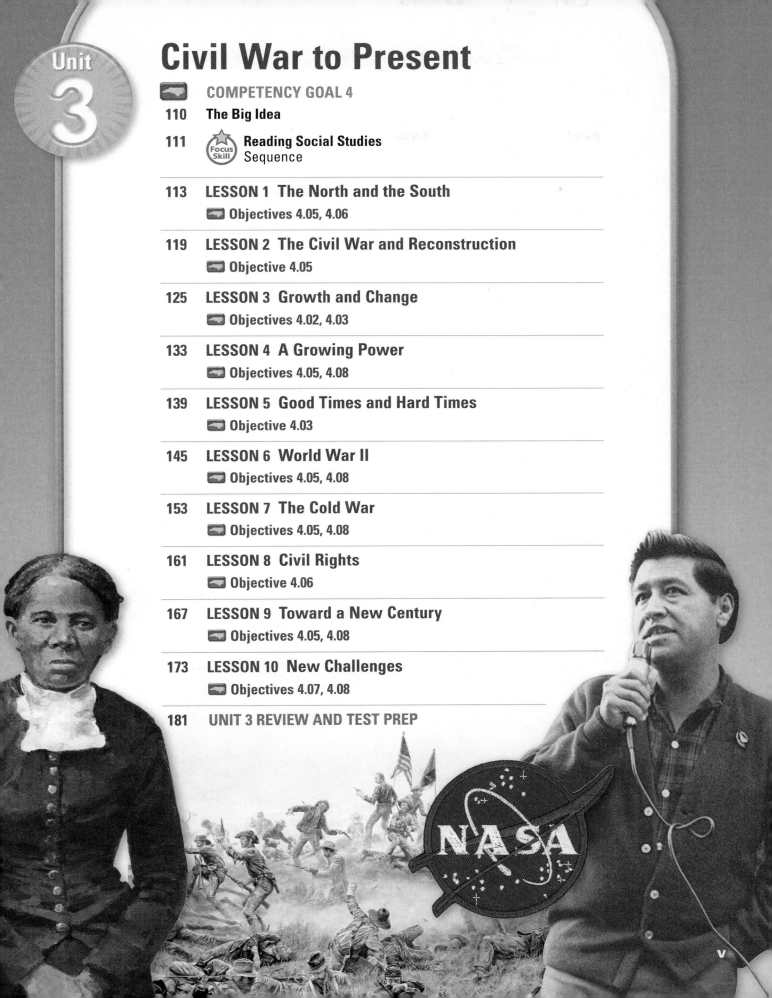

Unit 3

Civil War to Present

COMPETENCY GOAL 4

Unit 4

Government and Society

COMPETENCY GOAL 2

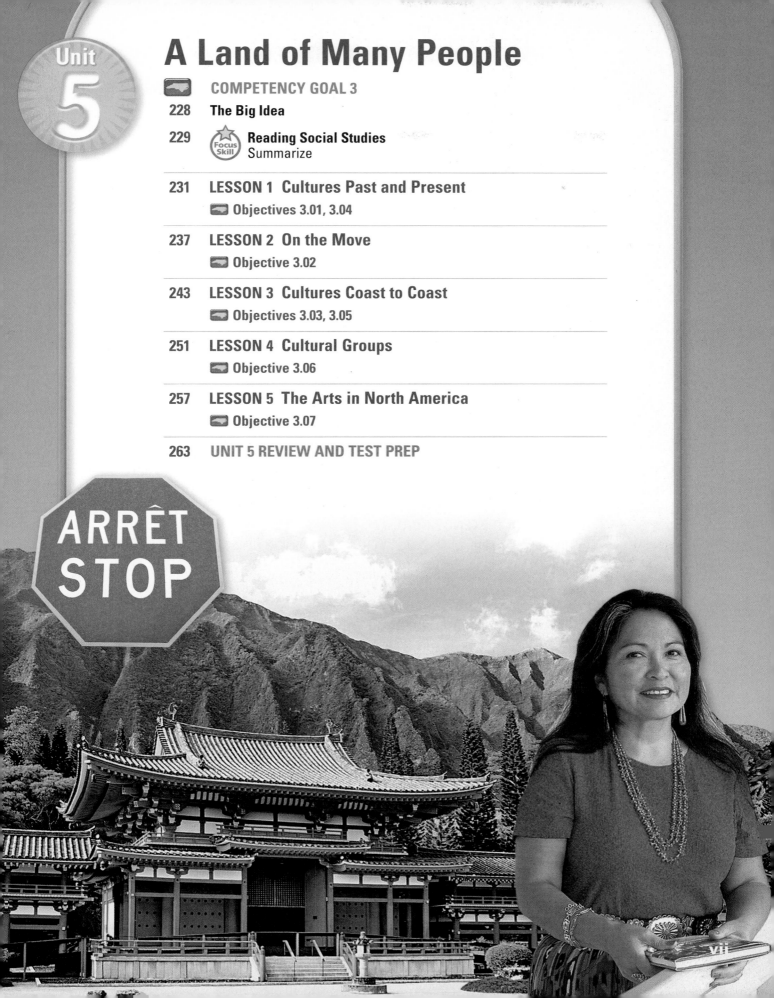

Unit 5

A Land of Many People

COMPETENCY GOAL 3

ARRÊT
STOP

vii

GEOGRAPHY REVIEW

The Five Themes of Geography

Learning about places is an important part of history and geography. Geography is the study of Earth's surface and the way people use it. When geographers study Earth and its geography, they often think about five main themes, or topics. Keeping these themes in mind as you read will help you think like a geographer.

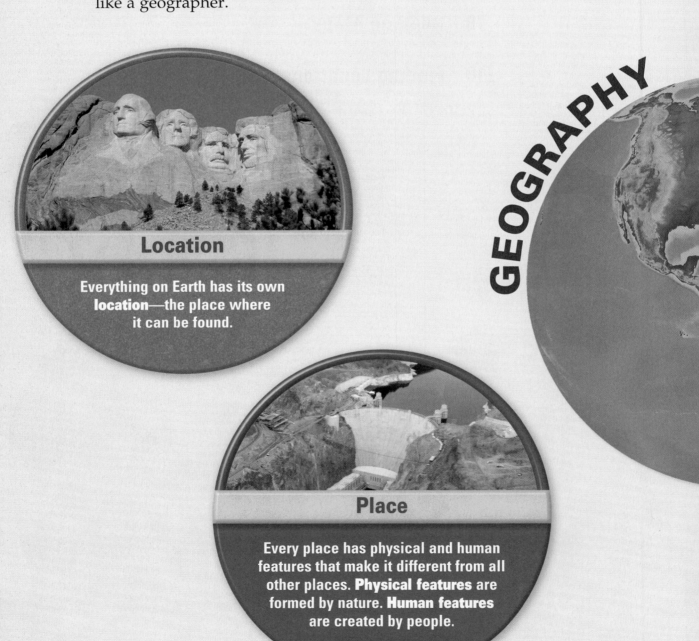

Location

Everything on Earth has its own **location**—the place where it can be found.

Place

Every place has physical and human features that make it different from all other places. **Physical features** are formed by nature. **Human features** are created by people.

GEOGRAPHY

Human-Environment Interactions

People and their surroundings interact, or affect each other. People's activities may **modify**, or change, the environment. The environment may affect people, requiring them to **adapt**, or adjust, to their surroundings.

THEMES

Movement

Every day, people in different states and countries exchange products and ideas.

Regions

Areas of Earth with main features that make them different from other areas are called regions. A **region** can be described by its physical features or its human features.

Looking at Earth

A distant view from space shows Earth's round shape. You probably have a globe in your classroom. Like Earth, a globe has the shape of a sphere, or ball. It is a model of Earth that shows Earth's major bodies of water and its seven **continents**, or largest land masses. Earth's continents, from largest to smallest, are Asia, Africa, North America, South America, Antarctica, Europe, and Australia.

Because of its shape, you can see only one-half of Earth at a time when you look at a globe. Halfway between the North Pole and the South Pole on a globe is a line called the **equator**.

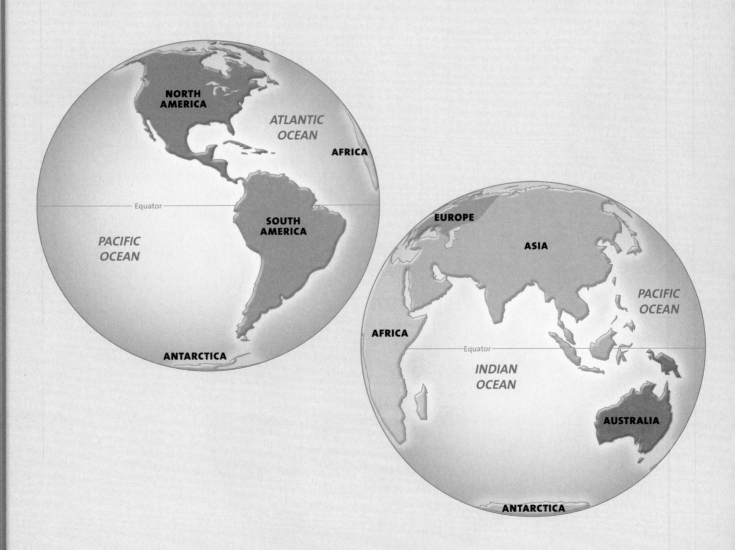

The equator divides Earth into two equal halves, or **hemispheres**. The Northern Hemisphere is north of the equator, and the Southern Hemisphere is south of it. Another line, the **prime meridian**, runs from the North Pole to the South Pole. It is often used to divide Earth into the Western Hemisphere and the Eastern Hemisphere.

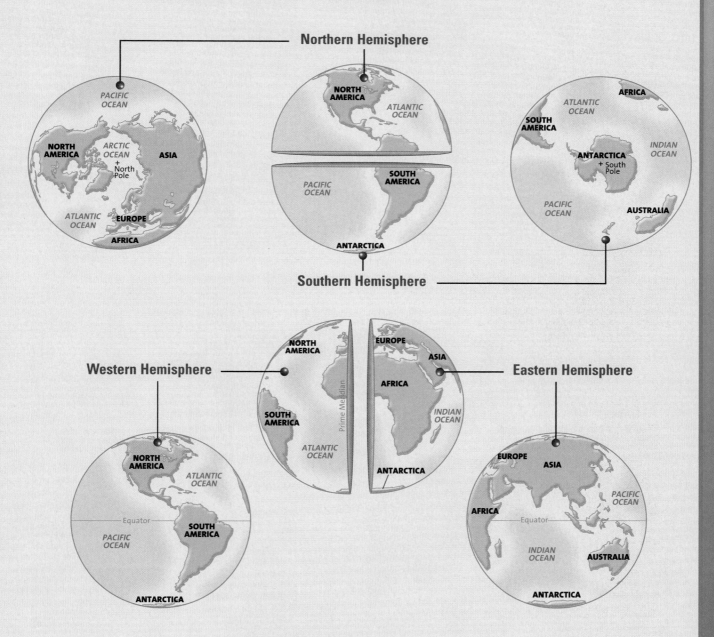

Geography Terms

1 **basin** bowl-shaped area of land surrounded by higher land
2 **bay** inlet of the sea or of some other body of water, usually smaller than a gulf
3 **canyon** deep, narrow valley with steep sides
4 **cape** point of land that extends into water
5 **channel** deepest part of a body of water
6 **coastal plain** area of flat land along a sea or ocean
7 **delta** triangle-shaped area of land at the mouth of a river

8 **fall line** area along which rivers form waterfalls or rapids as the rivers drop to lower land
9 **glacier** large ice mass that moves slowly down a mountain or across land
10 **gulf** part of a sea or ocean extending into the land, usually larger than a bay
11 **inlet** any area of water extending into the land from a larger body of water
12 **isthmus** narrow strip of land connecting two larger areas of land

13 marsh lowland with moist soil and tall grasses

14 mesa flat-topped mountain with steep sides

15 mountain pass gap between mountains

16 mountain range chain of mountains

17 mouth of river place where a river empties into another body of water

18 peninsula land that is almost completely surrounded by water

19 plain area of flat or gently rolling low land

20 plateau area of high, mostly flat land

21 savanna area of grassland and scattered trees

22 sea level level of the surface of an ocean or a sea

23 source of river place where a river begins

24 strait narrow channel of water connecting two larger bodies of water

25 swamp area of low, wet land with trees

26 tributary stream or river that flows into a larger stream or river

27 volcano opening in Earth, often raised, through which lava, rock, ashes, and gases are forced out

Reading Maps

Maps give important information about the world around you. A map is a drawing that shows all or part of Earth on a flat surface. To help you read maps, mapmakers add certain features to most of their maps. These features often include a title, a map key, a compass rose, a locator, and a map scale.

Sometimes mapmakers need to show certain places on a map in greater detail, or they must show places that are located beyond the area shown on the map. Find Alaska and Hawaii on

A **map title** tells the subject of the map. It may also identify the kind of map.
- A **political map** shows cities, states, and countries.
- A **physical map** shows kinds of land and bodies of water.
- A **historical map** shows parts of the world as they were in the past.

A **map key**, or legend, explains the symbols used on a map. Symbols may be colors, patterns, lines, or other special marks.

An **inset map** is a smaller map within a larger one.

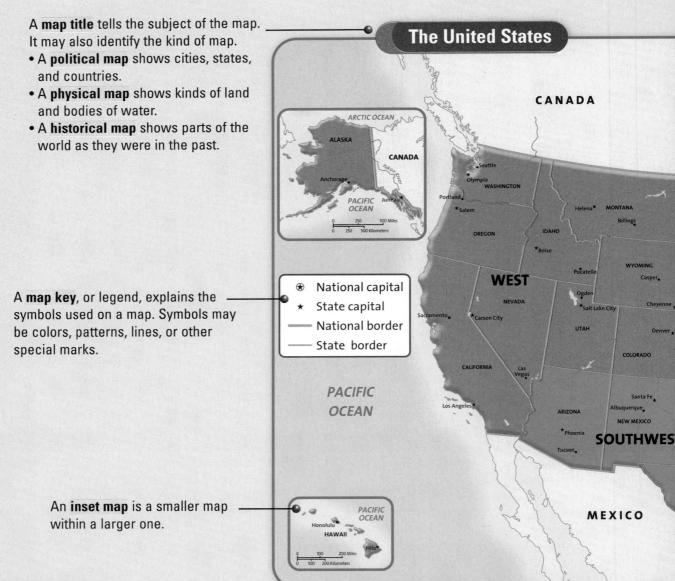

The United States

⊛ National capital
★ State capital
── National border
── State border

the map of the United States below. These two states are a long distance from the 48 contiguous (kuhn•TIH•gyuh•wuhs) states. The 48 contiguous states share at least one border with another state.

Because the United States covers such a large area, to show very much detail for Alaska and Hawaii and the rest of the country, the map would have to be much larger. Instead, here Alaska and Hawaii are each shown in a separate inset map, or a smaller map within a larger map.

A **locator** is a small map or globe that shows where the place on the main map is located within a larger area.

A **map scale**, or distance scale, compares a distance on the map to a distance on Earth. It helps you find the real distance between places on a map.

A **compass rose**, or direction marker, shows directions.
• The **cardinal directions** are north, south, east, and west.
• The **intermediate directions**, or directions between the cardinal directions, are northeast, northwest, southeast, and southwest.

Finding Locations

To help people find places on maps, mapmakers sometimes add lines that cross each other. These lines form a pattern of squares called a **grid system**.

Lines of latitude run east and west on a map. They are measured in degrees north or south from the equator.

Lines of longitude run north and south on the map. They are measured in degrees east or west from the prime meridian.

You can give the location of a place by first naming the line of latitude and then the line of longitude closest to it. For example, Washington, D.C., is near 40°N, 75°W.

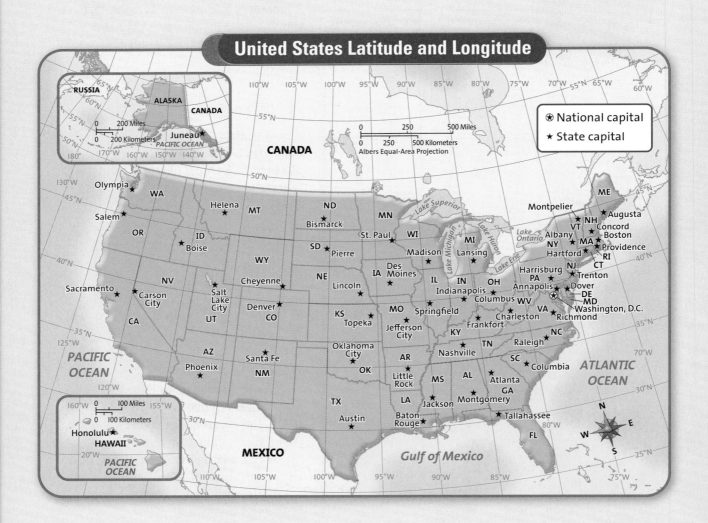

United States Latitude and Longitude

⊛ National capital
★ State capital

North America's Geography

THE RIO GRANDE
GORGE, IN TEXAS

Spotlight on Goals and Objectives

North Carolina Interactive Presentations

NORTH CAROLINA STANDARD COURSE OF STUDY

COMPETENCY GOAL 1 The learner will apply key geographic concepts to the United States and other countries of North America.

The Big Idea

How can geography help you understand the land and people of North America?

The study of Earth's surface and the way people use it is called **geography**. Geographers—scientists who study Earth and its geography—do much more than find places on maps. They apply key geographic concepts in order to learn all they can about a place and the people who live there. To do this, they often think about the five themes of geography.

THE FIVE THEMES OF GEOGRAPHY

Location Where is it?

Place What is it like there?

Regions How is this place like other places? How is it different?

Movement How and why do people, goods, and ideas move to and from this place?

Human-Environment Interactions How does this place affect people? How do people affect this place?

Draw a line to match each of the five themes of geography on the left with the correct description on the right.

Location	This place has mountains, as do the other places nearby. This place is part of an area that is different from other areas.
Place	It is often rainy and windy there.
Regions	People plow the rich soil there so that they can raise food crops.
Movement	This city is near the mountains, south of the border.
Human-Environment Interactions	People there use highways to travel. They use radios to communicate.

Reading Social Studies

⭐ (Focus Skill) Compare and Contrast

⟫ LEARN

When you **compare**, you tell how two or more things are alike, or similar. When you **contrast**, you tell how they are different. *Like, both, all, also, too, similar,* and *same* are words that are used to compare. *But, instead, unlike, however, different,* and *differ* are words that are used to contrast.

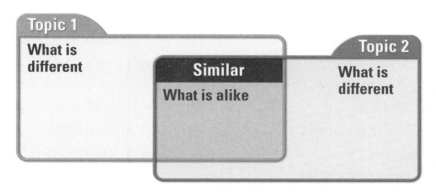

Topic 1
What is different

Similar
What is alike

Topic 2
What is different

⟫ PRACTICE

In each paragraph, circle the sentences that describe features that are similar. Underline those that describe features that are different. The first paragraph has been done for you.

North America has many types of landforms. Two tall mountain ranges are the Rocky Mountains and the Appalachian Mountains. Both of these ranges run north and south. The Rocky Mountains are much taller than the Appalachians. The tops of the Appalachian Mountains are more rounded than those of the Rockies.

Compare

Contrast

The Interior Plains region covers the central part of Canada and the United States. The land in this region is mostly flat. The southern part of the Interior Plains, in Canada, has rich soil. Wheat and other crops grow well there. However, the northern part has poor soil. There, it is too cold for farming.

Read the article. Then complete the activities below.

Climate Regions of North America

Because North America is so large, it has different climates. Two of North America's climate regions are desert and tundra.

North America has several deserts. A desert is an area that gets very little precipitation, or water that falls to Earth in the form of rain, sleet, or snow. All deserts are dry. Depending on their locations and the time of year, deserts can be hot or cold.

Death Valley is a desert located in southern California. It is the lowest point in North America. Death Valley also has some of the hottest temperatures in the United States. However, on winter nights, the temperatures can be very cold.

Even though it is a desert, many plants and animals can be found in Death Valley. Some animals that live there are rabbits, foxes, snakes, and lizards. Plants that need little water, such as the cactus, grow there.

In the far north of Canada is the Arctic Islands region. It is too cold there for trees to grow. The land is mostly tundra—a large, flat plain of frozen ground. During the winter, it is very cold and dark. In the summer, the top layer of soil melts, leaving the ground soggy. The tundra is windy, with very little precipitation.

Because the ground is frozen, only a few small plants grow on the tundra. Low-growing plants such as moss, lichen, and heath can be found there. Animals that live in this region include reindeer, foxes, polar bears, and seals.

1. **In the second paragraph, circle the sentence that describes how all deserts are alike. Then underline the sentence that describes how they can be different.**

2. **How do the temperatures differ in Death Valley?**

_____

_____

3. **Circle the sentences that tell how the Arctic Islands are similar to Death Valley. Underline the sentences that tell how they are different.**

North America's Land and Water

If someone asked you to describe the location of the United States, what would you say? You could give the country's **relative location**, or where it is compared to other places. You could say most of the United States lies south of Canada and north of Mexico.

Giving the relative location of a place is just one way to describe its location. You can also use the lines of latitude and the lines of longitude on a map or globe to give **absolute location**, or exact location. **What do you think you will learn about North America's land and water from reading this lesson?**

_____

_____

_____

NIAGARA FALLS

NORTH CAROLINA STANDARD COURSE OF STUDY

1.01 Describe the absolute and relative location of major landforms, bodies of water, and natural resources in the United States and other countries of North America.

❶ **LOCATION** Study the map on page 7. Describe the relative location of each landform.

Coast Mountains: _____

_____

_____

Central Valley: _____

_____

_____

❷ **LOCATION** Study the map on page 7. Give the absolute location of each landform. Write the closest line of latitude and line of longitude.

Mt. Logan: _____, _____

Yucatán Peninsula: _____, _____

▶ **THE COLORADO PLATEAU lies in Arizona, Colorado, Utah, and New Mexico.**

Landforms in North America

North America has many kinds of landforms. Mountains, hills, valleys, plains, and plateaus all make up parts of North America's land.

Mountains and Valleys

The United States and Canada share two large mountain ranges—the Appalachian (a•puh•LAH•chuhn) Mountains and the Rocky Mountains. The Appalachians run northeast from Alabama into eastern Canada. The Rockies run north from New Mexico across the United States, through Canada, and into Alaska.

Other mountains lie west of the Rockies. These are the Cascade Range and the Sierra Nevada. Along the Pacific Ocean are the Coast Ranges in the United States and the Coast Mountains in Canada.

Sandwiched between the Coast Ranges, the Sierra Nevada, and the Cascade Range are three large valleys. The largest is the more than 400-mile-long Central Valley in California.

Plains and Plateaus

The two largest landforms in area in the United States are plains. The Coastal Plain stretches inland from the Atlantic Ocean and the Gulf of Mexico. The Coastal Plain begins in Massachusetts and follows the coast into eastern Mexico.

The Interior Plains stretch across the middle of North America, from the Appalachian Mountains to the Rocky Mountains. The Interior Plains run north into southern Canada.

To the north of the Interior Plains is the Canadian Shield. This rocky, horseshoe-shaped area wraps around Hudson Bay.

The Mexican Plateau is Mexico's largest land-form. It is located in central Mexico. It is between two mountain ranges—the Sierra Madre Occidental and the Sierra Madre Oriental.

Landforms of North America

ARCTIC OCEAN

Brooks Range

Mt. McKinley
20,320 ft.

Alaska Range

Mt. Logan
19,550 ft.

Mackenzie Mts.

CANADIAN SHIELD

Coast Mountains

ROCKY MOUNTAINS

GREAT PLAINS

Puget Sound Lowland

Cascade Range

Willamette Valley

Coast Ranges

Sierra Nevada

Great Basin

Central Valley

Death Valley
-282 ft.

Mt. Elbert
14,433 ft.

INTERIOR PLAINS

Ozark Plateau

CENTRAL PLAINS

APPALACHIAN MOUNTAINS

COASTAL PLAIN

PACIFIC OCEAN

ATLANTIC OCEAN

Baja California

Sierra Madre Occidental

Mexican Plateau

Sierra Madre Oriental

COASTAL PLAIN

Gulf of Mexico

Tropic of Cancer

Pico de Orizaba
18,855 ft.

Yucatán Peninsula

Caribbean Sea

Sierra Madre del Sur

Isthmus of Panama

N
W   E
S

Legend

- △ Highest point
- ▽ Lowest point
- ▲ Other mountain peak
- —— National border

0   250   500 Miles
0   250   500 Kilometers
Lambert Azimuthal Equal-Area Projection

TextWork

3 Define the word *inlet* in your own words.

_____

_____

_____

4 The word *HOMES* can help you remember the names of the Great Lakes. Complete the list below by filling in the name of the lake that starts with the letter provided.

H _____

O _____

M _____

E _____

S _____

5 Scan the text. Circle the sentence that describes the relative location of Lake Nicaragua.

6 LOCATION Study the map on page 9. Circle the mouth of the Mississippi River. What is its absolute location?

_____

Which body of water is closest to 60°N, 110°W?

_____

Bodies of Water in North America

The Atlantic Ocean, Pacific Ocean, and Arctic Ocean surround North America. Many **inlets** give North America its shape. These smaller bodies of water cut into the land from a larger body of water. The largest inlets are called *gulfs*. The largest gulf is the Gulf of Mexico.

Lakes are inland bodies of water that are often made up of fresh water. The largest lakes in all of North America are together known as the Great Lakes. Four of these lakes—Superior, Huron, Erie, and Ontario—lie along the border between the United States and Canada. The fifth lake—Michigan—is entirely within the United States.

The largest lake south of the United States is Lake Nicaragua (ni•kuh•RAH•gwuh) in Nicaragua. It is a freshwater lake, but it has animals such as sharks and swordfish usually only found in oceans.

Rivers are bodies of moving water. Rivers flow from higher to lower ground. Every river flows into a larger body of water. The Mississippi River forms the largest *river system* in North America. Many smaller rivers flow into it. The Mississippi River system drains most of the Interior Plains.

The Continental Divide

An imaginary line called the Continental Divide divides the major river systems of North America. Most rivers east of the divide flow into the Atlantic Ocean. Most rivers west of the divide flow into the Pacific Ocean.

The Continental Divide runs along the Rocky Mountains, across the Mexican Plateau, and into Central America. Central America is made up of the seven countries of North America south of Mexico—Belize, Guatemala, Honduras, Nicaragua, El Salvador, Costa Rica, and Panama.

North America's Bodies of Water

ARCTIC OCEAN

Bering Sea

Beaufort Sea

Baffin Bay

PACIFIC OCEAN

Gulf of Alaska

Yukon River

Great Bear Lake

Great Slave Lake

Dubawnt Lake

Hudson Bay

Labrador Sea

Mackenzie River

Peace River

Lake Athabasca

Reindeer Lake

Saskatchewan River

Nelson River

Lake Winnipeg

Lake Nipigon

Gulf of St. Lawrence

Columbia River

Lake Superior

St. Lawrence R.

Snake R.

Missouri River

Mississippi River

Lake Huron

Lake Ontario

Hudson R.

Great Salt Lake

Lake Michigan

Lake Erie

Delaware River

Chesapeake Bay

Sacramento River

San Joaquin River

Colorado River

Ohio River

Roanoke River

ATLANTIC OCEAN

Arkansas River

Tennessee River

Savannah River

Red River

Mississippi River

Rio Grande

Gulf of California

Tropic of Cancer

Gulf of Mexico

Panuco R.

Lerma R.

Bay of Campeche

Gulf of Honduras

Caribbean Sea

Balsas R.

Lake Nicaragua

N
W E
S

0   250   500 Miles
0   250   500 Kilometers
Lambert Azimuthal Equal-Area Projection

—— Continental Divide
····· National border

Arctic Circle

70°N · 60°N · 50°N · 40°N · 30°N · 20°N · 10°N

170°W · 160°W · 150°W · 140°W · 130°W · 120°W · 110°W · 100°W · 90°W · 80°W · 70°W

10°W · 20°W · 30°W · 40°W · 50°W · 60°W

Natural Resources in North America

7 **REGION** Use the map on page 11 to compare and contrast natural resources. Identify two natural resources found in the United States but not in Mexico. Then find two found in both the United States and Mexico.

United States: _____

_____

United States and Mexico: _____

_____

8 **LOCATION** Give the relative location of most coal resources in Canada.

_____

_____

9 **LOCATION** Give the closest line of latitude and line of longitude to the gold deposit near Panama City, Panama.

_____

▶ **FISHERS bring in a lobster trap.**

North America has many important natural resources. A **natural resource** is something found in nature that people can use. There are two kinds of natural resources—renewable and nonrenewable. *Renewable resources* can be made again by people or nature. These include soil, water, and trees. *Nonrenewable resources* cannot be made again by people or would take thousands of years for nature to replace. Minerals, such as oil, coal, and metal ores, are nonrenewable resources.

Many Natural Resources

North America is rich in natural resources, but not every part of North America has every kind of resource. For example, along the rivers and lakes of North America, there is plenty of water. In the Sonoran Desert in northern Mexico, there is not much water. It is difficult for people, plants, and animals to live there.

The oceans are an important resource. Fish, crabs, lobsters, and other seafood provide food for people. Many people along the coasts work in the fishing industry. An **industry** is all the businesses that make or provide a product or service.

Soil is another important resource. The Interior Plains have very fertile soil. Farmers in the United States and Canada grow crops and raise animals on the Interior Plains. In Mexico, much of the farming takes place on the flat, fertile Mexican Plateau. In Central America, farmers take advantage of fertile soil in the valleys and on the sides of mountains. There they grow crops of coffee and bananas.

Minerals can be found in many parts of North America. In the Appalachian Mountains, coal is an important resource. It is used to make electricity. In Mexico, miners dig for silver and copper. Most of North America's silver comes from Mexico.

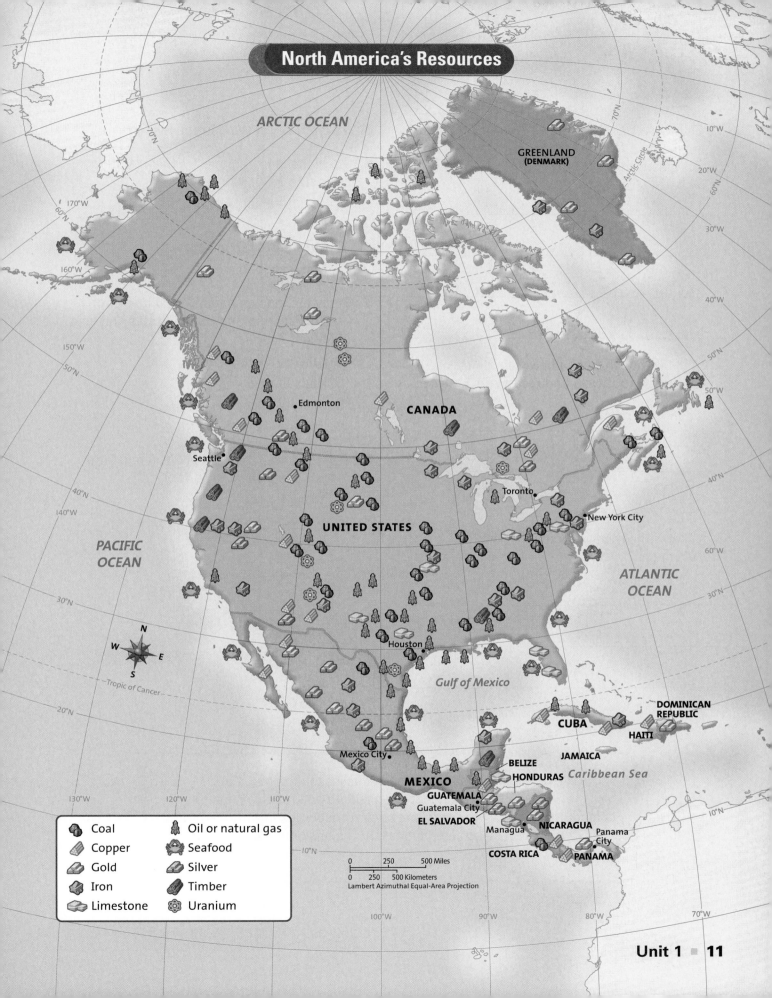

North America's Resources

ARCTIC OCEAN

GREENLAND (DENMARK)

CANADA

•Edmonton

•Seattle

UNITED STATES

Toronto•

•New York City

PACIFIC OCEAN

ATLANTIC OCEAN

Tropic of Cancer

Houston•

Gulf of Mexico

Mexico City•

MEXICO

CUBA

DOMINICAN REPUBLIC

HAITI

JAMAICA

BELIZE

HONDURAS

Caribbean Sea

GUATEMALA

Guatemala City

EL SALVADOR

Managua•

NICARAGUA

Panama City

COSTA RICA

PANAMA

Legend

Coal		Oil or natural gas	
Copper		Seafood	
Gold		Silver	
Iron		Timber	
Limestone		Uranium	

N W E S

0   250   500 Miles
0 250   500 Kilometers
Lambert Azimuthal Equal-Area Projection

1. **SUMMARIZE** What did you learn about finding locations in North America from reading this lesson?

_____

_____

_____

_____

2. What is the difference between the terms **absolute location** and **relative location**?

_____

_____

_____

3. What is the relative location of the Rocky Mountains?

_____

_____

_____

Circle the letter of the correct answer.

4. Study the map on page 7. Which landform is closest to 20°N, 90°W?

   A Yucatán Peninsula

   B Great Basin

   C Mackenzie Mountains

   D Mexican Plateau

5. Study the map on page 9. Which body of water is south of the United States and east of Mexico?

   A Lake Michigan

   B Hudson Bay

   C Gulf of Mexico

   D Rio Grande

6. Study the map on page 11. Which natural resource is closest to 40°N, 90°W?

   A gold

   B copper

   C timber

   D coal

writing

✎ **Write a Quiz** Use the maps in this lesson to write a quiz. Write five questions about the absolute and relative locations of landforms, bodies of water, and natural resources in North America. Then work with a classmate, and take turns answering each other's questions.

Living in North America

Some areas of North America have many people. Other areas have few people or none at all. Location influences, or affects, where people live. Because places have different climates, landforms, bodies of water, and natural resources, location also influences how people live. **Climate** is the kind of weather a place has over a long period of time. This means that people in North America, depending on where they live, have different ways of life. **What might you learn about where and how people live in North America by reading this lesson?**

_____

_____

_____

 OTTAWA, CANADA

**NORTH CAROLINA
STANDARD COURSE OF STUDY**

1.02 Analyze how absolute and relative location influence ways of living in the United States and other countries of North America.

1.05 Explain how and why population distribution differs within and between countries of North America.

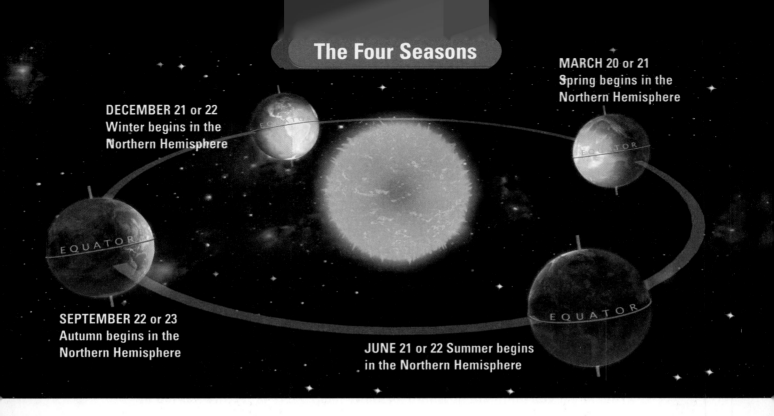

The Four Seasons

DECEMBER 21 or 22
Winter begins in the
Northern Hemisphere

MARCH 20 or 21
Spring begins in the
Northern Hemisphere

SEPTEMBER 22 or 23
Autumn begins in the
Northern Hemisphere

JUNE 21 or 22 Summer begins
in the Northern Hemisphere

EQUATOR

Climate Affects Ways of Life

Climate is different depending on location. In general, places near the equator, such as the countries of Central America, are warmer. Places farther from the equator, such as Canada and the northern parts of the United States, are cooler.

Climate can affect where people live. Much of northern Canada is very cold. Most people in Canada live within 100 miles of the United States border, where temperatures are warmer.

The climate of a place can also affect what people wear and what kinds of houses they build. People living far to the north wear warm clothes, such as parkas, thick gloves, and boots, in winter. In the southern parts of North America, it is warm all year. People there wear shorts to stay cool. Many homes have air-conditioning. Some have large windows to let in cool breezes.

The ways people earn a living may also depend on the climate. Farmers in Central America can grow bananas and other fruits that need a warm climate to grow.

TextWork

1 Study the illustration above. Seasons change as Earth orbits, or moves around, the sun. When does winter begin in North Carolina and the rest of the Northern Hemisphere?

_____

_____

2 Scan the text on this page. Circle the sentence that describes where most Canadians live.

Landforms Affect Ways of Life

Landforms can affect where people settle. Throughout history, people have settled on plains or other areas of flat land. It is easier to build roads, houses, and other buildings on flat land.

Today, most people still live in areas where the land is flat or mostly flat. Many of the largest cities in the United States are on the Coastal Plain or on the Interior Plains. Mexico's largest city and its capital—Mexico City—is on the Mexican Plateau. In fact, more than half of Mexico's people live on the Mexican Plateau.

Other landforms have discouraged people from settling in certain areas. In the past, people avoided settling in mountainous areas or wet marshlands. In such areas, it was more difficult to build houses and meet other needs. Even today, those areas have fewer people than other places.

Landforms can also affect what people do for fun. In the mountains, many people enjoy mountain climbing in summer and skiing in winter. Along the coasts, people enjoy collecting shells on beaches and swimming and surfing in the ocean.

TextWork

❸ Complete the sentences below to compare and contrast how landforms affect the ways people have fun in the mountains and along the coasts.

People in the mountains enjoy

_____

_____

_____

_____.

People along the coast enjoy

_____

_____

_____

_____.

❱ **MEXICO CITY** is located on the **Mexican Plateau.**

TextWork

4 Scan the text on this page. Underline the sentence that gives the relative location of Toronto, Canada.

5 Why do you think Toronto, Canada, was built at its present location?

_____

_____

_____

_____

_____

▶ **TORONTO, CANADA, is Canada's largest city.**

Living Near Bodies of Water

Having fresh water and transportation routes nearby helps people meet their needs. For this reason, many of North America's largest cities are located near bodies of water. In fact, the four largest cities in the United States are on or near a body of water.

Many cities were first built along the coasts because oceans served as transportation routes. Vancouver in Canada, Seattle in the United States, and Panama City in Panama are all on the Pacific Ocean. Oceans are important because they help connect the countries of North America to other parts of the world.

Other major cities have been built along large rivers and the Great Lakes. In Canada, the major cities of Quebec and Montreal lie along the St. Lawrence River. Canada's largest city, Toronto, is on Lake Ontario. The United States' largest city, New York City, is located where the Hudson River flows into the Atlantic Ocean. Today, as in the past, rivers and lakes make it easier for businesses to ship their goods.

❯ COFFEE grows well in the soil in Costa Rica.

Resources Affect Ways of Life

Natural resources also affect where people settle. Early people settled where they could gather fruits and nuts and hunt animals. Later, people settled where the soil was good for farming.

Natural resources still have an effect on people's ways of life. Natural resources can affect the kinds of jobs people have in certain areas. Many people along the coasts of North America earn a living by fishing. They sell fish and other seafood at markets.

Some natural resources lie under the seafloor. Off the coast of eastern Mexico and the southern United States, workers drill for oil beneath the Gulf of Mexico. The oil industry provides jobs for many people in Mexico, Texas, and Louisiana.

Soil is another important resource in North America. Many people in the Interior Plains work on farms. They grow crops and raise animals. In Honduras, the warm climate and fertile soil make farming an important industry. Many people there work on farms, growing bananas, coffee, and sugarcane.

TextWork

6 Circle the main idea sentence in the second paragraph. Underline the sentences that provide supporting details.

7 How does living along the coast affect how some people earn a living?

_____

_____

_____

_____

_____

8 The word *dense* means "crowded." Use this information to write a definition of *population density*.

_____

_____

_____

9 **HUMAN-ENVIRONMENT INTERACTIONS** Circle Mexico City on the map on page 19. What is the population density of Mexico City?

_____

_____

▶ **SYLVA, NORTH CAROLINA, has a low population density.**

Population in North America

As with the continent's natural resources, people are distributed, or spread out, unevenly over North America. Climate, bodies of water, natural resources, and landforms are some of the things that affect population distribution.

Different places in North America have different population densities. **Population density** is the average number of people living in an area of a certain size, usually 1 square mile. You can find population density by dividing the number of people living on a given amount of land by the area of that land. For example, if 2,000 people live on 10 square miles of land, the population density is 200 people per square mile.

Urban and Rural Areas

People may live in a large city, in a small town, or on a farm. **Rural**, or country, areas often have low population densities. **Urban**, or city, areas often have high population densities.

In general, most large urban areas are located along the coasts of North America or along some other large body of water. Chicago is one of the largest cities in the United States. It is located on Lake Michigan, one of the Great Lakes. Lake Michigan is an important source of fresh water for Chicago. It also serves as a shipping route.

People in North America live in inland areas, as well. Many of these areas are rural areas, with few large cities or towns. However, there are some exceptions.

Mexico City, North America's largest city, is located inland on the Mexican Plateau. San Salvador in El Salvador is one of the largest cities in Central America. It is located in a valley inland from the Pacific coast. The land there is mostly flat and very fertile. The Acelhuate River (ah•KEL•hway•teh) provides San Salvador with fresh water for drinking and growing crops.

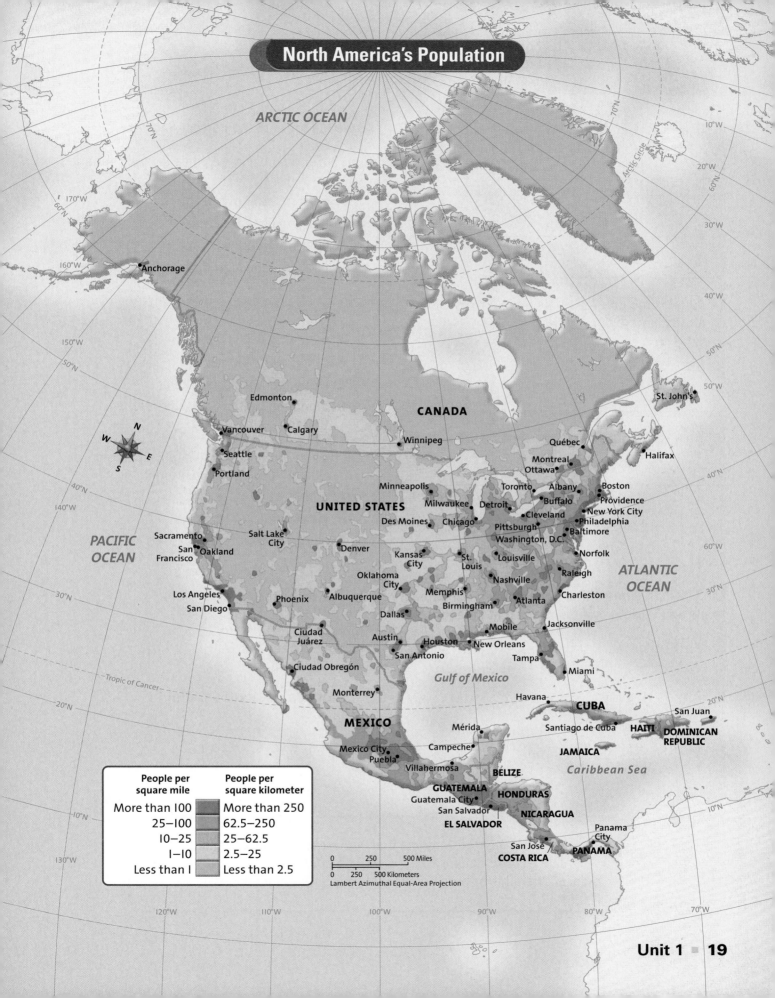

North America's Population

ARCTIC OCEAN

CANADA

UNITED STATES

PACIFIC OCEAN

ATLANTIC OCEAN

Anchorage

Edmonton
Vancouver Calgary
Seattle
Portland

Winnipeg

Sacramento
San Francisco Oakland
Salt Lake City
Denver

Los Angeles
San Diego
Phoenix Albuquerque

Ciudad Juárez

Ciudad Obregón

Monterrey

Minneapolis
Milwaukee Detroit
Des Moines Chicago

Kansas City
Oklahoma City
Dallas
Austin
San Antonio

St. Louis
Memphis
Birmingham

Louisville Nashville

Houston New Orleans
Mobile

Québec
Montreal
Ottawa
Toronto Albany Boston
Buffalo Providence
Cleveland New York City
Pittsburgh Philadelphia
Baltimore
Washington, D.C.
Norfolk
Raleigh
Charleston

Atlanta
Jacksonville

Tampa
Miami

Halifax
St. John's

MEXICO

Mérida
Campeche

Mexico City
Puebla
Villahermosa

Gulf of Mexico

Havana
CUBA
Santiago de Cuba

San Juan
HAITI **DOMINICAN REPUBLIC**
JAMAICA

Caribbean Sea

BELIZE
GUATEMALA
Guatemala City
San Salvador
EL SALVADOR

HONDURAS
NICARAGUA

Panama City
San José
COSTA RICA **PANAMA**

Tropic of Cancer

People per square mile	People per square kilometer
More than 100	More than 250
25–100	62.5–250
10–25	25–62.5
1–10	2.5–25
Less than 1	Less than 2.5

0 250 500 Miles
0 250 500 Kilometers
Lambert Azimuthal Equal-Area Projection

1. **SUMMARIZE** How does location affect the ways of life of people in North America?

_____

_____

_____

2. What is the difference between a **rural** and an **urban** area?

_____

_____

3. How is climate affected by a place's location?

_____

_____

Circle the letter of the correct answer.

4. Where are most large cities in North America located?

   A near the Gulf of Mexico

   B near bodies of water

   C near the Interior Plains

   D near the Mexican Plateau

5. In which area does the oil industry provide jobs for many people?

   A along the Gulf of Mexico

   B along the Great Lakes

   C along the Mississippi River

   D along the United States border with Canada

6. Which of the following is a physical feature that affects population distribution?

   A jobs

   B clothing

   C natural resources

   D cities

MATCHING Draw a line connecting each category on the left with the terms on the right that belong in that category.

7. landforms   soil, trees, oil, fish

8. bodies of water   mountains, valleys, plains

9. natural resources   lakes, rivers, oceans

writing

✏️ **Write a Letter** Imagine that you are writing to a friend who lives on the Pacific coast. Describe how your way of life may be different from his or hers because of your different locations.

North America is a large area with many differences. It has many kinds of regions. A **region** is an area with many things that are similar. A region can be a state, such as North Carolina, a country, such as Canada, or a group of countries, such as Central America.

Regions can also be based on physical characteristics, such as landforms, climate, or plant life. Cultural characteristics, such as language and history, can define a region as well. In a region, a group's ways of acting, speaking, and believing make up its **culture**, or way of life. **What will you learn about regions as you read this lesson?**

_____

_____

_____

ALBANY COUNTY, WYOMING

**NORTH CAROLINA
STANDARD COURSE OF STUDY**

1.03 Compare and contrast the physical and cultural characteristics of regions within the United States, and other countries of North America.

1.04 Describe the economic and social differences between developed and developing regions in North America.

❶ Circle the main idea in the third paragraph. Underline the details that support this main idea.

❷ **REGION** The map below shows the five regions of the United States. Circle the Northeast on the map. Then describe its relative location on the lines below.

_____

_____

_____

_____

_____

Regions of the United States

The United States is a large country with many different kinds of landforms. These landforms can be used to define regions. The Coastal Plain, the Appalachian Mountains, and the Central Valley are all examples of regions based on physical characteristics. The Mexican Plateau and the Canadian Shield are other examples in North America.

Because the United States is such a large country, geographers sometimes divide it into five other regions—the Northeast, the Southeast, the Midwest, the Southwest, and the West. These regions are named for their relative location within the United States.

The states in each region share many things. They share physical features, such as landforms and climate. Often the states share the same histories and cultures as well. Also, many people in a region work in the same kinds of industries. In North Carolina's Research Triangle Park, many people work in the computer industry.

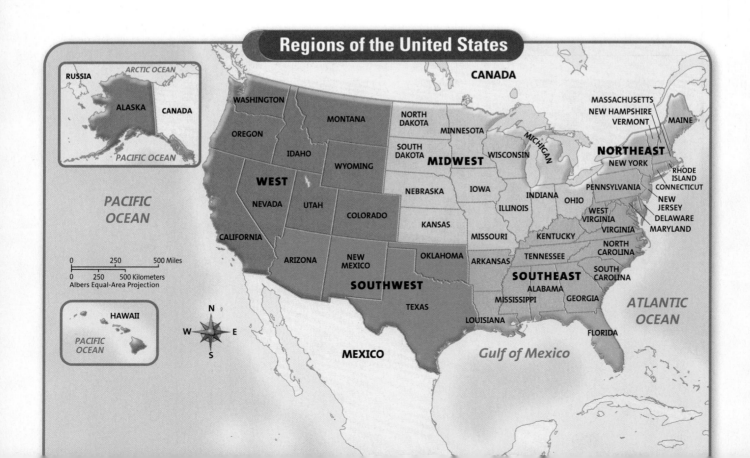

Regions of the United States

> AMERICAN INDIANS perform a corn dance at San Ildefonso Pueblo in New Mexico.

Cultures in the United States

During the late 1800s and early 1900s, millions of people came to the United States. Most came from Europe. They entered the United States through cities in the Northeast. Many settled in those cities. Others moved to cities in other regions.

Over time, more people arrived. Because of this, the United States is very diverse. Today, for example, Dearborn, Michigan, has one of the largest Arab American communities in the country. Festivals such as the Polish Fest in Wisconsin celebrate the diverse culture of the Midwest.

Music is important to the culture and history of the Southeast. African Americans there created jazz music. Country music grew out of music played by early European settlers.

American Indians and Hispanics have also shaped the culture in the United States, especially in the Southwest. Many cities there hold festivals to honor American Indian and Hispanic cultures.

In the West, Asian American culture can be seen in San Francisco's Chinatown and Japantown neighborhoods. Hawaii has two official languages—English and Hawaiian.

 TextWork

❸ Circle the word *diverse* each time it appears in this section. What does this word mean? Study the context clues below, and then write a definition.

• **People came to the United States from around the world.**

• **Festivals such as the Polish Fest in Wisconsin celebrate culture.**

• **The state of Hawaii has two official languages.**

Diverse: _____

_____

_____

_____

_____

▶ POPOCATÉPETL in Mexico is part of a region of volcanoes called the Ring of Fire.

❹ **REGION** On the map above, circle the names of the major volcanoes in North America that are part of the Ring of Fire.

❺ How is the land in Canada similar to the land in the United States?

_____

_____

_____

_____

_____

Other Regions

North America's other countries can be divided into regions. The people in each country often share a language, history, and traditions. **Traditions** are ways of life handed down from the past.

As in the United States, Canada's land is made up of mountains in the east and west and of plains in the middle. Both England and France explored and settled Canada. Today, Canada has two official languages—English and French.

In Mexico, much of the land is mountainous. In the north, the climate is dry and there are many deserts. In the south, there is much rainfall. The land there is covered by thick rain forests.

Like Canada's, Mexico's culture has been shaped by its history. Many people in Mexico trace their culture to the Maya and the Spanish. The Maya were an early American Indian group.

Central America, too, is mountainous. The cultures of Central America are similar to those in Mexico. As in Mexico, Spanish is the official language of most countries in Central America.

Economic Regions

Each country in North America has its own economy. An **economy** is the way the people of a region use their resources to meet their needs.

One way to study a country's economy is to look at its per capita income. This number tells how much money an average worker earns in a year.

Countries with a per capita income of $9,200 or more are called **developed countries**. Canada's per capita income is about $33,000 a year. The per capita income of the United States is $41,000.

In developed countries, most people work in jobs that pay well. They have money to buy goods such as televisions and cars. They also have access to schools and health care.

The economies of some North American countries are still being built up. These countries are called **developing countries**. Developing countries often have fewer resources than developed countries. Developing countries do not make many goods. Cuba, Guatemala, Haiti, and Jamaica all have per capita incomes under $5,000.

TextWork

6 Study the table below. Then use the information in the table to fill in the bar graph.

Economies of North America	
COUNTRY	PER CAPITA INCOME
Canada	$33,000
Guatemala	$4,700
Mexico	$10,000
Panama	$7,400
United States	$41,000

7 Which countries from the graph are developing countries?

_____

_____

Which are developed countries?

_____

_____

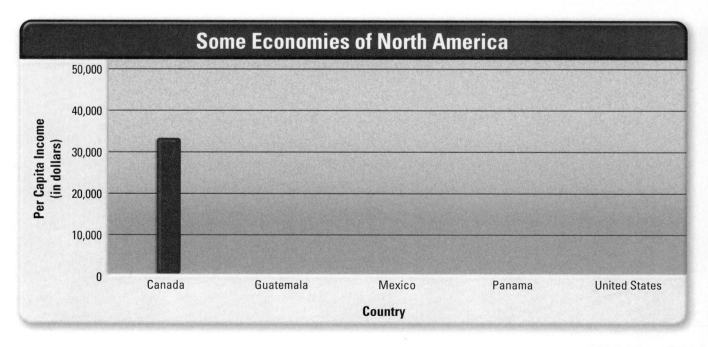

Some Economies of North America

Per Capita Income (in dollars)

50,000 — 40,000 — 30,000 — 20,000 — 10,000 — 0

Canada · Guatemala · Mexico · Panama · United States

Country

1. **SUMMARIZE** What features define regions in North America?

_____

_____

_____

2. Use the term **culture** in a sentence about **regions** in North America.

_____

_____

_____

3. Why are cities in the United States very diverse?

_____

_____

_____

Circle the letter of the correct answer.

4. Music is an important part of which region's cultural history?

   A the Southeast

   B the Midwest

   C the West

   D the Southwest

Draw a line connecting each country on the left with the region in that country on the right.

5. Canada   Central Valley

6. United States   Canadian Shield

7. Mexico   Mexican Plateau

activity

Make Flash Cards On one side of an index card, write the name of a country in North America. On the other side write a description of a physical, cultural, or economic characteristic of that country.

People and the Land

Different physical environments and the natural resources found in them affect the way people live in different regions of North America. A **physical environment** is the surroundings in which people, plants, and animals live. In turn, people and their activities affect the physical environment. Humans often change their ways of living and the physical environment around them in order to meet their needs. **What will you read in this lesson about how people are affected by their surroundings?**

_____

_____

BIKING NEAR THE ROCKY MOUNTAINS IN CANADA

 NORTH CAROLINA STANDARD COURSE OF STUDY

1.06 Explain how people of the United States and other countries of North America adapt to, modify, and use their physical environment.

People Adapt

People **adapt** by fitting their ways of life to the physical environment. There are many different kinds of physical environments in North America. People adapt to them in many different ways.

Adapting to Climate and Weather

Clothing is one way people often adapt. People who live in northern parts of North America often wear heavy clothing in winter to keep warm. People who live in warmer climates farther south wear lightweight clothing to help keep them cool.

Adapting to Landforms

People also adapt their houses. Houses in low-lying areas are often built high off the ground. In the low-lying areas of Belize, many houses are built on top of stilts. Stilts help keep houses there from being flooded in times of heavy rainfall.

In mountainous regions, such as the Rocky Mountains, houses may also be built on stilts. In these areas, stilts are used to keep the houses level against the steep sides of mountains.

❶ Locate the highlighted vocabulary word in the first paragraph. Circle it. Then underline the words in that sentence that help define the vocabulary word.

❷ Place an *X* on the photograph below that best shows people adapting to wet weather. Describe what you see in that photograph.

_____

_____

_____

_____

▶ **CLOTHING** is one way people adapt to weather.

Snow

Rain

Sun

Mark Twain

When Samuel Langhorne Clemens, better known as Mark Twain, was four years old, his family moved to Hannibal, Missouri. Hannibal is on the banks of the Mississippi River. As a boy, Twain watched steamboats on the river and dreamed of becoming a steamboat pilot.

After Twain grew up, he earned his pilot's license. When the Civil War shut down steamboat traffic on the Mississippi River, Twain traveled the country. He began writing the stories that made him a famous author.

Make It Relevant **How can where people live affect the kinds of work they do?**

People and Natural Resources

The kind of work people do often depends on the natural resources around them. Western Canada, for example, has thick forests. Some people there work in the timber industry. In the United States, the climate and soil in the eastern part of the Interior Plains are good for growing corn and soybeans. On the Great Plains, in the western part of the Interior Plains, the climate is drier. Farmers there grow wheat. Where the climate is too dry to grow crops, farmers raise cattle and sheep.

In the past, people could rely only on the natural resources in their region. For example, people who lived near forests made houses from wood. Where stone was available, people made stone houses. Early settlers on the Interior Plains had neither wood nor stone. They made houses from sod.

Today, natural resources do not have as large an impact on people's ways of life. Building materials, food, and other resources can be shipped almost anywhere on airplanes, trains, ships, or trucks.

TextWork

❸ Circle the sentences that compare and contrast what farmers grow in the eastern and western parts of the Interior Plains.

❹ How did early settlers on the Interior Plains adapt to their environment?

_____

_____

_____

_____

_____

The Panama Canal

NORTH
AMERICA
San Francisco • • New York

ATLANTIC
OCEAN

5,200 miles (8,368 km)

13,000 miles (20,921 km)

Caribbean
Sea

Panama
Canal

SOUTH
AMERICA

PACIFIC
OCEAN

N
W   E
S

0   750   1,500 Miles
0   750   1,500 Kilometers
Azimuthal Equal-Area
Projection

▶ THE PANAMA CANAL makes it easier for ships to
travel between the Atlantic Ocean and Pacific Ocean.

TextWork

5 MOVEMENT With your finger,
trace the route around the tip
of South America on the map.
Then trace the route through
the Panama Canal. How much
shorter in miles is the route
through the Panama Canal?

_____

6 After reading about the
Panama Canal, what do you
think about the importance of
travel and trade between the
Atlantic and Pacific coasts of the
United States?

_____

_____

_____

People Modify

In order to meet their needs or do their jobs,
people must often **modify**, or change, the physical
environment. They clear forests and drain swamps
to build houses, factories, and other businesses.
They clear and plow the land to plant crops. They
dig wells to find fresh water. Sometimes, people
blast tunnels through mountains and build bridges
so that roads and railroads can be built.

Modifying the Land

Before 1914, ships had to sail around South
America to get from the Atlantic Ocean to the
Pacific Ocean. A waterway dug across Panama in
Central America made this trip much shorter.

In 1904, workers began digging the Panama
Canal. They used heavy machines to clear the land.
So that ships could cross the land, workers built
locks. In a lock, a section of water is held by two
gates. When one gate is opened, the water raises or
lowers a boat to the level of the next lock. As the
land rises, locks help ships make the 8- to 10-hour
trip through the Panama Canal.

Modifying Waterways

People also modify waterways. They dig out the bottoms of rivers and harbors to make deep channels. These channels allow large ships to travel.

In 1959, Canada and the United States built channels and locks on the St. Lawrence River to make the St. Lawrence Seaway. Today, ships can use the St. Lawrence Seaway to carry goods between the Atlantic Ocean and the Great Lakes.

Another way people modify rivers is by building dams. Dams form *reservoirs* (REH•zuh•vwarz). These lakes, held back by a dam, provide water for cities, towns, and farms. In addition, water flowing through the dam can be used to turn large machines called generators that make electricity.

The Rio Grande, or Rio Bravo as it is called in Mexico, forms part of the border between the United States and Mexico. Cities, towns, and farms on both sides of the border depend on the river's waters. To make sure that there is enough water to meet everyone's needs, the United States built dams on the river. The United States and Mexico also signed an agreement to share the river's water.

TextWork

7 Underline the two sentences that describe things that dams provide for people.

8 Hoover Dam on the Colorado River supplies power to three states—Nevada, Arizona, and California. Circle the power plant on the diagram of the dam below. How do dams create electricity?

_____

_____

_____

_____

_____

_____

_____

The Hoover Dam

Reservoir

Power lines

Power plant

The force of the water turns the machines that make electricity.

Using the Land

Depending on where they live, people use Earth's surface in different ways. In the United States, about half of the land is used for farming. Most farming takes place on the plains and in the large valleys in the western part of the country.

9 What is much of the land in cities used for?

_____

_____

10 HUMAN-ENVIRONMENT INTERACTIONS Study the map on page 33. Circle Kansas City. What is the land around Kansas City mainly used for?

_____

11 HUMAN-ENVIRONMENT INTERACTIONS Study the map on page 33. How is the land in far northern Canada used? Why do you think this is so?

_____

_____

_____

Central American countries are mountainous and have many active volcanoes. Volcanic eruptions can destroy crops and buildings. However, the ash from the eruptions helps keep the soil fertile. Many people in Central America earn a living by farming. Farms there grow much of the world's coffee crop.

Over half of the land in Canada is covered by forests. The largest forest in Canada is the Boreal Forest. It covers 35 percent of Canada's land area. People in Canada use the forests for the country's timber industry.

Cities also take up large areas of North America. In cities, much of the land is used for businesses or housing. Businesses that need large numbers of workers are often located in or near cities. In cities, people often work in manufacturing or service industries, such as banking, education, or health care. Some of the land is also set aside for recreation. Many cities have large parks.

Public and Private Land

Much of the land in North America is private land. This land is owned by individual people or groups. Some land is public land. It is owned by all people in a nation. National governments control and take care of most public land.

Some of this public land is set aside for national parks and monuments. These places preserve, or protect, a country's historic sites and physical environment. In order to protect Mexico's history, many of the Mayan ruins there are protected by the government. Visitors come from around the world to see these ancient sites.

▶ LUMBERJACKS work in Canada's timber industry.

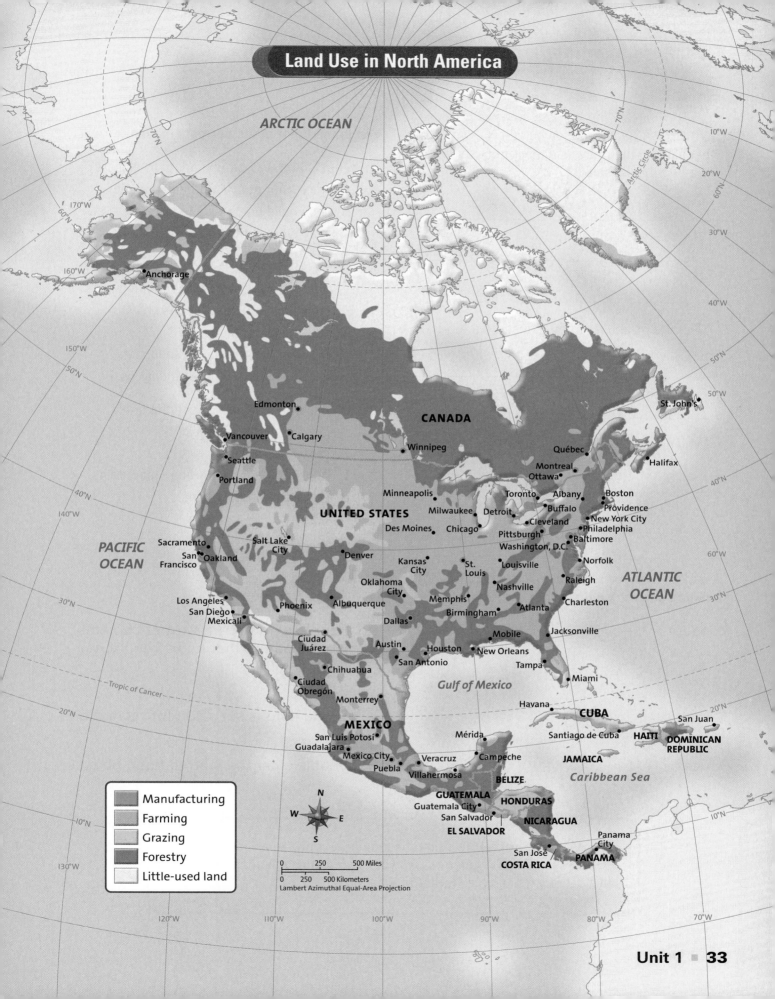

Land Use in North America

ARCTIC OCEAN

CANADA

Anchorage

Edmonton
Vancouver • Calgary
Seattle
Portland

Winnipeg

Québec
Montreal
Ottawa
Halifax

St. John's

UNITED STATES

Minneapolis
Milwaukee • Detroit
Des Moines • Chicago

Toronto • Albany • Boston
Buffalo • Providence
Cleveland • New York City
Pittsburgh • Philadelphia
Washington, D.C. • Baltimore

Sacramento
San • Oakland
Francisco

Salt Lake
City

Denver

Kansas
City

St.
Louis

Louisville

Norfolk

Los Angeles
San Diego
Mexicali

Phoenix

Albuquerque

Oklahoma
City

Memphis

Nashville

Atlanta

Raleigh

Charleston

PACIFIC OCEAN

Birmingham

Dallas

Austin

Houston
San Antonio

New Orleans

Mobile

Jacksonville

Tampa

Miami

ATLANTIC OCEAN

Ciudad
Juárez

Chihuahua

Ciudad
Obregón

Monterrey

Gulf of Mexico

Havana

CUBA

San Juan

— Tropic of Cancer —

MEXICO

San Luis Potosí
Guadalajara
Mexico City
Puebla

Mérida

Veracruz • Campeche
Villahermosa

Santiago de Cuba

HAITI

**DOMINICAN
REPUBLIC**

JAMAICA

Caribbean Sea

BELIZE

GUATEMALA
Guatemala City
San Salvador
EL SALVADOR

HONDURAS

NICARAGUA

Panama
City

San José
COSTA RICA

PANAMA

	Manufacturing
	Farming
	Grazing
	Forestry
	Little-used land

N
W • E
S

0   250   500 Miles
0 250 500 Kilometers
Lambert Azimuthal Equal-Area Projection

1. SUMMARIZE What did you learn about people and their physical environments from reading this lesson?

_____

_____

_____

2. Use **adapt** and **modify** in a sentence.

_____

_____

3. Why do people modify the land?

_____

_____

_____

Circle the letter of the correct answer.

4. What is one way people adapt to climate?

    A They wear heavy clothing in winter.

    B They build dams.

    C They work in the timber industry.

    D They dig wells.

5. What is one way people modify the land?

    A They build houses on stilts.

    B They build canals.

    C They work in the timber industry.

    D They live in the Rocky Mountains.

6. What is one way people use the land?

    A They build houses on stilts.

    B They build dams.

    C They blast tunnels through mountains.

    D They farm on the plains.

MATCHING Draw a line connecting each word on the left with the sentence describing that word on the right.

7. adapt

People who live in warmer climates wear clothing that helps keep them cool.

8. modify

Some land is set aside for recreation.

9. use

People clear the land to build houses.

writing

Write a Letter Imagine that you are writing to a friend who lives in Central America. Tell your friend how you adapt to your physical environment in North Carolina.

Movement in North America

In North America and around the world, people are constantly moving. As people move, so do ideas. Wherever they move to, people share their culture. In turn, they are influenced by the ways of life of their new home.

In order to get the things they need, people must also move goods from place to place. Sometimes they *trade*, or exchange, goods over long distances. Through trade, new goods and ideas are shared. The ways in which people, goods, and ideas move have changed over time. **What might you learn about the movement of people, goods, and ideas as you read this lesson?**

_____

_____

_____

▷ TRAFFIC IN ATLANTA, GEORGIA

 **NORTH CAROLINA
STANDARD COURSE OF STUDY**

1.07 Analyze the past movement of people, goods, and ideas within and among the United States, Canada, Mexico, and Central America and compare it to movement today.

① Circle the highlighted vocabulary word on this page. Underline the words that give a definition of this word.

② Circle the sentences that describe why early people migrated. Underline the sentence that describes why many people migrate today.

The Movement of People

Over time, people came from around the world to settle in North America. People have also moved from place to place within the continent.

Migration

People around the world often move from place to place. This movement of people is called **migration**.

Migration takes place for different reasons. People might move because conditions attract, or pull, them from their homeland to a new place. For example, early people often moved from place to place in search of food. When food ran out in one area, they moved to a new place. Today, many people move to find new opportunities, such as jobs.

Sometimes people move because they are pushed out of their homes. In the 1930s, a drought—a time with little or no rain—caused crops to fail in parts of the United States. Farmers in these areas could no longer provide for their families. Many families sold or left their farms to find work in other parts of the country.

❯ FAMILIES often move for a new job or other new opportunity.

 **IMMIGRANTS came to the United States in large numbers in the 1800s and 1900s.**

Immigration

Today, many people move to the countries of North America from other places around the world. Some move to one country in North America from another. This movement of people into a new place is called **immigration**.

Many *immigrants*—people who leave their home country to live in another—are pulled from their homelands. Others are pushed. During the 1800s, Ireland's potato crop failed for several years in a row. As a result, there was not enough food to feed everyone. Large numbers of Irish people starved to death. Many others moved to the United States.

In recent years, people from Africa and eastern Europe have come to the United States and other countries in North America. Many of these people have come to escape wars.

Even though the reasons people move have not changed much over the years, how they move has. In the past, people traveled by foot, in wagons, in boats, or on trains. Today, people can reach almost any place in North America. In automobiles and buses, people can travel long distances in only a few hours. On airplanes, they can cover the same distance in even less time.

TextWork

3 How are the reasons people immigrate and the reasons people migrate similar?

_____

_____

_____

_____

_____

_____

4 Underline the sentence that describes how people traveled in the past. Circle the sentences that describe how people travel today.

❺ Review the context clues below, and write down the subject they refer to.

• Created trade networks.

• Traded with people in nearby villages, who then traded with people in villages farther away.

_____

_____

Moving Goods and Ideas

Over the years, people in North America have developed new ways to trade and communicate. New inventions have made it possible to move goods and ideas faster and more easily.

Moving Goods

No one place has everything people want or need. People often must travel to get the goods they need. Many American Indian groups created trade networks. They traded with people in nearby villages. In turn, the people of those villages traded with villages farther away. In this way, goods moved long distances.

New inventions allowed people to carry goods more easily and to places farther away. In the 1700s, sailing ships carried goods from North America to other places all around the world.

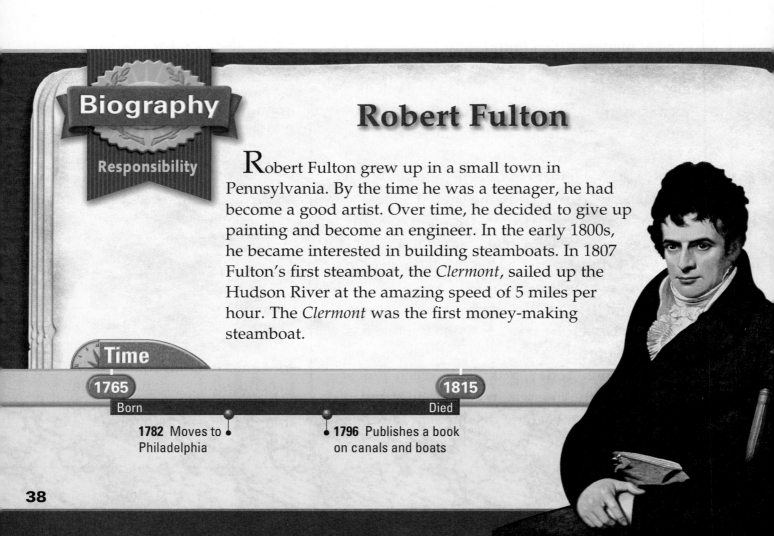

Biography

Responsibility

Robert Fulton

Robert Fulton grew up in a small town in Pennsylvania. By the time he was a teenager, he had become a good artist. Over time, he decided to give up painting and become an engineer. In the early 1800s, he became interested in building steamboats. In 1807 Fulton's first steamboat, the *Clermont*, sailed up the Hudson River at the amazing speed of 5 miles per hour. The *Clermont* was the first money-making steamboat.

Time

1765
Born

1782 Moves to Philadelphia

1796 Publishes a book on canals and boats

1815
Died

Advances in Communication

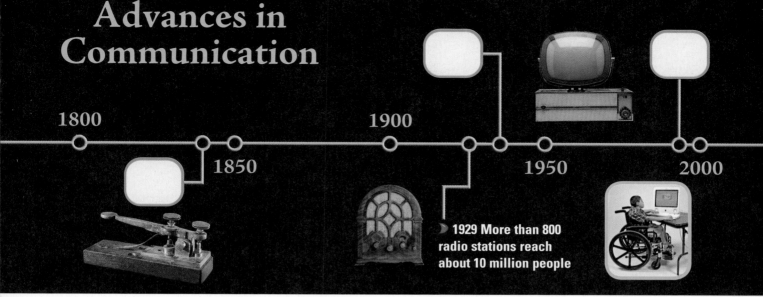

1800

1850

1900

1950

2000

1929 More than 800 radio stations reach about 10 million people

By 1807, steam engines were being used to power boats. By 1830, locomotives, or railroad engines, were pulling trains full of people and goods.

Automobiles and trucks made the movement of people and goods even easier and faster. Soon highways connected the different parts of North America. The Pan-American Highway runs from Canada through the United States, Mexico, and Central America, and into South America.

Airplanes made moving goods the easiest and fastest yet. Today, airplanes can carry goods quickly to almost anywhere in the world. This has enabled people to send fresh seafood and other foods to markets before they spoil.

Moving Ideas

Whenever people move or travel to a new place, they take their culture with them. They spread their beliefs, languages, foods, music, and other ideas. Through trade, American Indians exchanged ideas and beliefs with other villages and tribes. However, ideas spread in this way traveled slowly.

During colonial times, books, newspapers, and other printed materials were often used to spread new ideas. However, these materials had to be printed and then delivered by horse or wagon.

 **TextWork**

6 Use the events listed below to complete the time line above. Add the letter of the event to the appropriate box in the time line.

A. 1844—The first telegraph message is sent

B. 1991—The World Wide Web brings the Internet to people around the world

C. 1939—The first regular television broadcast in the United States takes place

TextWork

7 Skim the text. What is the topic of this section?

_____

_____

Moving Ideas Faster

Over time, new inventions have allowed ideas to spread more quickly. The telegraph and then the telephone allowed people to spread ideas over long distances instantly. The first radio broadcasts began in the 1920s.

Television first became popular in the 1950s. It has helped spread ideas quickly to large numbers of people.

Today, the Internet spreads ideas more rapidly than ever. Almost anyone with a computer can share ideas with people around the world through e-mail.

Lesson 5 Review

1. **SUMMARIZE** How has the movement of people, goods, and ideas changed over time?

_____

_____

_____

2. What is the difference between **migration** and **immigration**?

_____

_____

Circle the letter of the correct answer.

3. Which invention allowed people to transport goods faster and more easily?

   A the telegraph

   B the automobile

   C the Internet

   D trade networks

4. Which invention has allowed people to share ideas with others around the world rapidly?

   A the telegraph

   B the automobile

   C the Internet

   D trade networks

activity

Make a Time Capsule Gather together pictures and images of how people, goods, and ideas move today. Then write a paragraph to make predictions about how you think people, goods, and ideas will move in the future. Place your predictions and images in a box or other container. Share your images and predictions with the class.

Review and Test Prep

💡 The Big Idea

People can use the five themes of geography to help them study and understand the land and people of North America.

Summarize the Unit

⭐ **Focus Skill** **Compare and Contrast** Complete the organizer to show that you can compare and contrast landforms in North America.

Topic 1

Coastal Plain

_____

_____

_____

Similar

_____

_____

_____

_____

Topic 2

Interior Plains

_____

_____

_____

_____

Use Vocabulary

Fill in the missing term in each sentence, using the correct vocabulary term from the Word Bank.

1. The term _____ refers to the average number of people living in an area of a certain size.

2. The movement of people is called _____.

3. An _____ cuts into land from a larger body of water.

4. A _____ is a way of life handed down from the past.

5. All businesses that make one kind of product are an _____.

Word Bank

inlet p. 8
industry p. 10
population density p. 18
tradition p. 24
migration p. 36

Think About It

6. What is the relative location of the Canadian Shield?

_____

_____

7. What is the difference between developing and developed countries?

_____

_____

8. What is one way that people use the land in Central America?

_____

_____

Circle the letter of the correct answer.

9. How do farmers in the western part of the Interior Plains adapt to the region's dry climate?

  A They grow wheat.

  B They work in the timber industry.

  C They make their houses from sod.

  D They grow corn.

10. Which waterway was modified to allow ships to travel between the Great Lakes and the Atlantic Ocean?

  A the Rio Grande

  B the St. Lawrence River

  C the Pan-American Highway

  D the Panama Canal

Show What You Know

Writing Write a Travel Brochure

Write a travel brochure about a country in North America. Describe the country's landforms, bodies of water, climate, and natural resources.

Activity Make an Atlas

Make an atlas of North America. Include maps, fact sheets, graphs, charts, and illustrations for the countries of North America.

GO online To play a game that reviews the unit, join Eco in the North Carolina Adventures online or on CD.

The Early United States

> **PLIMOTH PLANTATION IN MASSACHUSETTS**

Spotlight on Goals and Objectives

North Carolina Interactive Presentations

NORTH CAROLINA STANDARD COURSE OF STUDY

COMPETENCY GOAL 4 The learner will trace key developments in United States history and describe their impact on the land and people of the nation and its neighboring countries.

The Big Idea

How can events in history have an impact on the land and the people?

Try to imagine what life was like for people who lived in the past. Why do you think people did the things they did? How do you think different events impacted, or affected, their feelings and beliefs?

By studying history, people today can better understand how the land and people's ways of life have changed over time and how they have stayed the same. They can see how past events have impacted both an area of land and the people living in it.

Think of an event that happened in your community during your lifetime. Describe how that event changed the land in your community and how it changed the people who live in your community.

What was the event? _____

_____

_____

_____

How did the event change the land? _____

_____

_____

_____

How did the event change the people? _____

_____

_____

_____

Reading Social Studies

Cause and Effect

⟩ LEARN

Understanding cause and effect can help you see why events happen. A **cause** is an event or an action that makes something else happen. An **effect** is what happens because of that event or action. Certain words and phrases, such as *because, since, so, for these reasons*, and *as a result*, are hints that can help you see cause-and-effect relationships. In some paragraphs, the effect may be stated before the cause.

Cause		Effect
An event or an action	➤	What happens

⟩ PRACTICE

Circle the cause in each paragraph and underline the effect or effects of that cause. The first paragraph has been done for you.

The Taino (TY•noh) were American Indians who lived on islands in the Caribbean Sea. They were a peaceful people. They had warlike neighbors, the Carib, who lived on nearby islands. The two groups did not get along. Because the groups did not get along, the Carib sometimes attacked Taino villages.

Cause
Effect

People from Europe soon came to North America. European explorers carried diseases and fought with American Indians. As a result, life changed for the Taino, Carib, and other American Indian groups. Many of them died because of diseases or fighting.

Read the article. Then complete the activities below.

From Strangers to Neighbors

In 1765, John Rutledge traveled from his home in South Carolina to New York City. He called it his first trip to another country. That says a lot about how people living in the British colonies viewed one another.

The 13 British colonies had been founded at different times and for different reasons. Each had its own mix of people. Each had its own businesses and its own government. For these reasons, the colonies really were like different countries.

Things were about to change, though. John Rutledge was going to New York City to meet with leaders from nine of the colonies.

They were to discuss a new tax law. The colonists thought that the tax was unfair. They wanted to figure out what to do about it.

While in New York City, Rutledge met with Sir William Johnson. Johnson was a rich British merchant who was friendly with the Iroquois. Johnson told Rutledge about how members of the Iroquois League worked together to solve problems.

Rutledge told other colonists about the Iroquois League. Like the Iroquois, the colonists soon began to work together. They started seeing each other not as people from other countries but as neighbors.

1. **In the third paragraph, underline the sentences that explain why John Rutledge traveled to New York City.**

2. **Why were the colonies like different countries?**

   _____

   _____

   _____

3. **Underline the sentences that explain how learning about the Iroquois League affected colonists.**

Early People

Lesson

1

Historians study the past. They look for hints in the objects and documents that people left behind. By doing this, they are better able to understand what the world was like when an event took place.

Studying history can help you see how the present and the past are connected. It helps you see how some things change over time and some things stay the same. **What ideas about early people will you learn by reading this lesson?**

_____

_____

_____

▶ **CANYON DE CHELLY in Arizona**

NORTH CAROLINA
STANDARD COURSE OF STUDY

4.01 Define the role of an historian and explain the importance of studying history.

4.02 Explain when, where, why, and how groups of people settled in different regions of the United States.

Early Ways of Life

Scientists are still not sure how the first people arrived in North America. One possible explanation is that there was once a "bridge" of land between Asia and North America. Many historians believe that thousands of years ago, early people crossed this land bridge from Asia to North America. They were the **ancestors**, or early family members, of present-day American Indians.

Civilizations Begin

Early people followed the animals they hunted. About 5,000 years ago, some people in the Americas began growing crops. Farming, or agriculture, gave these people a reason to stay in one place.

Over time, some groups began to form civilizations. A **civilization** is a group of people with forms of government, religion, and learning. Some groups founded large cities, such as Cahokia in what is today the state of Illinois.

① Write a definition for the word *civilization* in your own words.

_____

_____

_____

② **MOVEMENT** With your finger, trace the route on the map below that early people took to get to Central America over hundreds of years. Then underline the sentence that tells how, as many historians believe, people first got to North America.

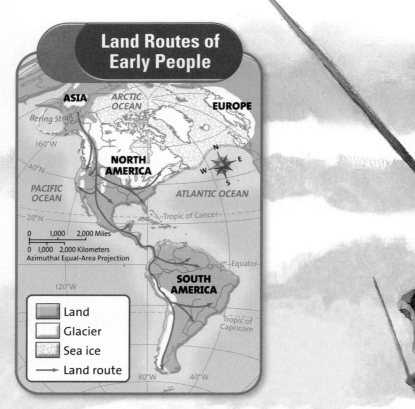

Land Routes of Early People

ASIA
ARCTIC OCEAN
EUROPE
Bering Strait
160°W
40°N
NORTH AMERICA
PACIFIC OCEAN
ATLANTIC OCEAN
20°N
Tropic of Cancer
0 1,000 2,000 Miles
0 1,000 2,000 Kilometers
Azimuthal Equal-Area Projection
0° Equator
120°W
SOUTH AMERICA
Tropic of Capricorn
80°W   40°W

Land
Glacier
Sea ice
Land route

Civilizations in North America

The Olmec civilization was one of the earliest in the Americas. From about 1500 B.C. to A.D. 300, the Olmec ruled most of what is now southern Mexico. The Olmec formed trade routes. They also made up ways of writing and counting.

Between A.D. 300 and A.D. 900, the Maya ruled what is now southern Mexico, Guatemala, and northern Belize. The Maya also made up ways of writing and counting.

Many early American Indian groups lived in what is now the eastern United States. There they built large earth mounds. Historians use the name Mound Builders for all these groups. But their cultures, or ways of life, were often different.

The Ancient Puebloans lived in the area where the present-day states of Utah, Arizona, Colorado, and New Mexico meet. They lived in houses called pueblos. Pueblos had many levels.

❯ HUNTERS AND GATHERERS crossed the land bridge to get to North America.

TextWork

❸ The years before the birth of Jesus Christ are labeled *B.C.* The years after Christ's birth are labeled *A.D.* On the time line below, mark the time period of the Olmec civilization. Mark the beginning date with an *X* and the end date with a dot.

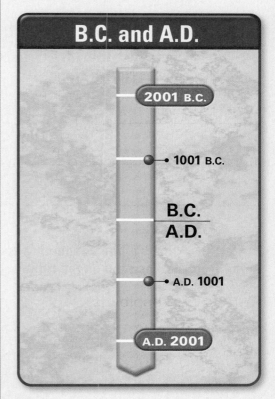

B.C. and A.D.

2001 B.C.

1001 B.C.

B.C.
A.D.

A.D. 1001

A.D. 2001

❹ Scan the text on this page. Circle the sentence that describes the location of the Ancient Puebloans.

1. **SUMMARIZE** Why is studying history important?

_____

_____

_____

2. Use the word **historian** in a sentence about early people in North America.

_____

_____

_____

Circle the letter of the correct answer.

3. What caused some early people to begin to settle in one place?

  A farming

  B a land bridge

  C building mounds

  D pueblos

4. Where was the Olmec civilization located?

  A in what is now southern Mexico

  B in what is now the United States

  C in what is now Cuba

  D in what is now Canada

MATCHING Draw a line connecting each early civilization on the left with its correct location on the right.

5. Ancient Puebloans

where the present-day states of Utah, Arizona, Colorado, and New Mexico meet

6. Maya

what is now the eastern United States

7. Mound Builders

what is now southern Mexico, Guatemala, and northern Belize

writing

Write a List of Questions Imagine that a historian is coming to your class to give a talk. Write a list of questions that you might ask a historian about his or her job and why studying history is important.

American Indians

Long ago, American Indians lived in almost every part of North America. Each American Indian group was different, and each group had its own way of life. Yet the lifeways and traditions of groups that lived in the same area were often similar. All the groups in a region were affected by the same climate and landforms. They also depended on the same kinds of natural resources to meet their needs. **How do you think this lesson will improve your understanding of American Indians?**

_____

_____

_____

AN INUIT fisher in a kayak

NORTH CAROLINA
STANDARD COURSE OF STUDY

4.02 Explain when, where, why, and how groups of people settled in different regions of the United States.

TextWork

1 What caused the Iroquois League to form?

_____

_____

_____

2 **LOCATION** Study the map on page 53. Circle the label for the Iroquois. Then describe the relative location of the Iroquois.

_____

_____

3 **LOCATION** Study the map on page 53. Circle the label for the Powhatan. Then describe the relative location of the Powhatan.

_____

_____

_____

The Eastern Woodlands

The Eastern Woodlands stretched east from the Mississippi River to the Atlantic Ocean. In the northeast, people hunted and gathered food. People farther south grew corn, beans, squash, and other plants. There were two main language groups—the Algonquian (al•GAHN•kwee•uhn) and the Iroquoian (ir•uh•KWOY•uhn).

Some Iroquoian groups lived in what is now Pennsylvania and New York and along Lake Ontario in Canada. Their homes were called _longhouses_. They could hold up to 50 people.

Different Iroquoian groups often battled each other over control of hunting areas. In 1570, the Iroquois League was formed. The Iroquois League acted as a **confederation**, or loose group of governments working together. The goal of the league was to settle conflicts peacefully.

Among the Algonquian groups were the Powhatan, Ottawa, and Miami. They lived on the Coastal Plain and near the Great Lakes. Some groups lived in longhouses. Others lived in round, bark-covered homes called _wigwams_. Fish was an important food for the Algonquians. The Algonquians made clothing mostly from deerskin.

▶ **THE EASTERN WOODLANDS** The many forests in the region provided people with wood to make homes, boats, and tools.

Early Cultures of North America

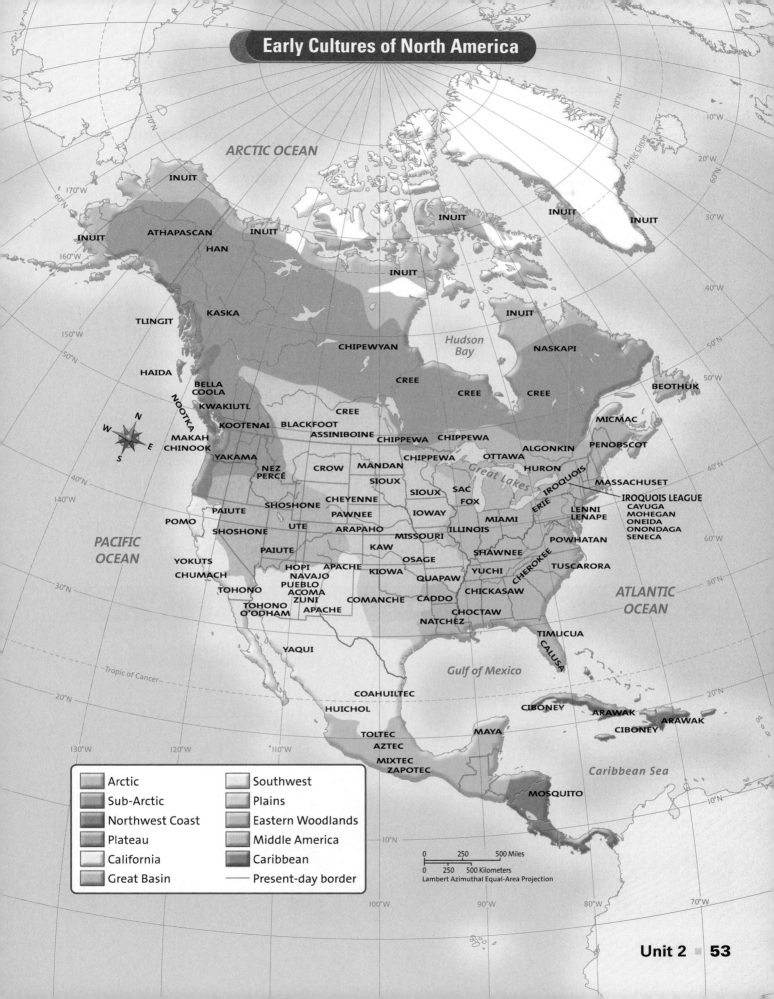

ARCTIC OCEAN

INUIT

INUIT

INUIT

INUIT

INUIT

INUIT

INUIT

ATHAPASCAN

HAN

INUIT

INUIT

KASKA

TLINGIT

CHIPEWYAN

Hudson Bay

NASKAPI

HAIDA

CREE

CREE

CREE

BEOTHUK

BELLA COOLA

KWAKIUTL

CREE

MICMAC

NOOTKA

KOOTENAI

BLACKFOOT

ASSINIBOINE

CHIPPEWA

CHIPPEWA

ALGONKIN

PENOBSCOT

MAKAH

CHINOOK

CHIPPEWA

OTTAWA

HURON

Great Lakes

MASSACHUSET

YAKAMA

NEZ PERCÉ

CROW

MANDAN

SIOUX

ERIE

IROQUOIS

LENNI LENAPE

IROQUOIS LEAGUE
CAYUGA
MOHEGAN
ONEIDA
ONONDAGA
SENECA

PACIFIC OCEAN

PAIUTE

SHOSHONE

CHEYENNE

SIOUX

SAC
FOX

POMO

SHOSHONE

UTE

PAWNEE

IOWAY

MIAMI

ARAPAHO

MISSOURI

ILLINOIS

POWHATAN

YOKUTS

PAIUTE

KAW

OSAGE

SHAWNEE

ATLANTIC OCEAN

CHUMACH

HOPI

APACHE

KIOWA

YUCHI

TUSCARORA

TOHONO

NAVAJO
PUEBLO
ACOMA
ZUNI

QUAPAW

CHICKASAW

CHEROKEE

TOHONO O'ODHAM

APACHE

COMANCHE

CADDO

CHOCTAW

NATCHEZ

YAQUI

TIMUCUA

CALUSA

Gulf of Mexico

Tropic of Cancer

COAHUILTEC

HUICHOL

CIBONEY

ARAWAK

ARAWAK

CIBONEY

TOLTEC
AZTEC

MAYA

MIXTEC
ZAPOTEC

Caribbean Sea

MOSQUITO

Arctic	Southwest	
Sub-Arctic	Plains	
Northwest Coast	Eastern Woodlands	
Plateau	Middle America	
California	Caribbean	
Great Basin	Present-day border	

0   250   500 Miles
0   250   500 Kilometers
Lambert Azimuthal Equal-Area Projection

The Plains

4 Why do you think many American Indian groups settled on the Interior Plains?

_____

_____

_____

_____

5 Underline the sentences that describe what American Indians made from buffaloes. Then use this information to complete the diagram below.

The Plains people lived on vast grasslands known as the Interior Plains. Millions of buffalo, or American bison, once lived in this part of North America. Plains groups hunted these animals. They used buffalo to make many things. From the horns, they made cups and spoons. From the skin, they made clothing, homes, shields, and drums. From the bones, they made tools, arrowheads, and pipes.

Some Plains groups were farmers as well as hunters and gatherers. They gathered plants and hunted deer, elk, and buffalo. They farmed the rich valleys of the Missouri River and the Platte River. These people lived in villages made up of large round earthen houses called *lodges*.

Plains groups living in the western part of the Interior Plains moved from place to place. They followed herds of buffalo. These people made homes that were easy to move, such as the tepee (TEE•pee). The *tepee* was a cone-shaped tent.

Among the Plains people, every man in the group was equal. Any man could become chief if he was a good warrior and leader.

American Indian Uses of the Buffalo

Horns

Skin

Bones

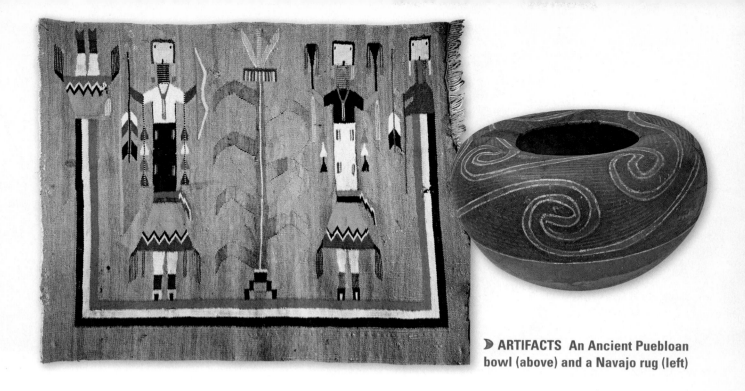

> **ARTIFACTS** An Ancient Puebloan bowl (above) and a Navajo rug (left)

The Southwest and the West

The desert Southwest was a hard place to live. The region has summer heat, winter cold, and little rain. Still, American Indian groups were able to adapt their ways of life to this land.

The Ancient Puebloans lived in villages that were called pueblos by later Spanish settlers. The Navajo (NA•vuh•hoh) moved into the Southwest in about A.D. 1025. In time, the Navajo began growing food and cotton as the Pueblo people did.

The Ancient Puebloans and the Navajo depended on trade for resources not found nearby. They sometimes traveled far to trade their pottery and baskets with other groups.

The West

Many different groups of American Indians lived on the lands that stretch from the Rocky Mountains to the Pacific Ocean. American Indians in the West depended on nearby natural resources. To get goods they could not make or find themselves, they formed large trade networks. These networks allowed them to get goods from faraway places.

 **TextWork**

6 Review the context clues below, and write down the subject to which they refer.

• **This region has summer heat, winter cold, and little rain.**

• **American Indian groups were able to adapt their ways of life to this land.**

_____

_____

7 Scan the text to find the date that the Navajo moved into the Southwest. Circle this date.

▶ **WHALE HUNT** The Makah hunted whales at sea using large dugouts.

TextWork

8 What resources were available to American Indians living in the Northwest Coast region?

_____

_____

_____

_____

_____

9 Circle the sentence that describes what caused Northwest Coast groups to develop a special language for trade.

The Northwest Coast

The Northwest Coast stretched along the Pacific Ocean. It included parts of what are today Washington and Oregon in the United States and British Columbia in Canada. Forests grow tall and thick there. The forests and rivers that run through the region are filled with fish and animals.

Many American Indian groups lived in this region. They met their needs by fishing and hunting and by gathering plants and nuts.

The rivers and coastal waters were an important resource. Salmon was the main food for most groups. Whales supplied not only food but also fat, which could be melted into oil to burn in lamps.

The giant trees that grow in the forests of the Northwest Coast provided wood for houses, tools, and boats. American Indians hollowed out logs to make boats called _dugouts_. They used the dugouts to hunt whales, to travel, and to trade.

To trade, people traveled on the area's bodies of water. Because groups spoke different languages, they made up a new language used for trade. It let them **barter**, or exchange goods.

The Arctic and the Sub-Arctic

The Arctic is the area near the North Pole. This land is mostly a flat plain where the land stays frozen year-round. One group, the Aleut (a•lee•OOT), lived along the coast of the Aleutian Islands. Another group, the Inuit (IH•noo•wuht), lived in what is now Alaska and northern Canada.

Because of the harsh climate, few plants grow in the Arctic. Groups there hunted animals such as foxes, seals, and whales. The people caught seals not only for their meat but also for their skins. The skins were made into clothes and tents. Whale oil was burned to light and heat houses. Animal bones were used to make tools.

South of the Arctic is the sub-Arctic region. It stretches from what is now eastern Canada to what is now Alaska. This area is also very cold much of the year. However, trees do grow in the sub-Arctic.

People of the sub-Arctic region, such as the Cree, hunted animals and gathered plants to meet their needs. The Cree used trees for wood. They used wood to make bows and arrows to hunt animals.

TextWork

10 Circle the names of the American Indian groups that lived in the Arctic.

11 What is one natural resource the people of the sub-Arctic had that the people of the Arctic did not have?

_____

_____

_____

➤ **INUIT** hunters carved designs into whale bone. The artifact (below) shows an Inuit whale hunt.

1. **SUMMARIZE** How did a region's natural resources affect its American Indian groups?

_____

_____

_____

2. Use the word **barter** to describe how American Indians traded.

_____

_____

3. Why do you think American Indians settled in the Northwest Coast region?

_____

_____

Circle the letter of the correct answer.

4. Which of the following groups lived in the Eastern Woodlands region?

   A Cree

   B Navajo

   C Powhatan

   D Inuit

5. How did the Plains people use the buffalo?

   A to plow farm fields

   B to pull wagons

   C to make many things

   D to ride

6. Which of the following groups lived in the sub-Arctic region?

   A Cree

   B Navajo

   C Powhatan

   D Inuit

MATCHING Draw a line connecting each group on the left with the region in which they lived on the right.

7. Iroquois   Arctic

8. Ancient Puebloans   Southwest

9. Aleut   Eastern Woodlands

writing

✎ **Write a Letter** Imagine that you could visit one of the American Indian groups described in this lesson. Write a letter that describes the group's daily life.

Exploration

In the 1400s, one of the best-known books was *The Travels of Marco Polo*. It tells of Marco Polo, an Italian trader, and his travels to Asia. European merchants wanted to buy and then sell Asian goods such as silks and spices. Soon European traders began traveling the long, difficult land routes to Asia.

Some traders wanted to find a faster water route to Asia. At that time, Europeans did not know that there were other continents beyond Europe, Africa, and Asia. **What might you learn about the European exploration of North America as you read this lesson?**

_____

_____

▶ **A MAP of the Western Hemisphere, 1595**

**NORTH CAROLINA
STANDARD COURSE OF STUDY**

4.03 Describe the contributions of people of diverse cultures throughout the history of the United States.

Navigational Tools

COMPASS

CHRONOMETER

ASTROLABE

TextWork

1 Scan the text on this page. Circle the names of the navigational tools mentioned.

2 What was one effect of Prince Henry's opening his school of navigation?

_____

_____

_____

_____

_____

Navigation Improves

By the 1400s, no Europeans had traveled to Asia by sea. They had no maps that showed the world correctly. Sailors did not have the knowledge and tools needed for such a long trip. Sailors and scientists began working to solve these problems.

In 1418, Prince Henry of Portugal opened a school of navigation. **Navigation** is the science of planning and following a route. At the school, sailors learned to sail ships called caravels. These lighter, faster ships could carry more goods. Prince Henry hired scientists to improve navigational tools. Sailors used the compass, the chronometer, and the astrolabe to figure out their place on Earth. People learned to draw better maps.

These and other developments made longer ocean explorations possible. Portuguese ships made expeditions in search of a sea route to Asia. An **expedition** is a trip taken with the goal of exploring. Prince Henry believed that the most direct sea route from Europe to Asia would be to sail south around Africa and then east. In time, the Portuguese found this route.

The Spanish Explore

The first Europeans to sail across the Atlantic Ocean were sent by Spain. They were seeking trade routes to Asia. What they learned was that two continents—North America and South America—lay between Europe and Asia.

Christopher Columbus

Christopher Columbus believed he could reach Asia by sailing west from Europe. He thought this route would be shorter than sailing around Africa.

The king and queen of Spain agreed to help pay for Columbus's voyage. On August 3, 1492, Columbus and his crew set sail. On October 12, they landed on an island in the Caribbean Sea. Columbus believed that he had reached the Indies, islands off the coast of Asia. This explains why he called the people he met there Indians.

Columbus returned to Spain. When the king and queen saw the gold, animals, plants, and people Columbus returned with, they paid for more expeditions. Columbus was expected to find more riches, start settlements, and spread the Catholic religion.

 **TextWork**

❸ Why did Columbus want to sail across the Atlantic Ocean?

_____

_____

_____

_____

❹ Scan the text. Circle the sentence that describes what the king and queen of Spain wanted Columbus to do on his next expeditions.

Children IN HISTORY

Diego Bermúdez

Some of the sailors on Columbus's expedition were as young as 12. That was the age of Diego Bermúdez. Diego was a page. Pages did the jobs that most sailors did not want to do, like cooking, cleaning, and keeping track of the time. Diego kept track of the time by using a half-hour glass. When all the sand had fallen to the bottom of the glass, Diego rang a bell and called out a short prayer. His actions let everyone know the time.

Make It Relevant What jobs do you have to do at home or at school?

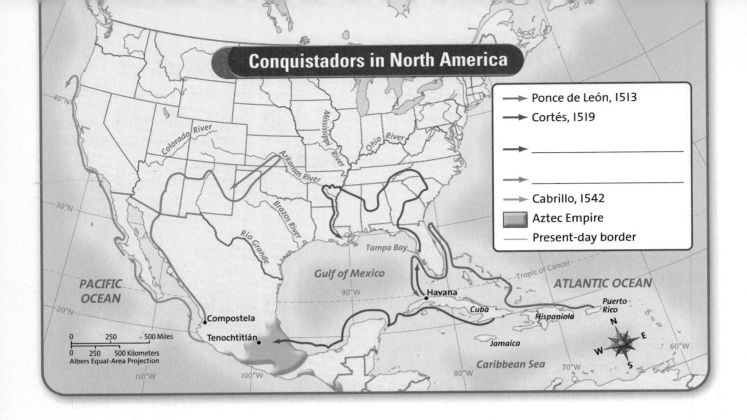

Conquistadors in North America

→	Ponce de León, 1513
→	Cortés, 1519
→	_____
→	_____
→	Cabrillo, 1542
▨	Aztec Empire
—	Present-day border

TextWork

5 MOVEMENT Use the information in the text to complete the map key above.

6 What caused Coronado to be sent to explore the Southwest?

_____

_____

_____

7 What was the effect of Coronado's expedition?

_____

_____

_____

_____

Conquistadors

More Spanish explorers and soldiers soon sailed to the Americas. They were known as *conquistadors* (kahn•KEES•tah•dawrz), or "conquerors."

Juan Ponce de León and Hernando de Soto explored the Southeast. In 1513, Ponce de León landed in Florida. From 1539 to 1542, de Soto explored nine states, including North Carolina.

In 1519, Spain sent Hernando Cortés to what is now Mexico. By 1521, Cortés had defeated the Aztecs, who ruled the area. The Spanish built Mexico City on the site of the Aztec capital. It became the capital of Spain's lands in the Americas.

After hearing stories about seven cities of gold, Spanish leaders in Mexico sent Francisco Vásquez de Coronado to find them. In 1540, he explored what is now the Southwest. He never found any gold, but he claimed more lands for Spain.

Spain also sent **missionaries**, or teachers of religion, to the Americas. Their goal was to *convert*, or change the beliefs of, American Indians to the Catholic religion.

Other Nations Explore

Other European countries wanted to find riches in North America. They also hoped to find a shortcut to Asia. Explorers began searching for a waterway through or around North America. They called this the Northwest Passage. The first to find it would control an important new trade route.

Verrazano and Cartier

The French king, Francis I, was one of the many European leaders who wanted to find the Northwest Passage. In 1524, he sent Giovanni da Verrazano to find it. Verrazano landed on the coast of what is now North Carolina. He explored much of the Atlantic coast. He did not find the Northwest Passage, but he did claim land for France.

In 1534, another French explorer, Jacques Cartier, also looked for the Northwest Passage. He reached the mouth of the St. Lawrence River and claimed all the land around it for France. In later expeditions, he explored what is now eastern Canada.

 **TextWork**

8 Add the letter for each entry below to the correct location on the time line.

A. Giovanni da Verrazano lands in what is now North Carolina.

B. Jacques Cartier reaches the mouth of the St. Lawrence River in what is now Canada.

9 Study your completed time line below. Did Cartier reach the mouth of the St. Lawrence River before or after Henry Hudson's first voyage to North America? How many years before or after?

_____

_____

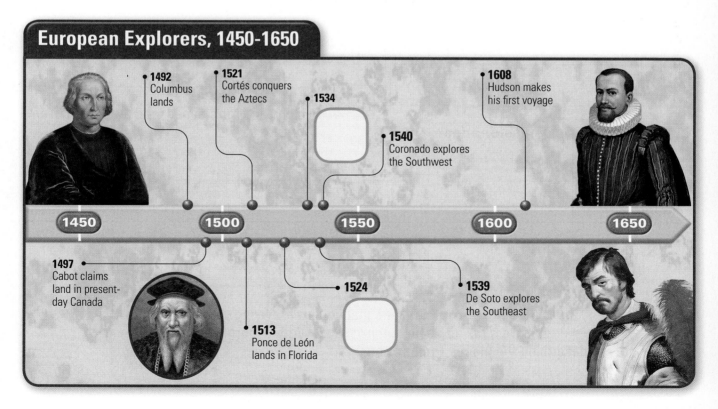

European Explorers, 1450–1650

1492 Columbus lands

1521 Cortés conquers the Aztecs

1534

1608 Hudson makes his first voyage

1540 Coronado explores the Southwest

1450   1500   1550   1600   1650

1497 Cabot claims land in present-day Canada

1524

1539 De Soto explores the Southeast

1513 Ponce de León lands in Florida

▶ **HENRY HUDSON meets with American Indians.**

Henry Hudson

By the 1600s, exploration was a big business. European trading companies also began sending explorers to look for the Northwest Passage.

An English explorer named Henry Hudson made four trips in search of the Northwest Passage. A company in England paid for his first two expeditions. A company in the Netherlands paid for his third and fourth expeditions.

Hudson claimed northern Canada and the Arctic Ocean for England. He claimed the Hudson River, in what is now New York, for the Netherlands.

Early European explorers never found the Northwest Passage. But, they learned much about North America. Their explorations led the way for settlement by Europeans.

Lesson 3 Review

1. **SUMMARIZE** Which countries sent explorers to claim land in North America?

_____

_____

2. Why did Spain send **missionaries**?

_____

_____

3. Which two explorers visited North Carolina?

_____

_____

4. Which explorer claimed land for two different countries?

_____

_____

writing

🖉 **Write a Journal** Imagine that you are traveling with one of the explorers talked about in this lesson. Write a journal entry describing the places you have been.

The First Colonies

▶ A MISSION in Trinidad, Cuba

By the early 1500s, several European nations had sent explorers to claim land in North America. These countries competed with each other to win control of as much of North America as possible.

Often more than one country claimed the same land. To help protect their claims in North America, European countries began forming colonies. A **colony** is a land ruled by another country. **What do you think you will learn about European colonies in North America in this lesson?**

_____

_____

**NORTH CAROLINA
STANDARD COURSE OF STUDY**

4.02 Explain when, where, why, and how groups of people settled in different regions of the United States.

4.03 Describe the contributions of people of diverse cultures throughout the history of the United States.

▶ SUGAR MILL Many enslaved Africans were forced to work in sugar mills.

 **TextWork**

❶ Review the graph below. About how many more Europeans were in the Western Hemisphere in 1750 than in 1650?

_____

Europeans in the Western Hemisphere, 1550–1750	
YEAR	**POPULATION**
1550	🧍🧍🧍
1650	🧍🧍🧍🧍🧍🧍🧍🧍🧍🧍
1750	🧍🧍🧍🧍🧍🧍🧍🧍🧍🧍🧍🧍🧍🧍🧍🧍🧍🧍🧍🧍

🧍 = 500,000 people   🧍 = 250,000 people

❷ Circle the sentence that tells why the Spanish settled borderlands.

New Spain

Spain founded the colony of New Spain in 1535. Most of New Spain's lands were in present-day Mexico, and New Spain's capital was Mexico City. New Spain also included many islands in the Caribbean Sea and lands in Central America.

By 1550, there were more than 100,000 Spanish colonists in the Americas. Many colonists started gold and silver mines and large ranches and farms. They forced American Indians into slavery. **Slavery** is the practice of holding people against their will and making them work without pay. They later brought enslaved Africans to the Americas.

The Borderlands

Few Spanish colonists lived on the lands north of Mexico City. These lands on the edge of New Spain were called **borderlands**. They were made up of what are today northern Mexico, and the present-day states of Florida, Texas, New Mexico, Arizona, and California. Spain's major goal in settling these areas was to protect its empire. Spanish soldiers built **presidios** (pray•SEE•dee•ohz), or forts, in the borderlands.

St. Augustine and Santa Fe

In 1565, explorer Pedro Menéndez de Avilés (may•NAYN•days day ah•vee•LAYS) and 1,500 soldiers, sailors, and settlers sailed from Spain. The same year, they reached the area that is now St. Augustine, Florida. There they built the first permanent, or long-lasting, settlement in what is today the United States.

Spanish missionaries also settled other parts of New Spain. In 1610, they helped settle Santa Fe in present-day New Mexico. There, missionaries built a religious settlement called a **mission**.

In missions, missionaries and American Indians lived very close to each other. Many American Indians were forced to work on mission farms and ranches. Some fought back, tearing down churches and other mission buildings.

The Spanish—and the animals they brought with them—changed life for many American Indians. Horses, long extinct in the Americas, once again roamed the land. Some American Indian groups learned to tame horses for use in hunting and in war. Some learned to raise sheep and to use their wool in making clothing.

TextWork

❸ List two effects of Spanish settlement on American Indians.

• _____

_____

_____

• _____

_____

_____

❹ **LOCATION** Over time, New Spain's settlements spread northward along El Camino Real, or the Royal Road. Spain also started settlements in other areas. Circle the settlements on the map below that were in the present-day United States.

Settlements of New Spain, 1650

> **JAMESTOWN** For one year, John Smith (left) served as the leader of Jamestown. Today, a reconstruction of Jamestown (above) stands near the original site.

Early English Colonies

5 Scan the text about the Virginia Colony. Circle the sentence that describes what caused the colonists at Jamestown to begin planting crops.

6 Write a main idea for the details listed below.

Details:

• **The colonists were soon growing tobacco as a cash crop.**

• **By 1619, the colony had more than 1,000 people.**

• **The colony set up the House of Burgesses to make laws.**

Main Idea: _____

_____

England's leaders saw that Spain had grown rich from its colonies. They wanted colonies of their own. They knew that they would gain from the natural resources in the colonies. England's first colony, on Roanoke Island in present-day North Carolina, failed in 1585.

The Virginia Colony

By the early 1600s, England was ready to try again to start a colony. In 1607, colonists landed in North America and founded Jamestown in present-day Virginia. Most colonists came to find gold. No one bothered to plant or gather food.

Jamestown might not have lasted without its new leader, Captain John Smith. Smith made an important rule—anyone who did not work did not eat. The colonists were soon busy planting crops.

For all of its troubles, Jamestown and the Virginia Colony grew. The colonists in Virginia were soon growing tobacco as a cash crop. A **cash crop** is a crop that people grow to sell. By 1619, the Virginia Colony had more than 1,000 people. The colony set up the House of Burgesses to make laws. It was the first *legislature*, or lawmaking body, in North America.

The Plymouth Colony

The Virginia Colony needed more people. The colony's founders agreed to pay for the trip of a group of English people now called the Pilgrims. The Pilgrims wanted to build a community where they could freely follow their religious beliefs.

In September 1620, the Pilgrims left from England on a ship called the *Mayflower*. They were blown off course and landed in New England. There they founded a colony called Plymouth.

To keep order, all the men aboard the *Mayflower* signed a *compact*, or agreement. It became known as the Mayflower Compact. It gave the colonists the right to govern themselves.

At first, the Pilgrims and the American Indians in the area were friendly. The American Indians showed the Pilgrims where to fish and how to plant squash, corn, and pumpkins. Later, as more English colonists came, the two groups fought over land and resources.

7 As you skim the text, write a question you have about the Plymouth Colony.

_____

_____

_____

How could you find the answer to this question?

_____

_____

_____

Biography

Trustworthiness

Tisquantum

In 1605, Tisquantum, or Squanto as the English called him, was captured and taken to England. There he learned to speak English. In 1619, Tisquantum returned to North America. On March 22, 1621, the chief of Tisquantum's tribe sent him to talk to the Pilgrims. That day, Tisquantum and the Pilgrims worked out a peace treaty. It said that the two groups would help each other.

Time

1585		1622
Born?		Died

1605 Is captured and taken to England

1619 Returns to North America

8 For whom was Louisiana named?

_____

_____

9 List two differences between French fur traders and English settlers.

- _____

_____

_____

- _____

_____

_____

▶ **FRENCH FUR TRADERS** and American Indians traded goods.

New France

In 1608, Samuel de Champlain (sham•PLAYN) founded Quebec along the St. Lawrence River in what is now Canada. Quebec was the first French settlement in North America. The French lands became known as New France.

In the 1630s, French missionaries began arriving in New France. These missionaries often lived with American Indians and learned their languages. Some French fur traders also lived with American Indians and learned their languages and ways of life. The fur traders spread west along the St. Lawrence River. They built trading posts rather than permanent settlements.

The king of France sent people to explore New France. With the help of American Indians, Jacques Marquette and Louis Joliet explored parts of the Mississippi River. In 1682, Sieur de la Salle traveled to the mouth of the Mississippi River. La Salle claimed all of the Mississippi River valley for France. He named the land Louisiana in honor of King Louis XIV. In 1722, the town of New Orleans became Louisiana's capital.

 **NEW AMSTERDAM** By 1643, more than 400 people lived in the town.

New Netherland

In the 1600s, the Dutch also began to settle a colony. They called it New Netherland. They settled in parts of what are now New York and New Jersey. Like the French, the Dutch set up the colony in order to make money from the fur trade.

The Dutch believed that they had bought Manhattan Island from the American Indians who lived there. The American Indians believed that the land was for all people to use and that nobody could own the land. They thought that the Dutch were paying to use what was on the land.

In 1626, the Dutch began laying out a town on the southern end of Manhattan Island. They called the settlement New Amsterdam. It was built next to a harbor where the Hudson River flows into the Atlantic Ocean. Ships could sail down the Hudson River to drop off furs and to get supplies. Ships waited in the harbor to carry the furs to Europe.

By the 1630s, New Amsterdam had about 200 people and 30 houses. It had warehouses for storing food and furs. For protection, the Dutch built a fort that had high walls made of stone.

![TextWork icon] **TextWork**

❿ Summarize information about New Netherland. Write two facts about the colony.

• _____

_____

_____

• _____

_____

_____

⓫ Scan the text on this page. Underline the sentence that tells where New Amsterdam was located.

1. **SUMMARIZE** Why did Europeans start colonies in North America?

_____

_____

_____

2. Write a sentence about New Spain using the words **presidio** and **borderlands**.

_____

_____

_____

3. How was the Virginia Colony different from the Plymouth Colony?

_____

_____

_____

_____

Circle the letter of the correct answer.

4. What was the first permanent Spanish settlement in what is now the United States?

   A Jamestown

   B New Amsterdam

   C Santa Fe

   D St. Augustine

5. Why did the Pilgrims want to settle in North America?

   A They wanted to make money.

   B They wanted to spread Christianity.

   C They wanted to gather natural resources.

   D They wanted to start their own religious community.

6. Which country claimed all of the lands of the Mississippi River valley?

   A England

   B France

   C Spain

   D the Netherlands

activity

Draw a Map Draw a map that shows the lands of Spain, England, France, and the Netherlands in North America. On the map, color in the land claims of each country in a different color. Show this information in a map key.

The Thirteen English Colonies

Virginia and Plymouth were England's first colonies in North America. The success and the survival of these colonies made more people move to North America. In time, 13 English colonies spread out along the eastern coast of the present-day United States. **What do you think this lesson will teach you about life in the Thirteen Colonies?**

_____

_____

_____

REENACTORS at Colonial Williamsburg in Virginia

**NORTH CAROLINA
STANDARD COURSE OF STUDY**

4.02 Explain when, where, why, and how groups of people settled in different regions of the United States.

Unit 2 ■ 73

TextWork

1 Why do you think that the Puritans did not want *dissent*?

_____

_____

_____

_____

_____

_____

2 LOCATION Study the map below. Circle the name of the settlement founded by Thomas Hooker.

The New England Colonies

In 1628 and 1630, the Puritans arrived in New England. The Puritans wanted to change the Church of England to make it more "pure." They lived in what became known as the Massachusetts Bay Colony.

The Massachusetts Bay Colony did not welcome people whose beliefs were different from their own. Its leaders thought that **dissent**, or disagreement, would hurt the colony. Roger Williams and Anne Hutchinson both disagreed with the colony's leaders. They were forced to leave Massachusetts. They left and started settlements in what became the Rhode Island Colony.

Thomas Hooker also left the Massachusetts Bay Colony because he disagreed with its leaders. He founded Hartford. In 1636, Hartford joined nearby settlements to form the Connecticut Colony.

In 1623, a Scottish settler named David Thomson started a fishing settlement called Portsmouth. In 1679, this settlement joined with others in the area to form the New Hampshire Colony.

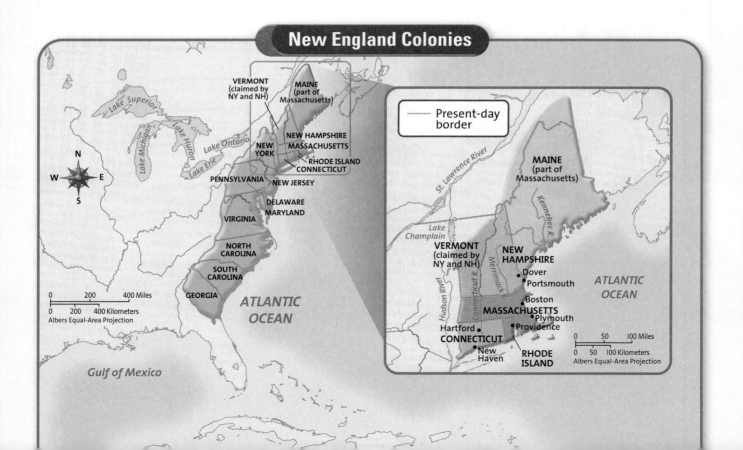

New England Colonies

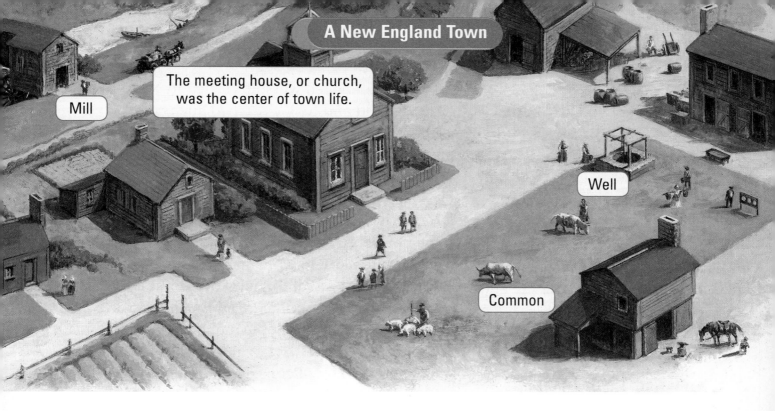

A New England Town

Mill

The meeting house, or church, was the center of town life.

Well

Common

Life in New England

Religion was the center of life in the New England Colonies. On Sunday, every person had to attend church. Many towns had schools so that children could learn to read the Bible.

Most people in New England lived in small towns. All town decisions were made at town meetings. Only male church members could vote.

Because of the rocky soil and cool climate, farming was not easy in New England. Many farmers raised dairy cows and sheep instead. Some colonists cut down trees and made lumber. Lumber was used to build houses and ships. Shipbuilding was a leading industry in New England.

The New England Colonies became leaders in shipping and trading. Colonial ships followed what became known as **triangular trade routes**. These routes connected the colonies to Europe, the Caribbean, and Africa. Trading ships carrying goods also carried people from Africa. These people were captured in Africa, forced across the Atlantic Ocean, and later sold into slavery. This cruel journey was called the **Middle Passage**.

 **TextWork**

❸ On the illustration, circle the building that was the center of town life. Why do you think the building was so important?

_____

_____

_____

_____

❹ How did colonists in New England use the land?

_____

_____

_____

_____

 **TextWork**

❺ Write a sentence about the Middle Colonies using the word *charter*.

_____

_____

_____

_____

_____

_____

❻ **LOCATION** Study the map below. Circle the colonies that were once New Netherland.

The Middle Colonies

In 1664, English warships sailed to New Netherland and took over the Dutch colony. New Netherland was then split into two new colonies—New York and New Jersey. The city of New Amsterdam became New York City.

Many of the early settlers who came to New Jersey were members of a religious group called the Quakers. In New Jersey, the Quakers hoped to find a safe place to worship.

King Charles II of England owed money to the father of William Penn, an English Quaker. Instead of paying back the money, he gave Penn a **charter**—a written approval to start a colony. Penn named his colony Pennsylvania. He also became the owner of the Delaware Colony.

People from many places came to the Middle Colonies. Many came as **indentured servants**. In exchange for the passage, or trip, to the colonies, they usually worked without pay. This period of work could last from 4 to 7 years. After that time, they were freed.

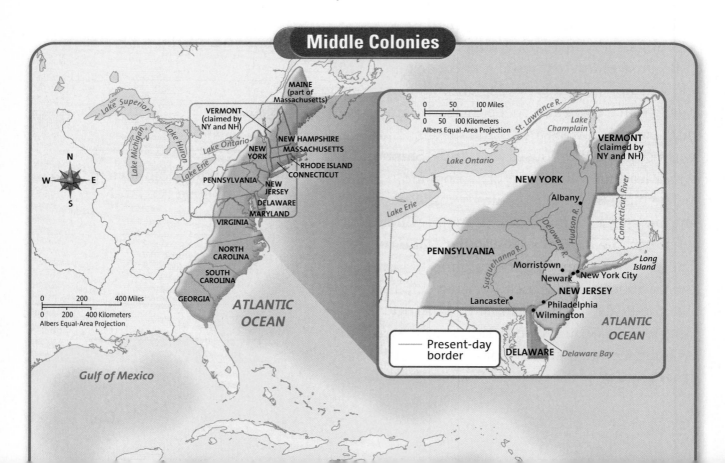

Middle Colonies

▶ FARMERS in the Middle Colonies often hired free Africans or used enslaved workers.

In the 1720s, a new religious movement called the Great Awakening began in the Middle Colonies. The number of church members in the colonies grew. **Religious toleration**, or the acceptance of differences in religion, also grew.

The Breadbasket Colonies

Unlike New England, the Middle Colonies had fertile soil and a climate that was better for growing crops. Farmers in the Middle Colonies grew so many crops used in making bread that the Middle Colonies were called the "breadbasket" colonies.

Farmers in the Middle Colonies went to market towns to sell or trade their livestock and crops. Every town had a gristmill, which ground grain into flour. New York City and Philadelphia were important port cities. There people could ship goods across the Atlantic Ocean to England.

Many colonists also worked in skilled trades. Young people learned skilled trades by becoming apprentices. An *apprentice* learned a trade from an experienced worker.

Women and girls had few chances to work outside the home. However, if a woman's husband died, she could take over his business.

TextWork

7 Scan the text about the Breadbasket Colonies. List one difference between the Middle Colonies and the New England Colonies.

_____

_____

_____

_____

8 Why do you think that most towns in the Middle Colonies had a gristmill?

_____

_____

_____

_____

TextWork

9 Underline the sentence that describes what caused the Calverts to start a new colony. Circle the name of this colony.

10 **LOCATION** Study the map below. Circle the towns in North Carolina. What was it about the location of these towns that you think made them important?

_____

_____

_____

_____

_____

_____

The Southern Colonies

In addition to Virginia, England started other colonies in the South. The Maryland Colony was founded by the Calverts, a wealthy English family. The Calverts were Catholic. They hoped to start a colony in North America that would be a safe place for Catholics.

In 1663, King Charles II gave land for a colony south of Virginia. The new colony was called Carolina. In 1712, Carolina's leaders split the colony into North Carolina and South Carolina.

James Oglethorpe had an idea for another colony. He wanted *debtors*, or people who had been put in prison for owing money, to settle the lands. The king of England liked Oglethorpe's idea and gave him a charter for the Georgia Colony.

The Southern Economy

The Southern Colonies depended on farming. Cash crops were grown on large farms called **plantations**. Much of the work on plantations was done by enslaved Africans.

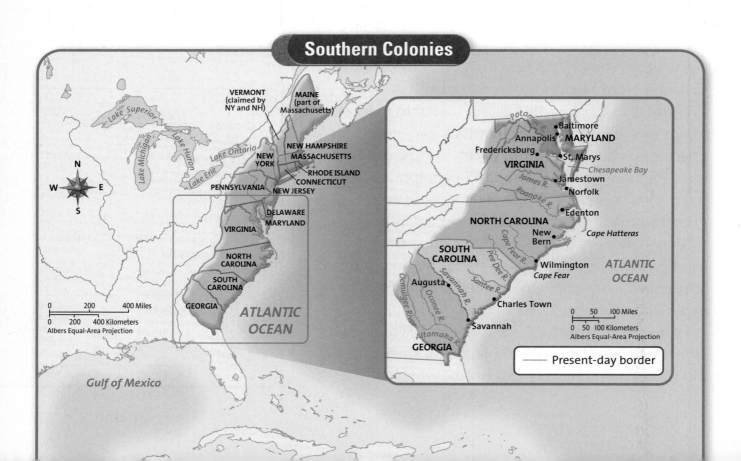

Southern Colonies

Most people in the Southern Colonies lived and worked on small farms. Few of these farmers had enslaved workers. Those who did often worked alongside their enslaved workers but did not treat them as equals.

In Maryland, Virginia, and North Carolina, tobacco was the main cash crop. In South Carolina and Georgia, the climate was too warm and wet for tobacco. Farmers there grew rice instead.

Rice did not grow well in areas where the land was higher and drier. There farmers found that they could grow indigo. Indigo is a plant that makes a blue dye used to color clothing.

As plantations got larger, more cash crops were shipped from the colonies. Cash crops were sent to port cities, such as Baltimore, Maryland, and Charles Town, South Carolina.

The Southern Colonies had other industries, too. Wilmington, North Carolina, became an important shipping center for lumber. Southern colonists made naval stores as well. **Naval stores** are goods used to make or repair ships. They include pine tar, turpentine, and pitch. Shipbuilding was also an industry in the Southern Colonies.

▶ **TRADE AND SHIPPING** Goods were often packed into large wooden barrels for shipping.

 TextWork

⓫ Study the illustration above. Why do you think crops and goods were packed in wooden barrels for shipping?

_____

_____

_____

_____

_____

_____

⓬ Scan the text on this page. Circle the Southern Colonies' main cash crops. Underline other industries in the Southern Colonies.

1. **SUMMARIZE** Where did colonists from England settle in North America?

_____

_____

_____

2. How did **dissent** in the Massachusetts Bay Colony lead to the founding of new colonies?

_____

_____

_____

3. List one similarity between present-day North Carolina and colonial North Carolina.

_____

_____

_____

Circle the letter of the correct answer.

4. What was an effect of the Great Awakening?

   A Religious toleration in the Middle Colonies grew.

   B There were fewer religious people.

   C There were fewer churches in the Middle Colonies.

   D Dissent in the Middle Colonies grew.

MATCHING Draw a line connecting each region on the left with the correct activities on the right.

5. The New England Colonies   grew lots of crops for making bread

6. The Middle Colonies   grew mainly cash crops, often on plantations

7. The Southern Colonies   raised many dairy cows and sheep

writing

✏ **Write a Diary Entry** Imagine that you are a colonist in the New England, Middle, or Southern Colonies. Tell which colony you live in, and then write a paragraph that describes your daily life.

The Colonies Unite

Both France and Britain, as England became known in 1707, claimed land in the Ohio River valley. In the 1750s, fighting broke out between the two countries over this land. This conflict was known as the French and Indian War. It ended in 1763. Britain won most of France's lands in North America.

After the French and Indian War, trouble grew between Britain and the American colonies. Britain expected people in the 13 colonies to obey all British laws. But many colonists grew unhappy with British rule. **What do you think this lesson will tell you about changes in the colonies?**

_____

_____

▶ **FANEUIL HALL in Boston, Massachusetts**

**NORTH CAROLINA
STANDARD COURSE OF STUDY**

4.04 Describe the causes and effects of the American Revolution, and analyze their influence on the adoption of the Articles of Confederation, Constitution, and the Bill of Rights.

Growing Problems

1 Why do you think that colonists wanted to settle in the backcountry?

_____

_____

_____

_____

2 Write a definition of the word *representation,* using your own words.

_____

_____

_____

_____

After the French and Indian War, many people began to move to the **backcountry**. This land was the land "in back of" the area settled by Europeans. These lands were home to many American Indian groups. As a result, fighting broke out.

To end the fighting, Britain's King George III made a *proclamation*, or formal announcement. The Proclamation of 1763 said that all lands west of the Appalachians belonged to American Indians. The Proclamation angered colonists who wanted to settle there.

Colonists Protest New Taxes

Britain needed money to pay for the French and Indian War. British leaders thought that the colonists should help. *Parliament*, the lawmaking branch of the British government, passed new tax laws to raise money. The colonists believed that Britain had no right to tax them. They had no **representation** in Parliament. No one in Parliament spoke for them.

▶ **THE BOSTON TEA PARTY** The colonists who took part in the Boston Tea Party refused to pay for the tea they had destroyed.

Many people **protested**, or worked against, these new taxes. Some colonists began to **boycott**, or refuse to buy, all British goods.

Fights often broke out between the colonists and British soldiers. One of the worst fights took place in Boston on March 5, 1770. Crispus Attucks, an African American sailor, and four other colonists were killed. This fight became known as the Boston Massacre. A *massacre* is the killing of many people who cannot defend themselves.

The Boston Tea Party

In 1773, Parliament passed the Tea Act. This law said that only the East India Company could sell tea to the 13 colonies. Colonists could either buy the tea—and pay the tax on it—or not drink tea.

In November 1773, three ships carrying tea reached Boston. On the night of December 16, 1773, about 150 colonists dressed as American Indians marched to Boston Harbor. They boarded the ships and threw more than 300 chests of tea overboard. Their angry protest became known as the Boston Tea Party.

TextWork

❸ What was one way that colonists *protested* new taxes?

_____

_____

_____

_____

❹ What was the cause of the Boston Tea Party?

_____

_____

_____

_____

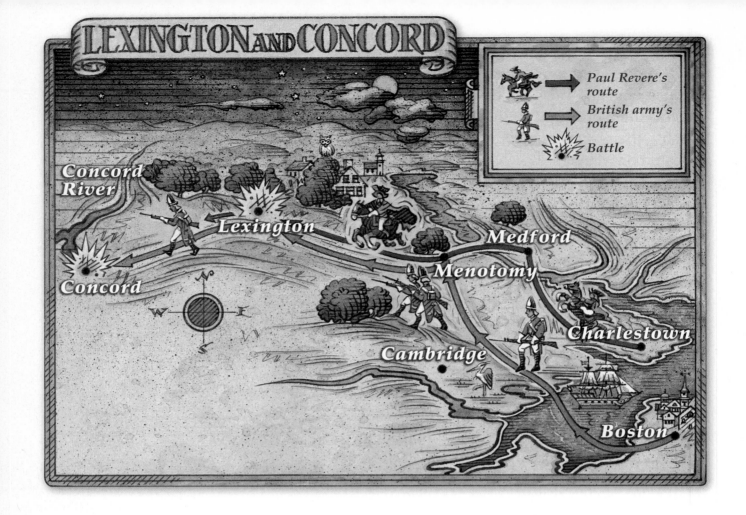

LEXINGTON AND CONCORD

Legend:
- Paul Revere's route
- British army's route
- Battle

Map labels: Concord River, Lexington, Concord, Medford, Menotomy, Cambridge, Charlestown, Boston

TextWork

5 MOVEMENT Study the map above. Circle the town in which Paul Revere's route began.

6 What caused Paul Revere to ride to Lexington to warn the townspeople?

_____

_____

_____

_____

_____

Colonists Join Together

In September 1774, colonial leaders met in Philadelphia. The meeting was later called the First Continental Congress. These leaders voted to stop most trade with Britain. They also asked the colonies to form *militias*, or armies of citizens. In Massachusetts, members of the militia were called **Minutemen**. They were said to be ready to fight at a minute's notice.

In April 1775, British soldiers marched toward Lexington and Concord, towns in Massachusetts. They planned to arrest colonial leaders and to take their weapons. The British wanted their march to Lexington to be a secret. Paul Revere found out about the plan. He rode to Lexington to warn the townspeople about the attack.

When the British arrived in Lexington, the Minutemen were waiting. No one knows which side fired first, but shots rang out. The British then moved on to Concord, where they met more resistance from Minutemen. After much fighting, the British decided to retreat, or fall back, to Boston.

The poet Ralph Waldo Emerson later called the first shot fired at Lexington "the shot heard 'round the world." The fighting in Lexington and Concord marked the beginning of a long war called the American Revolution. A **revolution** is a sudden, complete change of government.

The Road to War

The Second Continental Congress met on May 10, 1775. By June, colonial leaders agreed that the colonies should prepare for war.

The first step was for Congress to form an army. It was called the Continental Army. Congress chose George Washington as the leader of the Continental Army.

By the time Washington was chosen to lead the new Continental Army, the first major battle of the American Revolution had already been fought. On June 17, 1775, colonists fought with British soldiers on Breed's Hill, near Boston.

The fighting on the hill was much tougher than the British had expected. Twice they were forced back toward the Charles River. Eventually, though, the colonists had to retreat, and the British captured Breed's Hill.

The battle on Breed's Hill was wrongly named for nearby Bunker Hill. Although the British won the battle, they suffered heavy losses. More than 1,000 British soldiers had been killed or wounded. The British learned that fighting the colonists would not be as easy as they had thought. The British king promised to do anything that was necessary to crush the colonists' rebellion.

TextWork

7 Reread the text on this page. Circle the sentences that tell why the Battle of Bunker Hill was important.

8 Do you think the colonies could have made peace with Britain after the Battle of Bunker Hill? Why or why not?

_____

_____

_____

> **GEORGE WASHINGTON**

1. **SUMMARIZE** List one reason why the colonies decided to prepare for war.

_____

_____

_____

_____

2. In your own words, write a definition for the word **revolution.**

_____

_____

_____

3. List one effect of the French and Indian War on relations between the colonists and Britain.

_____

_____

_____

Circle the letter of the correct answer.

4. Why did King George III issue the Proclamation of 1763?

   A He wanted the colonists to take land from American Indians.

   B He wanted to stop the fighting between colonists and American Indians.

   C He wanted to give the land back to France.

   D He wanted to punish the colonists.

5. Why were the colonists angered by the new British tax laws?

   A They did not have to follow British laws.

   B They did not drink British tea.

   C They had no representation in Parliament.

   D They did not have money to pay taxes.

6. What was the first major battle of the American Revolution?

   A the Battle of Lexington

   B the Battle of Bunker Hill

   C the Battle of Concord

   D the Battle of Yorktown

activity

Draw a Cartoon Imagine that you are a colonist who is against British tax laws. Draw a cartoon that encourages others to boycott British goods.

The American Revolution

After the Battle of Bunker Hill, more colonists started to think that their problems with Britain could not be settled. They began to choose sides. They had to decide if they should stay loyal to Britain. More colonists began to call for *independence*—the freedom to rule themselves. **What might you learn about the American Revolution as you read this lesson?**

_____

_____

_____

▶ REENACTORS IN PHILADELPHIA

 NORTH CAROLINA
STANDARD COURSE OF STUDY

4.04 Describe the causes and effects of the American Revolution, and analyze their influence on the adoption of the Articles of Confederation, Constitution, and the Bill of Rights.

4.05 Describe the impact of wars and conflicts on United States citizens, including but not limited to, the Civil War, World War I, World War II, the Korean War, the Vietnam War, Persian Gulf War, and the twenty-first century war on terrorism.

▶ **PRESENTING THE DECLARATION** The Declaration of Independence was first presented in the Assembly Room of the Pennsylvania State House.

 **TextWork**

❶ Scan the text. Underline the sentences that tell why the Declaration of Independence is important.

❷ What effect do you think signing the Declaration had on the American Revolution and colonial leaders?

_____

_____

_____

_____

_____

Declaring Independence

On June 7, 1776, Richard Henry Lee slowly rose from his chair at the Second Continental Congress. He said that Congress should make a formal statement calling for independence. Congress decided to form a committee to write a *declaration*, or official statement, about independence. It would be sent to King George III. Thomas Jefferson, from Virginia, was to be the main writer.

On July 4, 1776, Congress voted to accept the Declaration of Independence. The colonies now thought of themselves as independent states. They were free to set up their own government.

By August 2, a copy of the Declaration was ready to be signed by the members of the Second Continental Congress. Signing the Declaration was dangerous. If the Americans lost the war, the British would punish the signers, maybe by death.

The Articles of Confederation

The Second Continental Congress had to decide how to unite the new states. It was decided that each state would govern itself but would work together on national issues. This first plan of government was the Articles of Confederation. It was a big change from being governed by a king.

Under the Articles, each state elected representatives to serve in a national legislature, called the Confederation Congress. Each state had one vote in the Confederation Congress. This Congress kept the states together during the American Revolution.

The national government was weak, however. Americans were fighting a war to win their independence. They feared that a strong national government might threaten their freedom. Because of this, the Articles of Confederation left most power with the states.

The national government had the power to declare war, make treaties, and borrow money. Still, it could not enforce laws, control trade, or collect taxes. It could ask for an army, but the states had to provide the soldiers.

❸ Why were the Articles of Confederation important?

_____

_____

_____

_____

❹ Scan the text on this page. Did Americans want a strong central government? Why or why not? Underline the sentences that tell you this.

❯ **JOHN DICKINSON helped write the Articles of Confederation.**

TextWork

5 Describe in your own words the meaning of the words *Patriot* and *Loyalist*.

- _____
- _____
- _____
- _____
- _____
- _____

6 Reread the text about personal hardships. Underline the sentences that describe hardships faced by Americans during the war.

▶ **LOSS OF PROPERTY** Colonists watch as British soldiers burn their home.

Americans and the Revolution

Colonists who supported independence were called **Patriots**. Those who remained loyal to Britain were called **Loyalists**. Some Loyalists fled to Canada, which was still loyal to Britain. About one-third of the colonists stayed *neutral*, or did not choose sides.

Personal Hardships

Americans faced many hardships. Towns were often attacked and burned by the British army. Some Patriots destroyed their own belongings and crops to keep them from being taken by the British.

Americans faced economic problems, too. One problem was a shortage of goods. British warships stopped trading ships from unloading goods at American ports. As the shortage of goods grew worse, prices rose.

Because there was a shortage of goods, some farmers and shopkeepers began charging extra-high prices for their crops or goods. Some states passed laws that limited how much people could charge. However, these laws were often broken.

▶ **AFRICAN AMERICANS in the First Rhode Island Regiment fought for the Patriots.**

African Americans

At the start of the war, one of every five people in the 13 colonies was of African descent. Some of the African Americans were free. However, most African Americans lived enslaved in the South.

About 5,000 enslaved African Americans fought for the Continental Army. Many were promised their freedom as a reward for their service. Peter Salem fought in the Battle of Bunker Hill. James Forten was just 14 years old when he joined the Continental Navy.

Women and the War

Women took on new roles during the war. Some raised money for the war and collected clothing for the soldiers. Others used their talents to support the Patriot cause. Mercy Otis Warren wrote poems and stories about people fighting for freedom.

Some girls and women joined the men in battle. Deborah Sampson dressed in men's clothes so that she could fight. Margaret Corbin was wounded after taking her husband's place in battle.

 **TextWork**

7 Scan the text on this page. Circle the sentence that describes how African Americans helped during the American Revolution.

8 Write two details relating to the main idea, Women and the War.

Details:

- _____

_____

- _____

_____

TextWork

9 Compare and contrast the American and British armies by listing one fact about each.

BRITISH: _____

_____

_____

AMERICAN: _____

_____

_____

10 Circle the sentences that tell why European countries decided to help the Americans.

Fighting for Independence

At first, the soldiers in the Continental Army had no uniforms. Many had no guns, so they carried spears and axes. Most soldiers were farmers who had enlisted, or signed up, to fight.

The British army was made up of experienced soldiers. The British army also used **mercenaries**, or hired soldiers. Even so, it was hard to fight a war 3,000 miles from home. The British had to wait a long time for supplies and soldiers to reach them.

At first, the British won many battles and captured many important cities. Then, in October 1777, the Continental Army won the Battle of Saratoga in New York. The British loss was a turning point in the war. A **turning point** is an event that causes an important change. After this victory, some European countries, including France, decided to help the Americans.

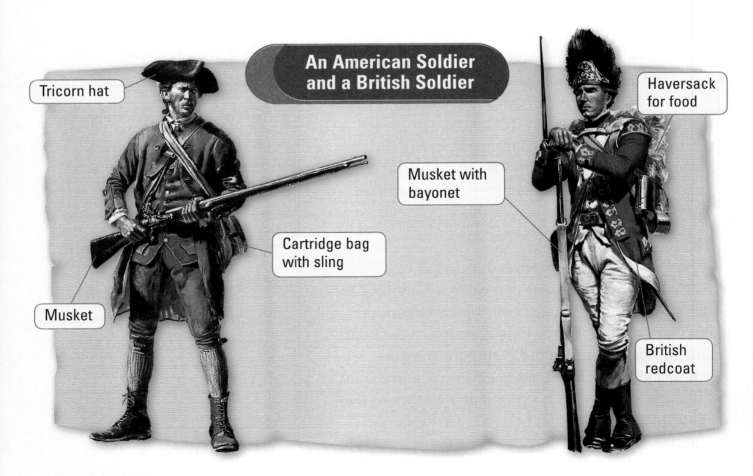

An American Soldier and a British Soldier

Tricorn hat

Haversack for food

Musket with bayonet

Cartridge bag with sling

Musket

British redcoat

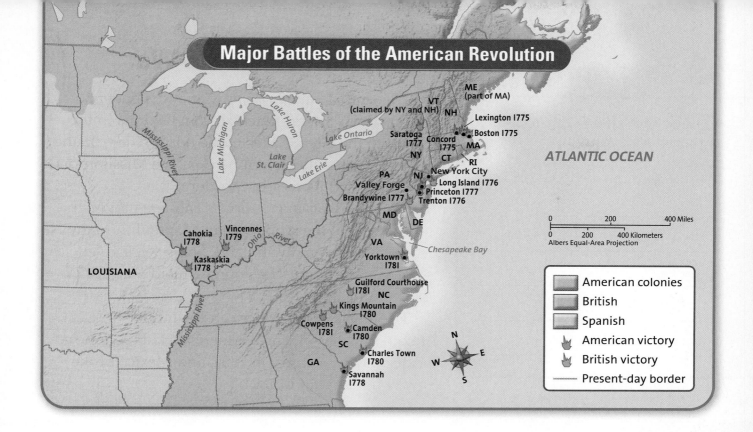

Major Battles of the American Revolution

The Americans still struggled. Washington's army spent the winter of 1777–1778 in Valley Forge, Pennsylvania. They did not have enough food or supplies. Finally, when the Americans received help, the army grew stronger.

Victory at Yorktown

In 1778, the British moved the fighting to the South. They hoped to beat the Americans before help from France could arrive. They also hoped to capture southern ports. The British won battles at Savannah, Georgia; Charles Town, South Carolina; and Guilford Courthouse, North Carolina. Still, the British had to use a lot of troops at the Battle of Guilford Courthouse. This weakened the British army.

By the summer of 1781, the British had set up their headquarters at Yorktown, Virginia. The Americans and the French made a plan to surround the British at Yorktown. After being surrounded for weeks, the British gave up on October 19, 1781.

TextWork

11 LOCATION Study the map above. Circle the battle that took place in North Carolina. How did this battle affect the British army?

_____

_____

12 How did the Americans defeat the British?

_____

_____

_____

 **TextWork**

Effects of the War

The United States was now an independent nation. Its borders stretched from Georgia in the south to the Great Lakes in the north. The Atlantic Ocean formed its eastern border. The Mississippi River formed its western border.

After the war, many former soldiers moved to areas west of the Appalachian Mountains. Many soldiers were paid with land. Some were given hundreds of acres. The young United States was slowly pushing west.

The ideals of the American Revolution spread to other places in North America. Haiti became an independent country in 1804, and Mexico broke away from Spain in 1821.

13 List two effects of the American Revolution.

- _____
_____
_____

- _____
_____
_____

Lesson 7 Review

1. **SUMMARIZE** How did the 13 colonies win their independence from Britain?

   _____
   _____
   _____

2. Use the word **mercenary** in a sentence about the American Revolution.

   _____
   _____

3. How did the American Revolution affect the daily lives of Americans?

   _____
   _____
   _____

4. What was the the turning point of the American Revolution?

   _____
   _____

 writing

 Write a Speech Imagine that you are in camp with the soldiers at Valley Forge. Write a speech to lift the soldiers' spirits.

The Young Nation

▶ INDEPENDENCE HALL in Philadelphia, Pennsylvania

After the American Revolution, high state taxes forced many people to borrow money. If they could not repay their debts, state courts sometimes took away their farms and homes.

In 1787, a group of farmers led by Daniel Shays tried to take over a weapons storehouse to protest the courts' actions. Because there was no national army, the state militia had to stop Shays. Shays's Rebellion made some people think that the national government could not keep order or protect them. **How will reading this lesson help you learn more about United States government?**

_____

_____

**NORTH CAROLINA
STANDARD COURSE OF STUDY**

4.04 Describe the causes and effects of the American Revolution, and analyze their influence on the adoption of the Articles of Confederation, Constitution, and the Bill of Rights.

1 What caused small states and large states to argue over representation?

_____

_____

_____

_____

2 Define the word *compromise* in your own words.

_____

_____

_____

_____

The United States Constitution

Many leaders believed that the country needed a stronger national government. In May 1787, leaders met at the Pennsylvania State House to create a new constitution. A **constitution** is a written plan of government. The meeting became known as the Constitutional Convention.

Compromises

The **delegates**, or representatives, disagreed about how each state would be represented in Congress. Delegates from large states wanted representation to be based on a state's population. Delegates from small states wanted each state to have the same number of representatives.

After a long debate, each side decided to **compromise**, or give up some of what it wanted. Congress would have two parts, or houses—the House of Representatives and the Senate. In the House of Representatives, representation would be based on population. In the Senate, each state would have two representatives. This agreement became known as the Great Compromise.

▶ **THE PENNSYLVANIA STATE HOUSE,** now called Independence Hall, is where delegates met in Philadelphia for the Constitutional Convention.

▶ NEWSPAPERS printed the Bill of Rights so that people could read it.

The delegates also disagreed about counting enslaved African Americans. Southern states wanted enslaved people to be counted as part of the population. Northern states said that enslaved people should not be counted.

The delegates finally agreed to count three-fifths of the total number of enslaved people in each state. This agreement later became known as the Three-Fifths Compromise.

Approving the Constitution

The Constitution was finished on September 17, 1787. Nine states had to **ratify**, or approve, it before it could go into effect.

Some states said they would be more willing to approve the Constitution if a *bill*, or list, of rights were added to it. This bill of rights would protect people's rights. Leaders promised to propose a bill of rights after the Constitution was ratified.

On June 21, 1788, New Hampshire became the ninth state to ratify the Constitution. As the leaders promised, the Bill of Rights was added to the Constitution in 1791.

 **TextWork**

❸ How did the delegates compromise about enslaved people?

_____

_____

_____

_____

❹ The table below shows the date and order in which each state ratified the Constitution. Which state was the ninth to ratify the Constitution?

_____

Why was this state important in approving the Constitution? Circle the sentence in the text that gives this information.

ORDER	STATE	DATE
Constitution Ratification Vote		
1.	Delaware	1787
2.	Pennsylvania	1787
3.	New Jersey	1787
4.	Georgia	1788
5.	Connecticut	1788
6.	Massachusetts	1788
7.	Maryland	1788
8.	South Carolina	1788
9.	New Hampshire	1788
10.	Virginia	1788
11.	New York	1788
12.	North Carolina	1789
13.	Rhode Island	1790

1. **SUMMARIZE** Describe one difference between the Articles of Confederation and the Constitution.

_____

_____

_____

_____

2. What is a **constitution**?

_____

_____

_____

3. How did the delegates compromise over representation in Congress?

_____

_____

_____

_____

Circle the letter of the correct answer.

4. Why did people want to write a new Constitution?

   A They wanted to make the national government stronger.

   B They wanted to give the national government less power.

   C They wanted to form a monarchy.

   D They wanted to give the states more power.

5. What was the compromise over how to count enslaved people called?

   A the Great Compromise

   B the Slavery Compromise

   C the Three-Fifths Compromise

   D the Representation Compromise

6. Why did some people want a bill of rights?

   A to protect the government's power

   B to explain the Constitution

   C to give more power to the states

   D to protect people's rights

7. Which was the first state to ratify the Constitution?

   A Rhode Island

   B Delaware

   C New York

   D North Carolina

writing

✎ **Write a Newspaper Article** Imagine that you are a newspaper reporter covering the Constitutional Convention. Write an article explaining how the delegates are writing the Constitution.

The United States grew rapidly in the 1800s. More immigrants arrived in the United States to find new opportunities. They wanted a chance to earn money and to own land.

The United States grew as more lands were added to the country. In time, the United States would stretch from the Atlantic coast to the Pacific coast. Soon new inventions and new ideas would change the ways Americans lived. **How will reading this lesson improve your understanding of the growth of the United States?**

_____

_____

WAGON TRAIN REENACTORS in North Dakota

NORTH CAROLINA STANDARD COURSE OF STUDY

4.03 Describe the contributions of people of diverse cultures throughout the history of the United States.

4.08 Trace the development of the United States as a world leader and analyze the impact of its relationships with Canada, Mexico, and selected countries of Central America.

❶ Scan the text on this page. Underline the sentences that give the reasons President Jefferson wanted to buy Louisiana from France.

❷ Study the time line below. Circle the date that Sacagawea joined the expedition. How did Sacagawea help the Corps of Discovery?

_____

_____

_____

_____

A Growing Nation

After the American Revolution, more pioneers wanted to move to lands west of the Appalachian Mountains. A **pioneer** is an early settler of an area. The Appalachians stood as a barrier to pioneers. Daniel Boone, a well-known pioneer, helped build the Wilderness Road through the Appalachians.

Lewis and Clark

President Thomas Jefferson wanted to make the United States bigger. He also wanted to have a port on the Gulf of Mexico. To do this, the United States bought Louisiana, including New Orleans, from France. The sale, called the Louisiana Purchase, more than doubled the size of the country.

Little was known about the lands of the Louisiana Purchase. Meriwether Lewis and William Clark led an expedition through the lands.

THE JOURNEY OF
LEWIS & CLARK

▶ Meriwether Lewis

MAY 1804

▶ William Clark

NOVEMBER 1804

▶ The Lewis and Clark expedition departs from St. Louis, Missouri

▶ Sacagawea joins the expedition and helps guide them west

▶ Meriwether Lewis keeps an expedition journal (above)

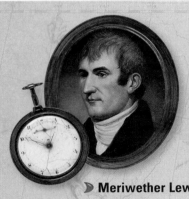

They put together a team of about 40 people that became known as the Corps of Discovery. Their expedition took more than two years. The Corps of Discovery learned many things about the new lands of the Louisiana Purchase.

The Indian Removal Act

In the early 1800s, many settlers moved to Cherokee lands in the Southeast. This caused conflicts between settlers and American Indians. In 1830, President Andrew Jackson signed the Indian Removal Act. It forced the Cherokee to move to Indian Territory, in what is now Oklahoma.

The Cherokee were forced to walk almost 800 miles, often in bad weather. One out of every four Cherokee died. The journey became known as the Trail of Tears. In time, the United States forced almost all American Indians east of the Mississippi River off their lands.

 **TextWork**

❸ Scan the text about the Indian Removal Act. Underline the sentences that describe what caused American Indians to be forced from their land.

❹ Where was the Indian Territory?

_____

_____

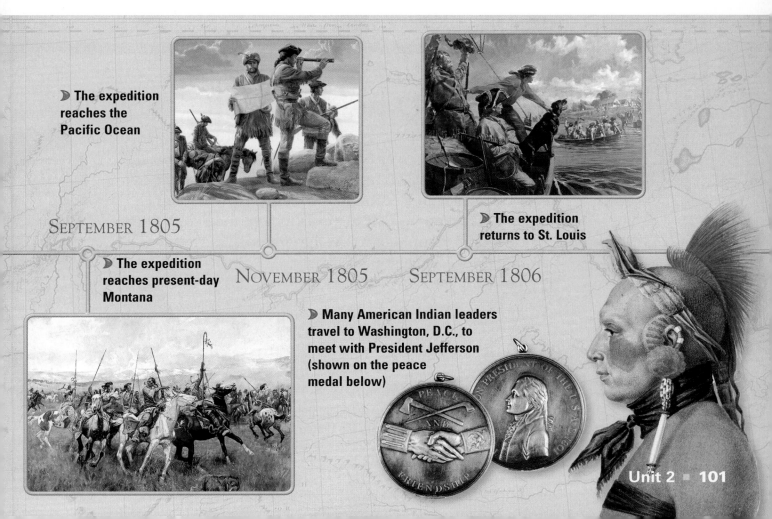

▶ **The expedition reaches the Pacific Ocean**

SEPTEMBER 1805

▶ **The expedition reaches present-day Montana**

NOVEMBER 1805

▶ **The expedition returns to St. Louis**

SEPTEMBER 1806

▶ **Many American Indian leaders travel to Washington, D.C., to meet with President Jefferson (shown on the peace medal below)**

TextWork

5 Scan the text on this page. Underline the sentence that describes why the Mexican government encouraged people to move to Texas.

6 Read Davy Crockett's biography below. What character trait would you use to describe Davy Crockett? Why?

_____

_____

_____

_____

The Mexican-American War

In 1821, Mexico won independence from Spain. Mexico took control of much of the Southwest, including Texas. Few people lived in Texas, so Mexico offered land there to encourage settlement. Many of these settlers were Americans.

Moving West

The Mexican government tried to stop further American settlement. General Antonio Lopez de Santa Anna, the leader of Mexico, sent troops to Texas to enforce Mexican laws. Fighting broke out. One group of Texans used a mission called the Alamo as a fort. They were defeated there after fighting for 13 days.

Texan leaders declared Texas independent and formed an army. In one battle, the Texan army captured Santa Anna. In return for his freedom, Santa Anna gave Texas its independence. Texas became a state in 1845.

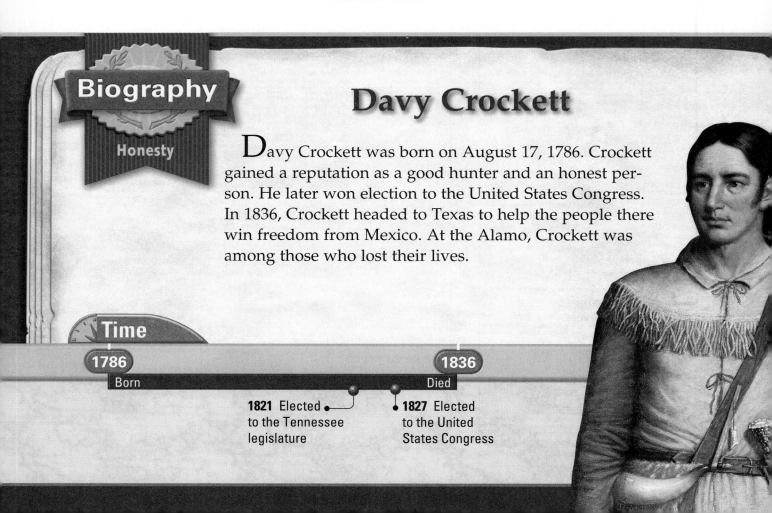

Biography

Honesty

Davy Crockett

Davy Crockett was born on August 17, 1786. Crockett gained a reputation as a good hunter and an honest person. He later won election to the United States Congress. In 1836, Crockett headed to Texas to help the people there win freedom from Mexico. At the Alamo, Crockett was among those who lost their lives.

Time

1786
Born

1836
Died

1821 Elected to the Tennessee legislature

1827 Elected to the United States Congress

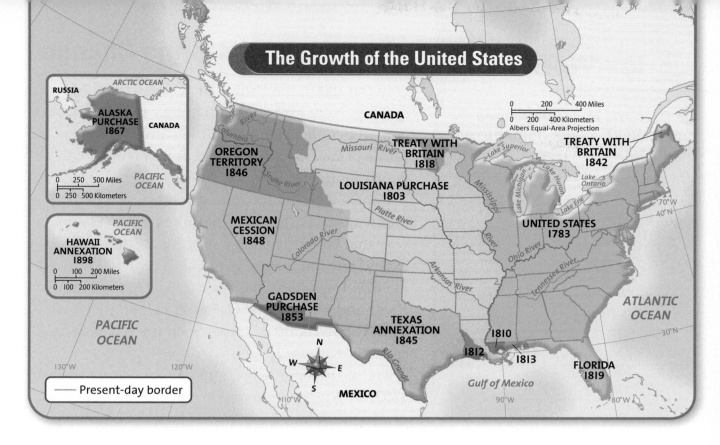

The Growth of the United States

Manifest Destiny

Many people in the United States believed in Manifest Destiny. **Manifest Destiny** is the idea that the United States should stretch from the Atlantic Ocean to the Pacific Ocean. Many settlers followed the Oregon Trail to Oregon. Other settlers traveled to Utah on the Mormon Trail.

Both the United States and Britain claimed Oregon. Arguments over Oregon almost caused a war. In 1846, the two countries agreed to fix the forty-ninth parallel as the border between the United States and Canada.

Mexico and the United States had never agreed about the Texas border. In 1846, the United States sent soldiers to the border. Fighting broke out.

After more than a year of fighting, the United States won the Mexican-American War. In exchange for peace, Mexico agreed to sell the United States a large area of land called the Mexican Cession. In 1853, the United States bought more land in the Gadsden Purchase.

TextWork

7 REGION Study the map above. Circle the lands gained by the United States in the Mexican Cession. In what year did the United States gain these lands?

_____

8 In your own words, explain the term _Manifest Destiny_.

_____

_____

_____

_____

9 Scan the text. Circle three new developments during this time period.

10 How was rail travel an improvement over travel by steamboats?

_____

_____

_____

_____

_____

▶ PASSENGERS and employees stand by a train on the DeWitt Clinton Railway.

Developments Bring Change

In the 1800s, the United States was growing quickly. New inventions and other developments helped people keep up with this growth. New forms of transportation let people travel and ship goods more easily.

Canals were built to get around river rapids and waterfalls. A *canal* is a human-made waterway that connects bodies of water. Canals can also extend natural waterways. The Erie Canal opened in 1825. It connects the Great Lakes to the Hudson River and the Atlantic Ocean. It helped make New York City a center of trade. Soon many states built canals.

The steam engine brought even more changes. In 1807, an American inventor named Robert Fulton used a steam engine to power a boat. Steamboats became the main form of travel on large rivers.

Steam power was also used in **locomotives**, or railroad engines. Rail travel was faster and cheaper than travel by steamboats. By 1850, more than 9,000 miles of railroad track crossed the country. Railroads made it easier for people to travel and ship goods.

> **FACTORIES** employed large numbers of workers.

The Industrial Revolution

During the 1800s, new inventions let people use machines to make goods. This change in the way goods were made came to be called the **Industrial Revolution**. Instead of working at home, more people moved to cities to work in factories.

In 1793, the first American textile mill opened in Rhode Island. That same year, Eli Whitney invented the **cotton gin**, a machine that could quickly remove seeds from cotton. The cotton gin let planters produce more cotton. Whitney also developed the idea of interchangeable parts. *Interchangeable parts* are parts that are exactly alike. With interchangeable parts, large amounts of goods could be made at one time.

In 1837, Samuel F. B. Morse invented the telegraph. It was a faster way to communicate. The telegraph sent messages from one machine to another along a wire.

Other inventions helped farmers. In 1832, Cyrus McCormick invented a mechanical reaper for harvesting grain. In 1837, John Deere invented a strong steel plow to cut through heavy soil.

 **TextWork**

11 Use the table to complete the picture graph.

Year	Number of Factories
1849	100,000
1859	150,000
1869	250,000

Increase in the Number of Factories in the United States, 1849–1869

1849

1859

1869

= 50,000 manufacturing businesses

1. **SUMMARIZE** List three ways the United States grew in the 1800s.

_____

_____

_____

_____

2. Use the word **pioneer** in a sentence about the growth of the United States.

_____

_____

3. List one way the Mexican-American War affected the United States.

_____

_____

_____

Circle the letter of the correct answer.

4. How did the Industrial Revolution affect the population of cities?

   A The population grew rich.

   B The population grew smaller.

   C The population grew larger.

   D The population stayed the same.

MATCHING Draw a line connecting the inventor on the left with the correct invention on the right.

5. Eli Whitney   telegraph

6. Samuel F. B. Morse   steel plow

7. John Deere   cotton gin

writing

Write a Persuasive Letter Imagine that you are an American in the 1840s. Write a letter to a friend, explaining why you are for or against Manifest Destiny.

Review and Test Prep

The Big Idea

All events in history are made up of people and places. These events often affect people and the land.

Summarize the Unit

(Focus Skill) **Cause and Effect** Complete the organizer to show that you understand the causes and effects of some key events in the history of North America.

Cause

Sieur de la Salle traveled to the mouth of the Mississippi River.

Effect

_____

_____

_____

_____

Minutemen were waiting for British soldiers when they arrived in Lexington.

Use Vocabulary

Fill in the missing word in each sentence, using the correct vocabulary word from the Word Bank.

1. The term _____ means "to approve."

2. Much of the work done on _____ was done by enslaved Africans.

3. A _____ is a loose group of governments working together.

4. Some _____ moved to Canada, which remained under British rule.

5. Many colonists _____ unfair taxes.

Word Bank

confederation p. 52

plantations p. 78

protested p. 83

Loyalists p. 90

ratify p. 97

Think About It

6. How did American Indians use the natural resources around them?

_____

_____

7. How did the discovery of new tools for navigation affect North America?

_____

_____

8. How did the Articles of Confederation make the national government weak?

_____

_____

Circle the letter of the correct answer.

9. Why did some enslaved African Americans fight for the Continental Army?

   A They did not like the British.

   B They were promised their freedom.

   C They were Loyalists.

   D They were mercenaries.

10. Why did President Thomas Jefferson want the United States to buy Louisiana from France?

   A to build the Mormon Trail

   B to stop Britain from buying it

   C to have a port on the Gulf of Mexico

   D to control Fort Mandan

Show What You Know

Writing Write a Scene
Imagine what the meeting between Sacagawea and Lewis and Clark might have been like. Write a scene for a play about this meeting. Tell why the meeting was important.

Activity Make a Museum Display
Make a museum display about North America's history to 1850. Decide which events, people, and places to include. Prepare a drawing, a map, a model, or a poster for your museum display.

GO online To play a game that reviews the unit, join Eco in the North Carolina Adventures online or on CD.

Civil War to Present

Spotlight on Goals and Objectives

North Carolina Interactive Presentations

NORTH CAROLINA STANDARD COURSE OF STUDY

COMPETENCY GOAL 4 The learner will trace key developments in United States history and describe their impact on the land and people of the nation and its neighboring countries.

▶ **THE LINCOLN MEMORIAL, IN WASHINGTON, D.C.**

 # The Big Idea

How can growth and change have an impact on the land and the people of a nation and its neighbors?

Over time, all of the countries of North America have grown and changed. Today, people live in almost every part of North America. As people spread out over the continent, they changed the land. By changing the land, people sometimes affected the people already living on that land. Over time, new inventions and discoveries have also brought growth and change to the land and the people of North America.

Study the two photos. What examples of growth and change do you see? Describe the ways that growth and change affected both the land and the people.

▶ Boston, Massachusetts, 1800s

▶ Boston, Massachusetts, today

How have growth and change affected the land and the people? _____

_____

_____

_____

Reading Social Studies

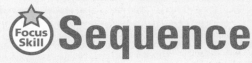

Sequence

⟫ LEARN

Sequence is the order in which events happen. Noticing the sequence of events helps you understand what you read. Dates help show sequence. So do certain words, such as *first, second, third, next, then, last, finally, later,* and *after*.

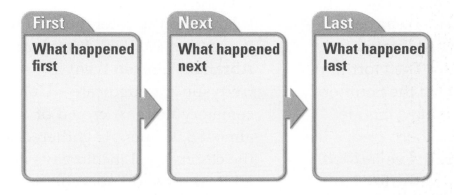

First	Next	Last
What happened first	What happened next	What happened last

⟫ PRACTICE

Underline the sequence hints in the paragraphs. The first paragraph has been done for you.

Slavery divided Americans, and many Americans wanted to see it ended. John Brown was one of them. He was willing to use violence against people to end slavery. First, Brown and a group of men went to Harper's Ferry, in what is now West Virginia, in October 1859. Next, they took guns from a government storehouse. Brown wanted to give the guns to enslaved people so they could fight for their freedom.

The plan failed. Two days later, Brown was captured. Most of his group was either killed or captured. Then, Brown was put on trial on October 27. He was found guilty on November 2. Finally, he was hanged one month later.

Sequence

Read the article. Then complete the activities below.

The Battle of Gettysburg

Slavery was just one of the many issues that divided the United States in the mid-1800s. First, many Southern states had separated from the United States to become their own country. Then, a war began between the Northern states and the Southern states. The Northern states fought to keep the Southern states from remaining separate.

In June 1863, Southern troops led by General Robert E. Lee headed north. They reached the town of Gettysburg, Pennsylvania, on July 1. There, they met a Northern army led by General George G. Meade.

The fighting at Gettysburg raged for three days. It was one of the deadliest battles of the war. During those three days, more than 3,000 Northern troops and almost 4,000 Southern troops were killed. In addition, more than 20,000 troops on each side were wounded or reported missing. The Northern army won the battle. After the battle, General Lee's army marched back to Virginia.

Four months later, on November 19, 1863, President Abraham Lincoln went to Gettysburg to dedicate a Union cemetery there. A crowd of almost 6,000 people gathered for the ceremony. Lincoln gave an address, or short speech, that day. His speech lasted for less than three minutes. Yet today, this speech is one of the most famous speeches in American history.

In his Gettysburg Address, Lincoln spoke about the ideas of liberty and equality on which the country had been founded. He honored the soldiers who died defending those ideas.

1. In the first paragraph, circle the words that show sequence.

2. Underline the sentence that tells when the Battle of Gettysburg began.

3. Circle the sentence that tells what happened immediately after the Battle of Gettysburg.

4. How many months after the battle did President Lincoln give the Gettysburg Address?

_____

The North and the South

In the 1850s, the North and the South were very different regions. In the North, most people worked in trade, in factories, or on small farms. In the South, the economy depended largely on agriculture. Enslaved Africans worked on plantations that grew mainly cotton and tobacco. The North and the South disagreed about slavery and other issues. In time, the disagreements led to war. **How will reading this lesson improve your understanding of United States history?**

_____

_____

A PLANTATION HOUSE near Vacherie, Louisiana

NORTH CAROLINA STANDARD COURSE OF STUDY

4.05 Describe the impact of wars and conflicts on United States citizens, including but not limited to, the Civil War, World War I, World War II, the Korean War, the Vietnam War, Persian Gulf War, and the twenty-first century war on terrorism.

4.06 Evaluate the effectiveness of civil rights and social movements throughout United States' history that reflect the struggle for equality and constitutional rights for all citizens.

TextWork

1 Write a sentence using the terms *free state* and *slave state*.

_____

_____

_____

2 Scan the text about the Missouri Compromise. Circle the sentence that explains the details of this compromise.

▶ **ARGUMENTS OVER TAXES** President Andrew Jackson believed the federal government could set taxes on trade. Many Southerners disagreed with this idea. Boston (below) was a center of trade in the North.

A Divided Nation

The Mason-Dixon line runs near the border between Pennsylvania and Maryland. It was the dividing line between free states and slave states. A **free state** did not allow slavery. A **slave state** did. For a time, there was an equal number of free states and slave states. This kept a balance between the North and the South in the United States Senate.

The Missouri Compromise

In 1819, Missouri wanted to join the United States as a slave state. Missouri would have upset the balance between free states and slave states. Congress debated the issue. Henry Clay of Kentucky came up with a compromise. He said that Missouri should join as a slave state and Maine should join as a free state. Clay's plan became known as the Missouri Compromise.

Many people in the South believed in states' rights. *States' rights* is the idea that each state should have the final say on laws that affect it. Many people in free states thought that the national government should have the final say on certain types of laws.

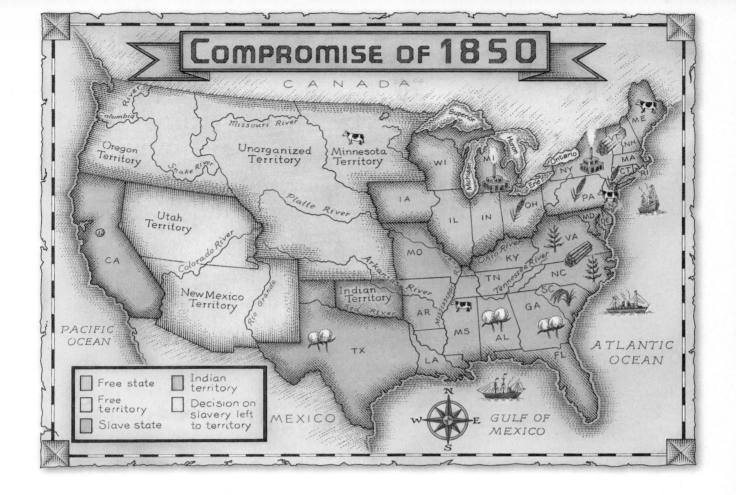

The Compromise of 1850

In 1850, California asked to join the United States as a free state. This would give the free states more votes in the United States Senate.

Henry Clay worked toward the Compromise of 1850. Under this plan, California became a free state. The other lands from the Mexican Cession would be divided into territories. The people living there would decide if they should have slavery.

The Fugitive Slave Act was also part of this compromise. A **fugitive** is someone who escapes from the law. The Fugitive Slave Act forced all Americans to turn in people who had escaped from slavery. Many Northerners did not like this law.

In 1854, the Kansas-Nebraska Act was passed. It let people living in Kansas and Nebraska decide if they wanted slavery. People for and against slavery moved to Kansas. Fighting broke out. After a vote, the people of Kansas decided not to allow slavery.

 TextWork

❸ Scan the text on this page. Underline the sentence that explains the Fugitive Slave Act.

❹ Read the events described below. Then write the event that comes next.

• **United States leaders agree to the Compromise of 1850.**

• **The Fugitive Slave Act is passed.**

• _____

_____

_____

UNDERGROUND RAILROAD ROUTES

Free states
Slave states
Major routes of the Underground Railroad

Working Against Slavery

Sometimes, enslaved people rebelled. In 1831, an enslaved man named Nat Turner led an attack that killed more than 50 people. Plantation owners in the area ended the rebellion. More than 100 enslaved people were killed.

Many white Northerners and free African Americans also worked against slavery. They were *abolitionists,* or people who wanted to end slavery.

Abolitionists often spoke out against slavery. Sojourner Truth gained her freedom in 1827. She traveled the country, speaking out against slavery. Frederick Douglass became well known for writing and speaking against slavery. He had escaped from slavery in 1838.

Other people worked to help enslaved people escape. The **Underground Railroad** was a system of secret escape routes. It led enslaved people to free lands in the North, Canada, the Caribbean, and Mexico. Conductors, or helpers, along the Underground Railroad led runaways to hiding places. Harriet Tubman, a former enslaved person, was one of the best-known conductors.

TextWork

5 **MOVEMENT** Study the map above. With your finger, trace the Underground Railroad routes that ended in Canada. Then circle the areas on the map where these routes began.

6 Scan the text about people who worked against slavery. List three people who worked against slavery.

_____

_____

_____

Dred Scott was an enslaved man who traveled with his owner. After his owner died, Scott went to court to win his freedom. He said that he should be free because he had once lived in a free state.

In 1857, the Supreme Court ruled against Scott. Many people had hoped that the Dred Scott case would settle the disagreements over slavery. Instead, the decision made the problem worse.

The Election of 1860

Some Southerners began to worry that the United States government would end slavery in all areas. The new Republican party was made up mainly of Northerners. It was against allowing slavery to spread into new places.

In 1860, the Republican party chose Abraham Lincoln of Illinois to run for President. Some Southerners said that they would **secede** from, or leave, the United States if Lincoln became President. Lincoln won the election, and seven Southern states soon seceded from the United States.

TextWork

7 What was the result of the Dred Scott court case?

_____

_____

_____

_____

_____

8 Scan the text about the election of 1860. What happened after Lincoln was elected President? Underline the sentence that gives this information.

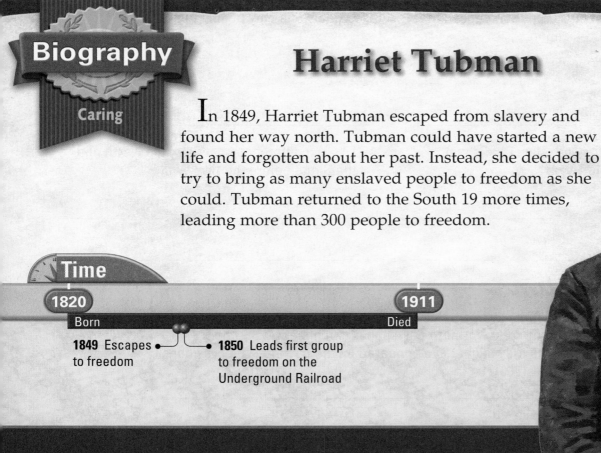

Biography

Caring

Harriet Tubman

In 1849, Harriet Tubman escaped from slavery and found her way north. Tubman could have started a new life and forgotten about her past. Instead, she decided to try to bring as many enslaved people to freedom as she could. Tubman returned to the South 19 more times, leading more than 300 people to freedom.

Time

1820		1911
Born		Died

1849 Escapes to freedom

1850 Leads first group to freedom on the Underground Railroad

The Civil War Begins

The Southern states that seceded formed their own government. It was called the Confederate States of America, or the Confederacy. The United States was known as the Union.

The Confederate states took over federal property in their states. However, the Union still had control over Fort Sumter in South Carolina. President Lincoln sent a ship to carry supplies to the fort. Confederate troops decided to attack the fort before the ship arrived.

The attack on Fort Sumter began a civil war. A **civil war** is a war between people in the same country. After the Battle of Fort Sumter, four more Southern states left the Union and joined the Confederacy.

▶ **FORT SUMTER** was the site of the first battle of the Civil War.

Lesson 1 Review

1. **SUMMARIZE** List one event that caused the United States to break apart.

2. How did arguments over slavery and states' rights lead to a **civil war**?

3. What is one way people fought against slavery?

4. List two differences between the North and the South before the Civil War.

writing

✏ **Write Newspaper Headlines** Write two newspaper headlines, one for a Northern newspaper and one for a Southern newspaper, as they might have appeared on the day after the presidential election of 1860.

The Civil War and Reconstruction

After the Battle of Fort Sumter, both the Union and the Confederacy made plans to win the Civil War. The Union's plan for winning the war was to first weaken the South and then attack it. The Confederacy's plan was to defend their lands from attack and to make the war last a long time.

The Civil War would last four years. It would cause the destruction of cities, the death of hundreds of thousands of soldiers, and a weakened economy. **How will reading this lesson improve your understanding of the Civil War?**

_____

_____

CIVIL WAR REENACTORS in Clinton, Georgia

NORTH CAROLINA STANDARD COURSE OF STUDY

4.05 Describe the impact of wars and conflicts on United States citizens, including but not limited to, the Civil War, World War I, World War II, the Korean War, the Vietnam War, Persian Gulf War, and the twenty-first century war on terrorism.

❶ Scan the text about early Civil War battles. Underline the sentence that explains how people's thoughts about the Civil War changed after the Battle of Bull Run.

❷ Write one effect for the cause given below.

Cause: Abraham Lincoln began to see that slavery had to end.

Effect: _____

_____

_____

❸ **REGIONS** Circle the border states on the map below.

Early in the Civil War

The first major battle of the Civil War was the Battle of Bull Run near Manassas Junction, Virginia. It was a long battle, but the Confederacy finally won. People soon understood that the war would last far longer than they had first thought.

In September 1862, the Confederates marched into the North. They were met by Union forces at Antietam in Maryland. More soldiers died in the Battle of Antietam than on any other day during the war. The Confederates were forced back into Virginia.

The Emancipation Proclamation

When Lincoln took office, he was not against slavery in the South. Lincoln did not want slavery to spread to the West. As the war continued, he began to see that slavery had to end. He decided to **emancipate**, or free, all enslaved people in areas still fighting against the Union. On January 1, 1863, President Lincoln signed the Emancipation Proclamation.

The United States in 1861

Legend:
- Union state
- Border state
- Confederate state
- Territory

Advantages in the Civil War	
NORTHERN ADVANTAGES	
More industry	
Advanced railroad system	
Strong navy	
SOUTHERN ADVANTAGES	
Large number of military leaders	
Troops experienced in outdoor living	
Familiar with the environment of the South	

Union Victories

In May 1863, Union General Ulysses S. Grant and his army attacked Vicksburg, Mississippi. The Union army kept people from bringing in food, water, and weapons to the city. After almost two months, Vicksburg finally gave up. Taking control of Vicksburg gave Union forces control of the Mississippi River.

On May 6, 1863, Confederate General Robert E. Lee won a major victory at Chancellorsville, Virginia. The Confederate army then decided to march into the North. Southern leaders thought that if they could win a major victory in a Northern state, people in the North would demand an end to the war.

In June 1863, General Lee's troops headed north. For three days, they fought the Union army at Gettysburg, Pennsylvania. About 7,000 soldiers were killed, and more than 20,000 on each side were wounded. The Union won the battle.

TextWork

❹ Study the table above. How would an advanced railroad system help the North?

_____

_____

_____

_____

_____

❺ Which event started first, the Battle of Vicksburg or the Battle of Gettysburg?

_____

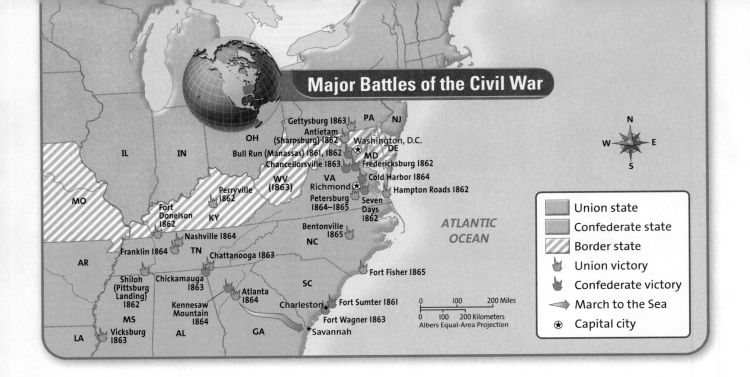

Major Battles of the Civil War

Gettysburg 1863
Antietam (Sharpsburg) 1862
Washington, D.C.
Bull Run (Manassas) 1861, 1862
Chancellorsville 1863
Fredericksburg 1862
Cold Harbor 1864
Richmond
Hampton Roads 1862
Petersburg 1864–1865
Seven Days 1862
Perryville 1862
Fort Donelson 1862
Bentonville 1865
Nashville 1864
Franklin 1864
Chattanooga 1863
Shiloh (Pittsburg Landing) 1862
Chickamauga 1863
Atlanta 1864
Kennesaw Mountain 1864
Charleston
Fort Sumter 1861
Fort Wagner 1863
Savannah
Fort Fisher 1865
Vicksburg 1863

IL, IN, OH, PA, NJ, MO, WV (1863), VA, DE, MD, KY, TN, NC, SC, AR, MS, AL, GA, LA

ATLANTIC OCEAN

N W E S

0   100   200 Miles
0   100   200 Kilometers
Albers Equal-Area Projection

Union state
Confederate state
Border state
Union victory
Confederate victory
March to the Sea
Capital city

TextWork

6 **PLACE** Study the map above. Who won the Battle of Chattanooga?

_____

7 Read the events described below. Then write the event that comes next.

• **General Robert E. Lee surrenders.**

• **The Civil War ends.**

• _____

_____

_____

_____

The War Ends

The Union victory at Gettysburg marked a turning point in the war. General Lee's army marched back to Virginia. It would never again be able to carry out a major attack on the Union.

In 1864 and 1865, the Union army kept winning battles. William Tecumseh Sherman and his army marched across the South to the sea. They destroyed land and property. In April 1865, Union soldiers took over Richmond, the Confederate capital.

General Lee's army was starving and out numbered. On April 9, 1865, General Lee surrendered to General Grant in the Virginia village of Appomattox (a•puh•MA•tuhks) Court House. Soon, other Confederate generals gave up. After four years, the Civil War was over.

Just five days after Lee's surrender, President Lincoln was **assassinated**, or murdered, by John Wilkes Booth. Booth supported the Confederacy. Lincoln's death shocked the nation.

Reconstruction

Before Lincoln was killed, he had started to make plans for the **Reconstruction**, or rebuilding, of the nation. Lincoln wanted to bring the nation back together quickly. He did not want to punish the people of the South.

After Lincoln's death, Andrew Johnson became President. Johnson, too, wanted to help the nation come together quickly. He allowed most Confederates to become full citizens again. They had to say they were loyal to the United States. Confederate states could rejoin the Union after they abolished slavery.

Many members of Congress had a different plan for Reconstruction. Congress put the Southern states under military rule. Union army officers acted as governors, and soldiers kept order. Southern states had to write new constitutions that gave African American men the right to vote.

After the war, the nation approved three amendments. The Thirteenth Amendment ended slavery. The Fourteenth Amendment gave equal rights to all citizens. The Fifteenth Amendment gave African American men the right to vote.

▶ **RECONSTRUCTION** Many cities, such as Richmond, Virginia, had to be rebuilt after the Civil War.

TextWork

8 Scan the text. Circle two results of Congress's Reconstruction plan.

9 Study the chart below. Then write one difference between Johnson's plan and Congress's plan.

_____

_____

_____

_____

Reconstruction Plans

Johnson's Plan	Congress's Plan
• Southern states not treated too harshly	• Wanted to strictly punish the Southern states
• Supported the 13th Amendment to abolish slavery	• Supported the 13th Amendment to abolish slavery
• Southern states could have elections	• Southern states would be under military rule
• State laws could limit rights of African Americans	• Supported the 14th Amendment
• States should decide who could and could not vote	• Supported the 15th Amendment

Reconstruction Ends

The **freedmen**—people who had been enslaved—wanted to start new lives. However, finding a job was difficult. Congress set up the Freedmen's Bureau to help. It gave food and supplies to former enslaved people and taught them to read and write.

Many enslaved people went back to work on plantations. Landowners paid workers by letting them keep a share of the crops they harvested. This system, called sharecropping, did not let African Americans earn much money.

Over time, white Southerners took back control of their state governments. They passed laws to keep African Americans from voting. In 1877, Reconstruction ended. African Americans soon lost many of the rights they had gained.

> **VOTING** This illustration shows African American men voting. A soldier is protecting the voters.

Lesson 2 Review

1. **SUMMARIZE** How did the Union defeat the Confederacy in the Civil War?

_____

_____

2. Use the word **Reconstruction** in a sentence about the Civil War.

_____

_____

3. Which battle was the turning point of the Civil War? Explain.

_____

_____

4. What happened to African Americans after Reconstruction ended?

_____

_____

writing

Write an Editorial Imagine that you are the editor of a newspaper in Kentucky. Write an editorial that argues why this border state should secede or why it should stay in the Union and find a peaceful solution to the slavery issue.

Growth and Change

⟩ **STEEL MILL in Homestead, Pennsylvania**

After the Civil War, many more Americans moved to the West. They often settled on lands that American Indians were using. As a result, American Indians were forced to move to different areas.

New industries created new jobs. Immigrants came to the United States to look for jobs and opportunities. Many African Americans moved to cities in the North and the Midwest for the same reasons. **What do you think you will learn about growth and change in the United States from reading this lesson?**

_____

_____

_____

**NORTH CAROLINA
STANDARD COURSE OF STUDY**

4.02 Explain when, where, why, and how groups of people settled in different regions of the United States.

4.03 Describe the contributions of people of diverse cultures throughout the history of the United States.

TextWork

❶ Scan the text on this page. Underline the sentence that describes the effect of the Homestead Act.

❷ List two reasons why living on the Great Plains was difficult.

_____

_____

_____

_____

_____

▶ **SOD HOUSES** Many homesteaders used sod to build their houses, but sod houses were difficult to keep clean.

The Last Frontier

In the 1800s, discoveries of gold and silver drew more people to the West. When people discovered gold or silver in a place, miners moved into the area and set up mining camps. Towns sometimes grew around the camps. After a few years, the deposits often ran out. Miners then moved to other places. Entire towns were abandoned.

As cities in the East grew, the demand for beef also grew. Large-scale cattle ranching had begun in Texas in the early 1800s. At first, ranchers sent cattle to cities near the Gulf of Mexico, such as Galveston, Texas. When railroads were built, by the 1870s, ranchers drove cattle to towns that grew up around railroads, such as Abilene, Kansas.

In 1862, Congress passed the Homestead Act. This law opened the Great Plains to settlement. Thousands of Americans and about 100,000 immigrants from Europe settled on the Great Plains. They started ranches and farms.

Living on the Great Plains was very difficult. There were few streams and few trees for wood. Droughts and dust storms were common there.

In the winter, snow and cold temperatures often covered the region. Insects were also a problem for farmers there. In 1874, grasshoppers came by the millions and ate all the crops.

Conflicts with American Indians

As more people moved to the West, they forced American Indians off their lands. The United States government wanted to move all American Indians to **reservations**. These were areas of land set aside by the government for use only by American Indians. Much of the reservation land was not as good as the American Indians' original lands.

In the 1860s, members of the Sioux Nation lived in the Black Hills in what is now South Dakota. After gold was discovered there, the United States sent soldiers to move all the Sioux to reservations. Some Sioux fought back, but they were later defeated and forced to move.

Other groups fought back as well. However, by 1880, almost all American Indians in the United States lived on reservations.

 TextWork

❸ What happened as more people moved west?

_____

_____

_____

_____

_____

❹ Underline the sentence that gives a definition of the term *reservation*.

TextWork

5 Underline the names of the two railroad companies that built the Transcontinental Railroad.

6 **LOCATION** Study the map below. Circle the name of the town where the two tracks of the Transcontinental Railroad met.

Transcontinental Railroad

- Promontory
- Sacramento
- Omaha

— Transcontinental Railroad

New Industries

After the Civil War, new inventions helped industries grow and change. Inventors came up with new ways to help businesses work better and faster. Sometimes, inventions helped create whole new industries.

The Transcontinental Railroad

The population of the West was growing quickly. The United States needed a way to connect its East and West coasts. In 1862, the United States Congress gave two railroad companies—the Union Pacific and the Central Pacific—the right to build a **transcontinental railroad**. This railroad would cross North America, linking the East and the West.

The Union Pacific built its railroad west from near Omaha, Nebraska. The Central Pacific built east from Sacramento, California. Thousands of Chinese and Irish immigrants were hired to lay the tracks.

On May 10, 1869, the two railroads met in Promontory, Utah. Many more railroads were built across the United States. People could now sell their goods in markets around the country.

▶ **CHINESE WORKERS** on the Central Pacific Railroad cut 15 tunnels through the solid rock of the Sierra Nevada.

Steel and Oil

Iron rails were first used for train tracks. As larger trains began to carry more goods, the rails needed to be replaced with something stronger. Steel rails were stronger, but they were expensive.

In 1872, a Scottish immigrant named Andrew Carnegie learned about a new way to make steel. He started a steel mill in Pittsburgh, Pennsylvania.

Steel was used for many things. Steel frames made it possible to build longer bridges and taller buildings. These new buildings seemed to touch the sky, so they were called *skyscrapers*. Skyscrapers became common in large cities.

In 1887, iron ore was found west of Lake Superior. This helped the steel industry spread to cities along the Great Lakes, such as Cleveland, Ohio, and Chicago, Illinois.

The oil industry also developed in the late 1800s. In 1863, John D. Rockefeller set up an oil refinery near Cleveland, Ohio. A *refinery* is a factory that turns *crude*, or raw, oil into goods that people can use. Over time, Rockefeller bought more refineries. By 1882, he controlled the oil industry.

▶ **THE BROOKLYN BRIDGE** in New York was the first steel-wire suspension bridge.

7 Why did railroads begin using steel rails?

_____

_____

_____

_____

_____

8 Did Andrew Carnegie open his first steel mill before or after John D. Rockefeller set up an oil refinery near Cleveland, Ohio?

_____

Rose Cohen

At the age of 12, Rose Cohen came from Russia to New York City. Rose got a job sewing coats to earn money.

Rose worked in a dark, crowded place called a sweatshop. Sweatshops were clothing factories where workers made dresses, shirts, and coats. The women and girls worked from before sunrise until long after dark. Rose earned $3 a week.

Later, Rose stopped working in sweatshops. She became a union leader.

Make It Relevant: Compare and contrast Rose's childhood with yours.

 **TextWork**

❾ What was Thomas Edison's most famous invention?

_____

❿ Circle the term *labor union*. Underline the context clues that give a definition of this term.

A Changing Economy

In the late 1800s, the United States economy began to change. New inventions helped the economy grow, and workers gained more rights.

Inventions

In the late 1800s, Thomas Alva Edison opened a laboratory in New Jersey. His best known invention was the first practical lightbulb. An African American engineer named Lewis Lattimer, who worked for Edison, helped improve the lightbulb. Lattimer also directed the building of Edison's first central electric power station.

In 1876, Alexander Graham Bell produced a new telephone. In 1877, he started the first telephone company in the United States.

Labor Unions

In the late 1800s, most workers received low pay for long hours. Many people worked 10- or 12-hour days. Workers began to form labor unions. A *labor union* is a workers' group that tries to get better working conditions. These groups began to ask for better wages and an 8-hour workday.

Cities and Immigration

Between 1860 and 1910, about 23 million immigrants arrived in the United States. Many came to make a new life. Some wanted to escape violence and poverty in their home countries.

Immigrants from Europe arrived at Ellis Island in New York Harbor. Immigrants from Asia arrived at Angel Island in San Francisco Bay.

Immigrants were often poor. Many lived in crowded, poorly built apartment buildings called **tenements**. Some immigrants found jobs in new industries. Others had a hard time finding jobs and learning English. Some children had to work full-time to help their families.

Many Americans did not like the new immigrants. Some Americans felt that because some immigrants had little education, they should not take part in a democracy. Others worried that newcomers would take their jobs.

 **TextWork**

11 List two reasons immigrants came to the United States.

_____

_____

_____

_____

_____

12 Scan the text. Underline the reasons many Americans were opposed to new immigrants.

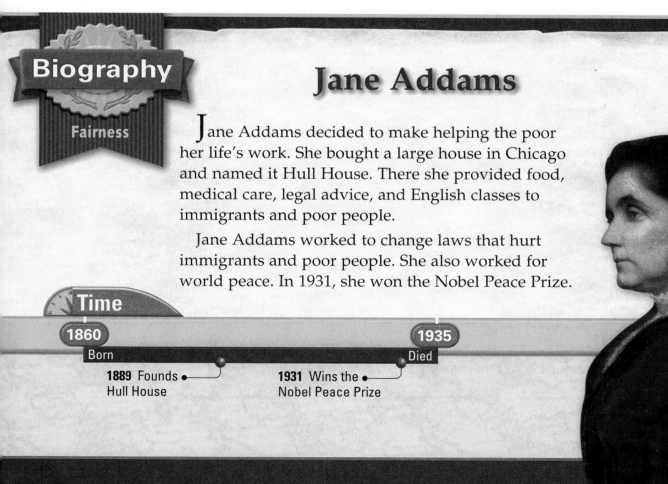

Biography

Fairness

Jane Addams

Jane Addams decided to make helping the poor her life's work. She bought a large house in Chicago and named it Hull House. There she provided food, medical care, legal advice, and English classes to immigrants and poor people.

Jane Addams worked to change laws that hurt immigrants and poor people. She also worked for world peace. In 1931, she won the Nobel Peace Prize.

Time

1860			1935
Born			Died

1889 Founds Hull House

1931 Wins the Nobel Peace Prize

African Americans Migrate

▶ THE GREAT MIGRATION brought thousands of African Americans to northern cities such as Chicago, New York City, and Detroit.

In the early 1900s, thousands of African Americans began moving from the South to northern cities. They moved to find better jobs and opportunities than they had in the South. This movement of people was so large that it became known as the Great Migration. Many African Americans found jobs in factories in northern cities.

Before the early 1900s, nearly nine of every ten African Americans lived in the South. After the Great Migration, more than half of all African Americans lived in the Northeast and the Midwest.

Lesson 3 Review

1. **SUMMARIZE** How did the United States grow and change in the late 1800s?

_____

_____

_____

2. Use the word **tenement** in a sentence about immigrants.

_____

_____

3. How did people moving west change the lives of American Indians?

_____

_____

_____

4. What problems did immigrants face?

_____

_____

activity

Create a Chart Make a chart showing the inventors mentioned in this lesson and their inventions. Illustrate your chart.

A Growing Power

By the late 1800s, the United States was a leader in industry and agriculture. In time, the United States gained control of lands in other parts of the world. The United States was becoming a world power. Its control and power now reached far beyond its own lands. **What might you learn about the United States as you read this lesson?**

_____

_____

THE USS *WYOMING*, a United States Navy ship

NORTH CAROLINA STANDARD COURSE OF STUDY

4.05 Describe the impact of wars and conflicts on United States citizens, including but not limited to, the Civil War, World War I, World War II, the Korean War, the Vietnam War, Persian Gulf War, and the twenty-first century war on terrorism.

4.08 Trace the development of the United States as a world leader and analyze the impact of its relationships with Canada, Mexico, and selected countries of Central America.

UNITED STATES POSSESSIONS, 1900

THEODORE ROOSEVELT

Russia

Alaska
1867

☐ U.S. possession
1857 Date acquired

1867
Aleutian Islands

Canada

NORTH
AMERICA

ASIA

China

Japan

PACIFIC OCEAN

United States

ATLANTIC
OCEAN

Midway
Islands 1867

1898 Wake
Island

1898 Hawaiian
Islands

Mexico

1898 Cuba

Philippine
Islands

1898

Johnston
Island 1858

Guam

Howland
Island 1857

1858 Kingman Reef

1898 Palmyra Island

1898

Puerto
Rico

1898

Baker
Island 1857

1857 Jarvis Island

N

W   E

S

SOUTH
AMERICA

1899 American Samoa

AUSTRALIA

TextWork

❶ PLACE Study the map above. Circle the Hawaiian Islands. When did the United States get possession, or control, of the Hawaiian Islands?

---

❷ Scan the text on this page. Underline two areas the United States gained control of in the late 1800s.

New Lands

In the late 1800s, the United States added new lands that were far from the rest of the country. In 1867, the United States bought Alaska from Russia. In 1898, Hawaii became a part of the United States. Both Alaska and Hawaii became states in 1959.

The Spanish-American War

In the 1890s, two of Spain's colonies were fighting for independence. They were Cuba, in the Caribbean Sea, and the Philippines, in the Pacific.

Many Americans supported Cuba. In January 1898, President William McKinley sent the battleship *Maine* to Havana, Cuba. He wanted to protect Americans who were living there. In February, the *Maine* exploded. More than 260 American sailors died. The cause of the explosion was not clear, but many Americans blamed Spain.

On April 21, President McKinley ordered a **blockade** of Cuba. United States Navy ships kept other ships from entering or leaving Cuba.

Congress declared war on Spain on April 25, 1898. The Spanish-American War lasted less than four months. On August 12, 1898, Spain signed an **armistice**, or agreement to stop fighting.

After the Spanish-American War, the United States became a world power. Spain agreed to give the United States control of Cuba, Puerto Rico, Guam, and the Philippines. Cuba and the Philippines later became independent countries, but Puerto Rico and Guam remain territories of the United States.

The Panama Canal

The United States stretched from the Atlantic Ocean to the Pacific Ocean. It took a long time and a lot of money to transport goods across the country by train. It took even longer to sail all the way around the tip of South America.

In 1901, Theodore Roosevelt became President. He wanted to build a canal across the Isthmus of Panama in Central America. The canal would link ports on the Atlantic coast of the United States and those on the Pacific coast. In 1904, work on the Panama Canal began. Ten years later, the Panama Canal opened.

TextWork

3 Use the word *armistice* in a sentence.

_____

_____

_____

_____

4 Scan the text about the Panama Canal. Circle the reason Theodore Roosevelt wanted to build the Panama Canal.

▶ **TUGBOATS** pull the SS *Kroonland* through the Panama Canal.

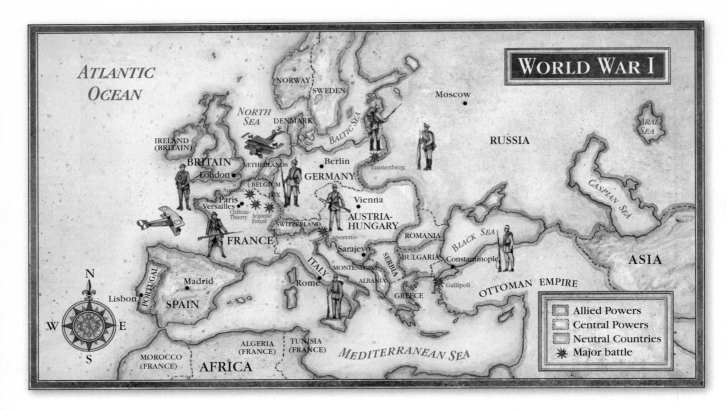

ATLANTIC OCEAN

WORLD WAR I

NORWAY
SWEDEN
Moscow

NORTH SEA
DENMARK
BALTIC SEA
RUSSIA

ARAL SEA

IRELAND (BRITAIN)
BRITAIN
London
NETHERLANDS
Berlin
GERMANY
Tannenberg

CASPIAN SEA

Somme
BELGIUM
LUX.
Paris
Versailles
Château-Thierry
Argonne Forest
SWITZERLAND
Vienna
AUSTRIA-HUNGARY

FRANCE

Caporetto
Sarajevo
ROMANIA
BLACK SEA

ASIA

PORTUGAL
Madrid
ITALY
Rome
MONTENEGRO
ALBANIA
SERBIA
BULGARIA
Constantinople
Gallipoli
OTTOMAN EMPIRE

Lisbon
SPAIN
GREECE

N
W E
S

MOROCCO (FRANCE)
ALGERIA (FRANCE)
TUNISIA (FRANCE)
MEDITERRANEAN SEA

AFRICA

Allied Powers
Central Powers
Neutral Countries
✳ Major battle

TextWork

5 Underline the sentences that describe the reasons many Americans changed their minds about entering World War I.

6 Write a number—1, 2, or 3—next to the description of the events below to place them in the correct order.

_____ Germany announces it will attack and sink all ships in the Atlantic.

_____ A Serbian rebel shoots and kills Archduke Francis Ferdinand of Austria-Hungary.

_____ President Wilson asks Congress to declare war on Germany.

World War I Begins

By 1914, most nations in Europe had joined one of two alliances. An **alliance** is an agreement among groups or individuals to help each other. On one side were the Allied Powers—Britain, France, Russia, Italy, and Serbia. On the other side were the Central Powers—Germany, Bulgaria, Austria-Hungary, and the Ottoman Empire.

On June 28, 1914, a Serbian rebel shot and killed Archduke Francis Ferdinand of Austria-Hungary. Austria-Hungary declared war on Serbia. The Allies and the Central Powers were drawn into the war. The war later became known as World War I.

At first, most Americans did not want the United States to fight in the war. Then, in 1915, a German submarine sank the British ship *Lusitania*. About 1,200 people drowned, including 128 Americans.

In 1917, Germany announced it would attack and sink all ships in the Atlantic. President Woodrow Wilson asked Congress to join the Allies and declare war on Germany.

Fighting the War

The United States had a small army. Congress passed a law to set up a **military draft**. This is a way to add people into the military. All men between the ages of 21 and 30 had to sign up.

The United States had to supply the Army quickly. The government took over parts of many industries. Factories began making war supplies. Many men left their jobs to join the Army. The need for more workers created new opportunities, especially for women and African Americans.

Most American soldiers went to France. The fighting there was **trench warfare**. The Allies and the Central Powers both dug deep trenches in the ground to protect themselves. Each side tried to move into the area between the trenches. New weapons, such as machine guns and barbed wire, made these moves dangerous. Tanks, poison gas, and airplanes also made the fighting more deadly.

The American troops helped the Allies win the war. On November 11, 1918, Germany signed an armistice. After four years and millions of deaths, the war was over.

TextWork

7 Why did the United States government take over parts of many industries?

_____

_____

_____

_____

_____

8 Circle two ways in which fighting in World War I was different from fighting in previous wars.

➤ **PILOTS AND MECHANICS** test planes at an airfield in France.

1. **SUMMARIZE** What caused the United States to become a world power?

_____

_____

_____

_____

2. Explain the word **alliance** in your own words.

_____

_____

_____

_____

3. Why do you think Americans supported Cuba in its fight for independence from Spain?

_____

_____

_____

_____

4. What was the result of the Spanish-American War?

_____

_____

_____

_____

Circle the letter of the correct answer.

5. Which American President wanted to build the Panama Canal?

  A Franklin D. Roosevelt

  B Herbert Hoover

  C Theodore Roosevelt

  D Woodrow Wilson

6. What event caused Austria-Hungary to declare war?

  A the assassination of Archduke Francis Ferdinand

  B the sinking of the *Lusitania*

  C the invasion of France

  D the formation of the Central Powers

writing

✏ **Write a Letter** Imagine that you are living during World War I. Write a letter to a soldier in the war. Tell what life at home is like.

Good Times and Hard Times

The 1920s were good times for many Americans. Factories no longer had to make war supplies. Americans were able to buy many kinds of new goods. Diverse cultures helped start new forms of art and music. New forms of entertainment, such as radio and movies, gave people more ways to spend their free time. However, the good times after World War I did not last forever. Soon, Americans were again faced with hard times. **What do you think you will learn about life in the United States after World War I?**

_____

_____

▶ **RUSH-HOUR TRAFFIC in Chicago, Illinois, 1926**

**NORTH CAROLINA
STANDARD COURSE OF STUDY**

4.03 Describe the contributions of people of diverse cultures throughout the history of the United States.

1 When did women gain suffrage in national elections? Did this happen before or after the end of World War I?

_____

2 Circle the consumer goods mentioned in the text. Then give a definition, in your own words, of the term *consumer goods*.

_____

_____

_____

_____

▶ **MARCHING FOR SUFFRAGE** After the war, President Wilson supported woman's suffrage.

After the War

World War I brought many changes to people at home in the United States. American women had been working for equal rights since the 1840s. By 1915, some states had given women **suffrage**, or the right to vote, in some state and local elections. Women still could not vote in national elections.

During the war, more women worked outside the home. They worked in offices and factories. Because of this, more people supported woman's suffrage. In 1920, the Nineteenth Amendment was ratified, and women got full voting rights.

When World War I ended, there was no longer a need for factories to make war supplies. Factories started to make *consumer goods* such as vacuum cleaners, washing machines, refrigerators, toasters, and radios. Many of these goods were popular because more people had electricity in their homes.

People bought many goods after the war. Perhaps the one that people wanted most was the automobile. By 1923, companies were making more than 3 million automobiles each year.

PRESIDENT WILSON SAYS:
"This is the time to support Woman Suffrage."

PRES
"I urge the peo
for Woman Suffra

▶ JAZZ Louis Armstrong (above left) was a famous jazz artist.

Entertainment

Artists in the 1920s were looking for new ways to express themselves. This new spirit of artistic freedom changed many art forms. Among them was a kind of music called jazz. Jazz grew out of African American music from the South.

New forms of entertainment gave Americans new ways to spend their free time. Radio stations began airing shows in the 1920s. By 1929, more than 800 stations reached about 10 million families. The most popular activity of the 1920s was going to the movies. By 1929, almost 90 million Americans went to the movies each week.

The Good Times End

During the 1920s, many Americans put money in the stock market. The **stock market** is a place where people can buy or sell *stocks,* or shares of companies. If more people want to buy than to sell, the price of a stock goes up.

In 1929, stock prices suddenly fell. People tried to sell all their stocks. On October 29, 1929, the stock market crashed. Many people who owned stocks lost all of their money.

TextWork

❸ What were two new forms of entertainment in the 1920s?

_____

_____

❹ In your own words, define the term *stock market.*

_____

_____

_____

_____

_____

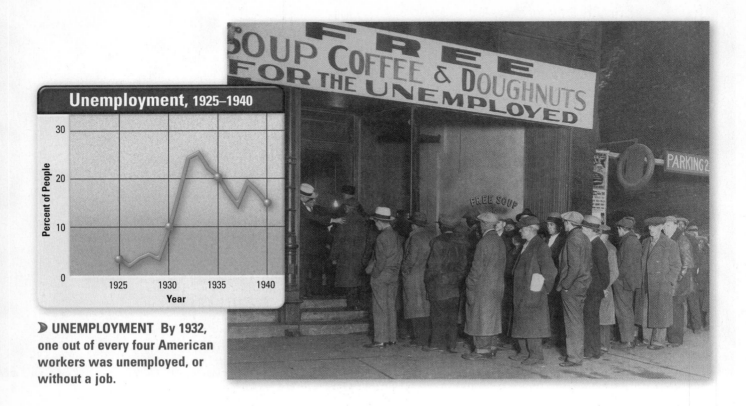

Unemployment, 1925–1940

Percent of People

0, 10, 20, 30

1925 1930 1935 1940

Year

▶ UNEMPLOYMENT By 1932, one out of every four American workers was unemployed, or without a job.

![TextWork]

5 Study the graph above. How did the percent of unemployed people change from 1930 to 1935?

_____

_____

6 List two effects of the Great Depression on Americans.

_____

_____

_____

_____

The Great Depression

The stock market crash caused many businesses to close. People lost their jobs. Many people raced to banks to get their savings. However, banks did not have enough money to give people. Thousands of banks closed. People lost their savings.

The 1930s was a period of hard times called the Great Depression. A **depression** is a time of little or no economic growth. Many people lose jobs and have little money.

The Great Depression was a time of suffering for many Americans. Many families did not have enough money for food. Families lost their homes and farms when they did not have the money to pay for them. People suffered even more because there were no government programs to help them.

The New Deal

In 1933, Franklin D. Roosevelt became President. Roosevelt promised Americans programs he called the New Deal. He believed that these programs would help end the Great Depression.

In 1935, Congress passed the Social Security Act. Social Security pays money to people after they retire. Another law created the Tennessee Valley Authority, or TVA. Many people worked for the TVA. They built dams in the Southeast.

Other laws created the Civilian Conservation Corps (CCC), as well as the Works Progress Administration (WPA). The CCC gave jobs to unemployed young people. CCC workers planted trees, made hiking trails through the woods, and made shelters for hikers all across the United States. The WPA helped build roads, hospitals, and parks. It also gave jobs to artists and writers. The WPA hired actors to put on plays and musicians to write music and put on concerts.

Not all of the New Deal programs worked. By the end of the 1930s, thousands of people were still without jobs and short of money. However, the New Deal gave people hope. It also gave the federal government more power. In addition, it made the federal government larger.

 **TextWork**

7 How did the Tennessee Valley Authority help workers in the southeastern United States?

_____

_____

_____

_____

8 Scan the text. What did the WPA do? Underline the sentences that give this information.

▶ **NEW JOBS** The CCC and the WPA put more than 11 million men and women back to work.

1. **SUMMARIZE** How did the Great Depression change life in the United States?

_____

_____

_____

2. Use the word **suffrage** in a sentence.

_____

_____

_____

3. How did the New Deal change the government?

_____

_____

_____

Circle the letter of the correct answer.

4. Which President started the New Deal?
   - **A** Woodrow Wilson
   - **B** Theodore Roosevelt
   - **C** Herbert Hoover
   - **D** Franklin D. Roosevelt

MATCHING Draw a line connecting each New Deal program on the left with the correct description on the right.

5. Tennessee Valley Authority

planted trees, made trails, and built shelters

6. Works Progress Administration

built dams in the south-eastern United States

7. Civilian Conservation Corps

built roads, hospitals, and parks

writing

✏ **Write a Newspaper Article** Imagine that you are a reporter living in the 1930s. Write a newspaper article explaining how the Great Depression has changed life in the United States.

World War II

During the 1930s, much of the world faced economic troubles. In Europe, many people were still rebuilding their countries after World War I. In Asia, some countries were running out of resources needed to make their economies grow. Powerful new leaders in some European and Asian nations promised to solve their countries' problems by force. These countries would soon threaten the United States and the rest of the world. **What do you think this lesson will teach you about World War II?**

_____

_____

▶ **NATIONAL WORLD WAR II MEMORIAL in Washington, D.C.**

**NORTH CAROLINA
STANDARD COURSE OF STUDY**

4.05 Describe the impact of wars and conflicts on United States citizens, including but not limited to, the Civil War, World War I, World War II, the Korean War, the Vietnam War, Persian Gulf War, and the twenty-first century war on terrorism.

4.08 Trace the development of the United States as a world leader and analyze the impact of its relationships with Canada, Mexico, and selected countries of Central America.

▶ ADOLF HITLER (center) prepares to address German soldiers.

Before the War

After World War I, Germany did not have enough money to pay for war damages. Its economy suffered. In the 1920s, Adolf Hitler became the leader of a political party called the Nazis. He had fought for Germany in World War I. He wanted to make Germany a powerful nation again.

The Nazis, or National Socialists, grew in power. Nazi soldiers used force to silence anyone who disagreed with them. In 1933, the Nazi party took control of Germany. Hitler began ruling as a *dictator*, or a leader with complete control.

Dictators also rose to power in several other countries. In 1922, Benito Mussolini took power in Italy. In 1924, Joseph Stalin took control of the Soviet Union (U.S.S.R.). The Soviet Union had been formed from many countries following a revolution in Russia in 1917.

In Japan, a group of military officers took control of the government. To get the resources Japan's industries needed, these military leaders decided to take over other nations in Asia. Italy and Germany also began taking over other countries.

![TextWork]

❶ List two countries in Europe that had dictators in the 1920s and 1930s.

_____

_____

❷ Skim the text. What did the governments of Italy, Germany, and the Soviet Union have in common?

_____

_____

_____

In 1939, nearly two million German troops marched into Poland. They attacked with tanks on land and planes in the air. The Germans called this fighting style *blitzkrieg*, or "lightning war." Two days later, Poland's allies, Britain and France, declared war on Germany. World War II had begun.

By the end of 1941, much of Europe was under German control. Only Britain, the Soviet Union, and a few small nations that did not take sides remained free from German control.

The United States Enters the War

Germany's invasions shocked and angered most Americans. However, many Americans did not want to fight in another war in Europe.

On December 7, 1941, Japanese planes bombed Pearl Harbor, a United States Navy base in Hawaii. Americans were angry about the attack. They wanted to go to war against Japan, Germany's ally.

The next day, the United States joined the war on the side of the Allies—Britain, France, and the Soviet Union. They fought against the Axis Powers—Germany, Italy, and Japan.

 **TextWork**

❸ Read the description of the event below. Then write the event that came next.

• **In 1939, German troops invaded Poland.**

• _____

_____

_____

❹ Study the illustration below. Circle the USS *Arizona*. Today, the sunken remains of this ship are a memorial to the soldiers and sailors who lost their lives defending Pearl Harbor.

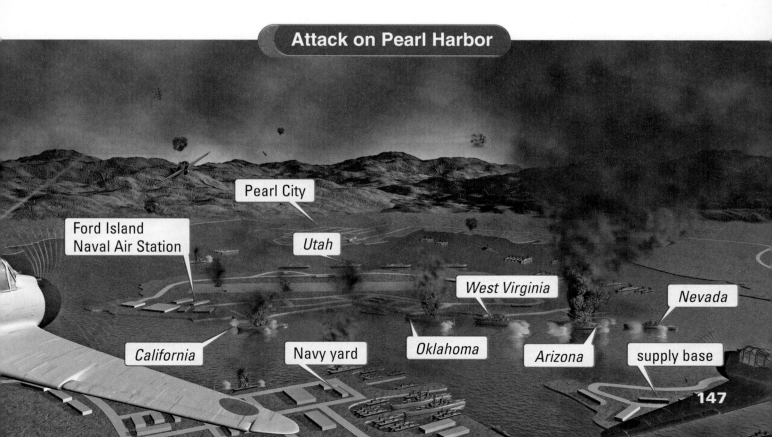

Attack on Pearl Harbor

Pearl City

Ford Island Naval Air Station

Utah

West Virginia

Nevada

California

Navy yard

Oklahoma

Arizona

supply base

5 Use the word *rationing* in a sentence about World War II.

_____

_____

_____

_____

6 How did World War II affect Japanese Americans?

_____

_____

_____

_____

_____

▶ **INTERNMENT CAMPS** About 110,000 Japanese Americans were held in internment camps.

Americans and the War

During World War II, the United States government took over many factories to make war supplies. Americans went to work in factories, shipyards, and aircraft plants. Many workers were women. They replaced the men who left to fight in the war. The war effort created many jobs and finally ended the Great Depression.

The government wanted to make sure that there were enough goods for all the soldiers. New rules called for **rationing**, or limiting what people could buy. People had to have coupons to buy goods such as butter, sugar, meat, and gasoline. They could buy only a certain amount of these goods.

World War II led to terrible problems for Japanese Americans. Many of them had been born in the United States and were citizens. But some people feared that Japanese Americans might help Japan invade the United States.

In February 1942, President Franklin D. Roosevelt ordered soldiers to put most Japanese Americans in **internment camps**. The camps, located mostly in western states, were enclosed by barbed wire and guarded by soldiers.

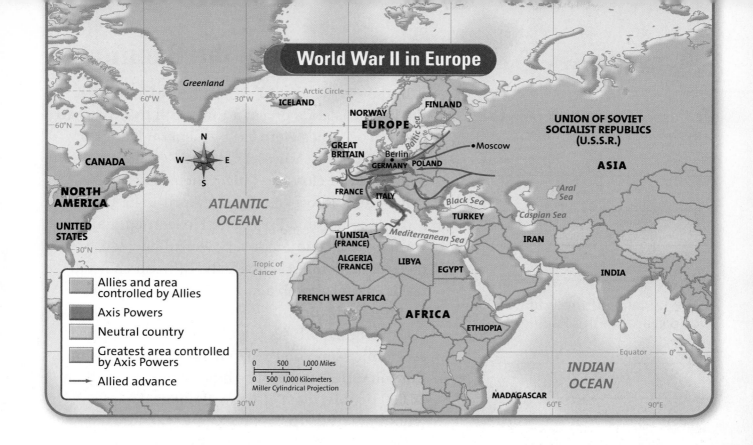

World War II in Europe

The War in Europe

The Allies planned to take control of the Mediterranean Sea. To do this, they needed to beat the Germans and Italians in North Africa. In 1942, American troops, led by General Dwight D. Eisenhower, invaded North Africa. By 1943, the Allies had won North Africa. The fighting then moved to Italy, where it lasted until June 1944.

The Allies also planned to take over France. On June 6, 1944, the date known as D day, Eisenhower led the Allies in the largest water-to-land invasion in history. About 2,700 ships sailed from Britain, with more than 175,000 troops aboard. They landed in Normandy, in northern France.

Many soldiers died, but the plan was successful. The Allies moved inland, pushing the German army back from the west. The Soviet Union pushed the Germans back from the east. On May 8, 1945, the Allies accepted Germany's surrender. The war in Europe was over.

 TextWork

❼ **LOCATION** Study the map above. Circle the labels for the United States and Europe on the map. How do you think the location of the United States was helpful to the country in the war?

_____

_____

_____

❽ What name was given to the date of the Allied invasion of France? When did it happen?

_____

_____

9 Describe the Allied plan to win the war in the Pacific.

_____

_____

_____

_____

10 What caused the end of World War II in the Pacific?

_____

_____

_____

_____

The War in the Pacific

In the Pacific, the Allies planned to take back the Pacific islands one at a time until they reached Japan. The Allies were led by General Douglas MacArthur and Admiral Chester W. Nimitz. As the Allies moved closer to Japan, their losses grew.

President Roosevelt died in April 1945. Harry S. Truman became President. He learned that the United States had made a powerful new weapon, the atomic bomb. He made the difficult choice to use an atomic bomb against Japan. He wanted to end the war quickly.

On August 6, 1945, the United States dropped an atomic bomb on the Japanese city of Hiroshima (hir•uh•SHEE•muh). The bomb killed more than 75,000 people, most of them civilians. Japan still would not give up.

On August 9, the United States dropped another atomic bomb on the city of Nagasaki (nah•guh•SAH•kee). Japan finally surrendered. On August 15, World War II ended.

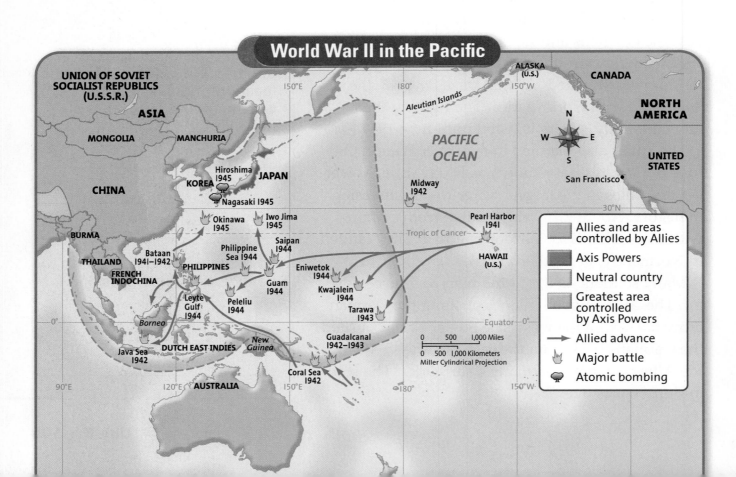

World War II in the Pacific

The Holocaust

Not until the war in Europe was over did people fully understand everything that Hitler and the Nazis had done. The Nazis had put millions of people in prisons called **concentration camps**. As Allied troops marched across Europe, they freed people in the camps. The Allies learned that the Nazis had murdered millions of men, women, and children in those camps.

The Nazis killed people for many reasons. They killed many for their religious and political beliefs. Others were killed because they were ill or disabled. The largest group of people killed were Jews. Hitler blamed them for Germany's problems.

During the war, Hitler ordered the murder of more than 6 million Jewish people. This terrible mass murder of more than two-thirds of all European Jews became known as the **Holocaust**.

Beginning in 1945, the Allies brought Nazi leaders to trial. They were charged with war crimes. Many of them were convicted and sentenced to death for their crimes.

❯ **PRISONERS** Before being imprisoned, many Jewish people were forced to wear a yellow Star of David (above) to make them stand out.

 **TextWork**

⓫ Circle the main idea of the second paragraph. Then underline the sentences that support the main idea.

⓬ Explain in your own words the word *Holocaust*.

_____

_____

_____

_____

_____

1. SUMMARIZE List one cause and one effect of World War II.

_____

_____

_____

2. Use the term **internment camp** in a sentence.

_____

_____

_____

3. How did World War II help people get back to work?

_____

_____

_____

Circle the letter of the correct answer.

4. What caused the United States to enter World War II?

   A the Japanese attack on Pearl Harbor

   B the German invasion of Poland

   C the Japanese invasion of China

   D the German invasion of France

MATCHING Draw a line connecting each country on the left with the dictator who ruled it on the right.

5. Italy   Adolf Hitler

6. Germany   Joseph Stalin

7. Soviet Union   Benito Mussolini

activity

Make a Time Line Make a time line that shows the important events of World War II.

The Cold War

SOVIET MILITARY PARADE in
Moscow, 1964

During World War II, the United States fought on the same side as France, Britain, and the Soviet Union. After the war, the Allies decided to divide Germany into four parts. France, Britain, and the United States set up West Germany. The Soviet Union set up East Germany.

World leaders also wanted to start a group that would help prevent future wars. In April 1945, delegates from 50 countries met to form the United Nations, or UN. The headquarters of the UN is in New York City. **What will you learn about life in the United States following World War II?**

_____

_____

**NORTH CAROLINA
STANDARD COURSE OF STUDY**

4.05 Describe the impact of wars and conflicts on United States citizens, including but not limited to, the Civil War, World War I, World War II, the Korean War, the Vietnam War, Persian Gulf War, and the twenty-first century war on terrorism.

4.08 Trace the development of the United States as a world leader and analyze the impact of its relationships with Canada, Mexico, and selected countries of Central America.

TextWork

❶ Define the term *cold war* in your own words.

_____

_____

_____

_____

❷ REGIONS Study the map below. What was the name given to the border between the communist and noncommunist countries?

_____

The Cold War Begins

The Soviet Union set up communist governments in the eastern European countries it took over during World War II. **Communism** is a political and economic system in which the government owns all industries and property. People in these countries had few rights and little freedom.

The **free world**, or countries that were against communism, did not want communism to spread. Hostility, or unfriendliness, grew between the free world and communist nations. This hostility became known as the Cold War. A **cold war** is fought mostly with words and money instead of soldiers.

The Berlin Airlift

After World War II, West Germany became a democracy. East Germany became a communist nation. Berlin, Germany's capital, was in East Germany. The Western Allies—Britain, France, and the United States—controlled West Berlin. The Soviets controlled East Berlin.

Europe and the Cold War

- Communist country
- Noncommunist country
- —— Iron Curtain

▶ **MISSION CONTROL** People from NASA kept track of space missions from Mission Control in Florida and Texas.

In June 1948, the Soviets cut off all land travel between Berlin, including West Berlin, and West Germany. They wanted to force the Western Allies out of the city. The Western Allies then started bringing goods and food into Berlin on airplanes.

Beginning in the summer of 1948, American and British planes brought more than 2 million tons of goods and food to West Berlin. The Berlin Airlift was the first showdown of the Cold War. In May 1949, the Soviets finally ended the blockade.

The Space Race

The Soviet Union and the United States also competed in space exploration. In 1957, the Soviet Union launched the first satellite, called *Sputnik* (SPUT•nik). A *satellite* is something that orbits Earth. People in the United States were afraid that the Soviet Union was getting ahead in science.

In January 1958, the United States launched its own satellite into space. In October 1958, the National Aeronautics and Space Administration, or NASA, was set up by Congress. The rocket and satellite programs already taking place were continued, and more space missions were planned.

TextWork

❸ Write the events of the Berlin Airlift in the order in which they happened.

In June 1948, _____

_____

_____

Beginning in the summer of

1948, _____

_____

_____

In May 1949, _____

_____

_____

The Cold War Heats Up

The Cold War started an arms race between the two countries. An **arms race** is a contest between countries to build new weapons. At that time, the United States and the Soviet Union were the only countries with nuclear weapons.

The Korean War

The Asian country of Korea was divided after World War II. North Korea was communist, and South Korea was democratic.

In June 1950, North Korean soldiers invaded South Korea. North Korea had received weapons and help from the Soviet Union. Led by the United States, the United Nations quickly took action. It voted to send soldiers to stop the invasion.

The UN forces pushed the North Koreans back all the way to the border between North Korea and China. China, a communist country, joined the fight. The UN forces were outnumbered and pushed back.

4 Scan the text about the Korean War. Underline the sentence that describes how the Korean War started.

5 LOCATION Study the map below. Why do you think North Korea was helped by China and the Soviet Union?

_____

_____

_____

_____

❯ THE KOREAN WAR MEMORIAL in Washington, D.C.

A Divided Korea

0   100   200 Miles
0   100   200 Kilometers
Lambert Azimuthal
Equal-Area Projection

CHINA

Tumen R.

SOVIET UNION

42°N
132°E

Yalu River

NORTH KOREA

Sea of Japan (East Sea)

40°N

⊛ Pyongyang

Cease-fire line 1953

N
W   E
S

38°N

⊛ Seoul
Inchon ⊛

Yellow Sea

SOUTH KOREA

36°N

122°E   124°E   126°E   130°E

128°E

⊛ National capital

34°N

Korea Strait

JAPAN

THE CUBAN MISSILE CRISIS, 1962

Florida
Miami
Key West
Guanajay Missile Site
San Cristobal Missile Site
Havana
Sagua la Grande Missile Site
Bay of Pigs
CUBA
CARIBBEAN SEA
Guantanamo Bay
BAHAMAS
ATLANTIC OCEAN
N W E S

In 1953, both sides agreed to a cease-fire. A **cease-fire** is a temporary end to the fighting. On July 22, 1953, an armistice was signed to stop the fighting. South Korea remained a free country.

The Cuban Missile Crisis

Fidel Castro had taken control of Cuba in 1959. With help from the Soviet Union, he had formed a communist government there. In October 1962, the United States learned that the Soviet Union had built launch sites for missiles in Cuba. Cuba is only 90 miles from Florida. President John F. Kennedy ordered a blockade of Cuba's ports.

These events became known as the Cuban Missile Crisis. A *crisis* is a very difficult or danger-ous situation. The Cuban Missile Crisis lasted 13 days. Americans worried about a possible nuclear war with the Soviet Union. Finally, the Soviet Union agreed to take the missiles out of Cuba. In return, Kennedy agreed to order the Navy ships to leave. He also promised not to try to take control of Cuba.

TextWork

6 LOCATION Study the map above. Circle the missile sites on the map. Which missile site was closest to Havana?

_____

7 Scan the text. Underline the reason President Kennedy ordered a blockade of Cuba.

8 Scan the text. Circle the results of the Cuban Missile Crisis.

TextWork

9 Scan the text. Circle the year that the number of American soldiers in Vietnam reached 500,000. Why do you think people's opinions of the war changed?

_____

_____

_____

_____

10 LOCATION Study the map below. Circle the capital of North Vietnam and the capital of South Vietnam.

▶ **HELICOPTERS** carried soldiers and supplies during the Vietnam War.

The Vietnam War

In 1954, Vietnam was also divided. North Vietnam was communist. South Vietnam had a government friendly to the United States.

In the late 1950s, a group of South Vietnamese communists called the Vietcong tried to take over the government. They were helped by North Vietnam, the Soviet Union, and China. The United States helped the government of South Vietnam.

In 1964, President Lyndon Johnson sent more soldiers to Vietnam. By 1968, there were more than 500,000 American soldiers there. Early on, most Americans supported the war. Later, more people turned against the war.

Richard Nixon became President in 1969. His plan to end the war was to build up the South Vietnamese army. However, South Vietnam's army was never able to protect its country.

In 1973, the United States agreed to a cease-fire. The last troops came home. Two years later, North Vietnam took control of South Vietnam.

A Divided Vietnam

CHINA

BURMA

NORTH VIETNAM
⊛ Hanoi

LAOS

Gulf of Tonkin

Red River

Mekong River

THAILAND

CAMBODIA

SOUTH VIETNAM

⊛ Saigon

Gulf of Thailand

Mekong Delta

South China Sea

⊛ National capital

0   100   200 Miles
0   100   200 Kilometers
Lambert Azimuthal Equal-Area Projection

 MOSCOW SUMMIT Ronald Reagan and Mikhail Gorbachev meet during the Moscow Summit.

The 1970s and 1980s

In November 1972, Nixon was reelected President. During the election campaign, people working to help Nixon, who was a Republican, had done things that were against the law. One of the things they had done was to break into an office of the Democratic party in the Watergate building in Washington, D.C. When Nixon learned about this act, he tried to cover it up.

The Watergate scandal ended Nixon's presidency. A *scandal* is an action that brings disgrace. On August 9, 1974, Nixon became the first American President to resign.

Ronald Reagan became President in 1981. He said that the Cold War was a "struggle between right and wrong, good and evil." In 1985, Mikhail Gorbachev (mee•kah•EEL gawr•buh•CHAWF) came to power in the Soviet Union. President Reagan said he would welcome the chance to meet the new Soviet leader in "the cause of world peace."

In 1986, Reagan and Gorbachev met in Iceland. Soon the United States and the Soviet Union agreed to treaties limiting nuclear weapons.

TextWork

11 Scan the text. How did Nixon react to the Watergate scandal? Underline the sentence that gives this information.

12 What was the result of the meeting between Reagan and Gorbachev in Iceland?

_____

_____

_____

_____

The Cold War Ends

Gorbachev wanted the Soviet people to have more freedoms. Changes in the Soviet Union led to new freedoms in other communist nations.

In November 1989, East Germany opened the Berlin Wall. The Berlin Wall had been put up in 1961 to divide East and West Berlin. East Germans poured into West Berlin. People from both sides of the wall used hammers to break down the wall. The following year, Germany was reunited.

The early 1990s marked the end of communism in eastern Europe. In 1991, Russia outlawed the Communist party. Once communism was gone, there was little to unite the many different people of the Soviet Union. Soon, the 15 Soviet republics declared independence.

▶ **CITIZENS OF BERLIN** helped tear down the Berlin Wall.

Lesson 7 Review

1. **SUMMARIZE** How did the Cold War affect the United States?

_____

_____

2. Explain the term **arms race** as it relates to the **Cold War**.

_____

_____

3. Why do you think the United States fought in the Korean War and the Vietnam War?

_____

_____

4. List one effect of the fall of communism and the end of the Cold War.

_____

_____

writing

🖊 **Write a Diary Entry** Imagine that you are living in East Germany in 1991. The Cold War has just ended. Write a diary entry about how you feel.

Civil Rights

After the Civil War, several constitutional amendments were passed that gave African Americans more rights. The Thirteenth Amendment ended slavery. The Fifteenth Amendment gave African American men the right to vote. However, many Southern states soon passed laws that kept African American men from voting and enjoying their new rights. Beginning in the 1950s, such laws were overturned. Many people continued to work to bring equality to all people. **What do you think you will learn about civil rights in this lesson?**

_____

_____

▶ THE MARCH ON WASHINGTON in Washington, D.C., 1963

**NORTH CAROLINA
STANDARD COURSE OF STUDY**

4.06 Evaluate the effectiveness of civil rights and social movements throughout United States' history that reflect the struggle for equality and constitutional rights for all citizens.

1 Scan the text. Underline the outcome of *Plessy* v. *Ferguson*.

2 For what did Thurgood Marshall argue in *Brown* v. *Board of Education of Topeka*?

_____

_____

_____

A Supreme Court Ruling

In 1896, the United States Supreme Court had made a ruling in a case called *Plessy* v. *Ferguson*. It said that separate public places for white people and African Americans were not against the law. They had to be equal, but they almost never were.

In the early 1950s, Linda Brown of Topeka, Kansas, wanted to go to school with other children in her neighborhood. Linda Brown's family and 12 other African American families decided to fight **segregation**, or the separation of the races, in schools.

The National Association for the Advancement of Colored People, or NAACP, agreed to help. One of its lawyers, Thurgood Marshall, presented the case before the Supreme Court. The case became known as *Brown* v. *Board of Education of Topeka*. Marshall called for **integration**, or the bringing together of people of all races, in public schools.

In 1954, the Supreme Court ordered an end to segregation in public schools. Still, many schools remained segregated.

Children IN HISTORY

Linda Brown

When Linda Brown was 12 years old, the Supreme Court ruled that segregation in schools was not legal. As a result, Linda and other African American children in her neighborhood were allowed to attend—with white students—the school closest to their homes.

However, not all schools followed the Supreme Court's ruling. Years later, in 1979, Linda Brown continued to fight segregation. She helped reopen the *Brown* v. *Board of Education of Topeka* court case, saying that schools in Topeka, Kansas, were still segregated.

Make It Relevant **How would you feel if you were forced to go to a different school?**

▶ CIVIL RIGHTS PROTESTERS
in Greensboro, North Carolina

The Civil Rights Movement

In the 1950s, more and more African Americans fought for their full civil rights. **Civil rights** are the rights that all people have under the Constitution.

The Fight for Civil Rights

On December 1, 1955, an African American woman named Rosa Parks got on a bus in Montgomery, Alabama. She sat in the middle of the bus. Under Alabama law, African Americans could sit in the middle part only if no white passengers wanted those seats. As the bus filled up, the driver told Parks to go to the back of the bus. She refused to move and was arrested.

African Americans in Montgomery decided to act. They began a boycott of the city's buses. It lasted for more than a year. Later, in November 1956, the Supreme Court ruled that segregation had to end on all public transportation.

At that time, many places in the United States were still segregated by race. Across the country, African Americans fought against segregation. Often they were met with violence.

TextWork

3 Circle the term *civil rights*. Underline the sentence that gives a definition of this term.

4 Write a number—1, 2, or 3—next to each description of an event below to place the events in the correct order.

_____ African Americans in Montgomery, Alabama, organize a bus boycott.

_____ The Supreme Court rules that segregation has to end on public transportation.

_____ Rosa Parks refuses to move from her bus seat.

5 Use the word *nonviolence* to describe the Civil Rights movement.

_____

_____

_____

_____

_____

_____

6 How was Malcolm X different from Dr. Martin Luther King, Jr.? Underline the sentences that describe these differences.

Leaders Work for Civil Rights

A minister named Dr. Martin Luther King, Jr., became a civil rights leader. He believed in using **nonviolence**, or peaceful ways, to bring change.

In 1963, King gave a speech in Washington, D.C. He said, "I have a dream that my four little children will one day live in a nation where they will not be judged by the color of their skin, but by the content of their character."

Malcolm X wanted change to happen faster. In speeches, he called for a separation between white people and African Americans. Only in this way, he said, could African Americans truly be free. Later in his life, his views changed.

Malcolm X was killed in 1965. Three years later, Dr. King was also killed. African Americans lost two important leaders, but they kept working for civil rights.

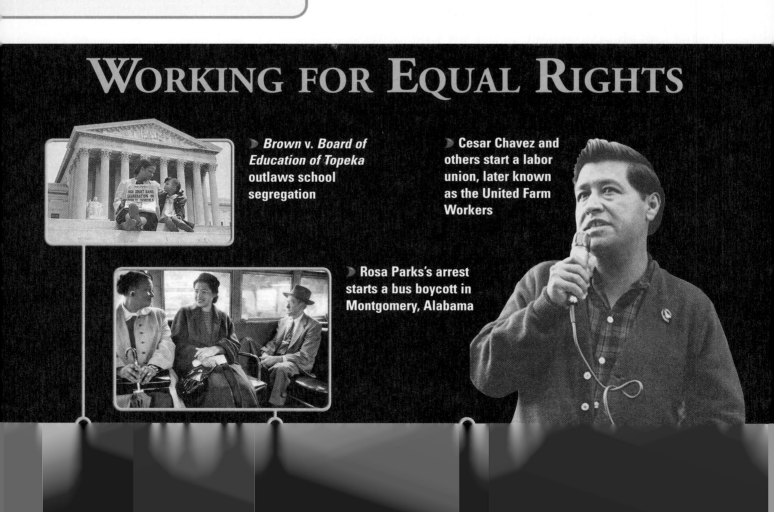

WORKING FOR EQUAL RIGHTS

⟩ *Brown v. Board of Education of Topeka* outlaws school segregation

⟩ **Rosa Parks's arrest** starts a bus boycott in Montgomery, Alabama

⟩ **Cesar Chavez** and others start a labor union, later known as the United Farm Workers

Civil Rights for All

In 1964, Congress passed a new Civil Rights Act. This law says that all Americans have the right to use public places and services. It also says that people cannot refuse to hire people because of their race, religion, gender, or place of birth.

Other groups also fought for civil rights. Cesar Chavez and Dolores Huerta helped start a group that would become the United Farm Workers (UFW). It worked to get better wages and working conditions for farmworkers.

By the 1960s, many women had jobs outside the home. But they often earned less pay than men. Women began to work together for equal rights.

New laws were passed that said businesses had to treat men and women the same. Since then, women have worked in jobs that were once held only by men. In 1981, Sandra Day O'Connor became the first female Supreme Court justice.

TextWork

7 Underline the sentences that describe two things protected by the Civil Rights Act of 1964.

8 What groups, other than African Americans, were helped by the Civil Rights movement?

_____

_____

_____

▶ Dr. Martin Luther King, Jr., and about 250,000 others march on Washington, D.C., to support civil rights laws

▶ The Civil Rights Act of 1964 is passed

▶ Malcolm X is assassinated

▶ Sandra Day O'Connor is appointed to the Supreme Court

1. **SUMMARIZE** What was the major goal of the Civil Rights movement?

_____

_____

_____

_____

2. Explain the term **civil rights** in your own words.

_____

_____

_____

3. How did *Brown* v. *Board of Education of Topeka* affect civil rights?

_____

_____

_____

_____

4. How did the Civil Rights movement help groups other than African Americans?

_____

_____

_____

Circle the letter of the correct answer.

5. What was a result of the Montgomery Bus Boycott?

   A The Supreme Court ruled that segregation must end in public schools.

   B Rosa Parks became the first female Supreme Court justice.

   C Cesar Chavez formed the UFW.

   D The Supreme Court ruled that segregation must end on public transportation.

6. Which minister and civil rights leader believed in the idea of using nonviolence?

   A Rosa Parks

   B Dr. Martin Luther King, Jr.

   C Malcolm X

   D Cesar Chavez

activity

Deliver a Speech Read with your classmates the "I Have a Dream" speech by Dr. Martin Luther King, Jr. Then take turns reading parts of the speech aloud. Discuss the meaning of the speech as a class.

Toward a New Century

> **THE BLUE ANGELS flying over Annapolis, Maryland**

In the late 1980s, the United States saw the end of the Cold War. But the nation soon faced new problems. In the early 1990s, the United States went to war with Iraq. The United States has also faced violence in the form of terrorism. **Terrorism** is the use of violence to promote a cause. **What might you learn about the United States as you read this lesson?**

_____

_____

_____

 NORTH CAROLINA STANDARD COURSE OF STUDY

4.05 Describe the impact of wars and conflicts on United States citizens, including but not limited to, the Civil War, World War I, World War II, the Korean War, the Vietnam War, Persian Gulf War, and the twenty-first century war on terrorism.

4.08 Trace the development of the United States as a world leader and analyze the impact of its relationships with Canada, Mexico, and selected countries of Central America.

1 What were two effects of Reagan's tax cuts?

_____

_____

_____

_____

2 How did President Reagan plan to win the Cold War?

_____

_____

_____

_____

President Ronald Reagan

In 1981, Ronald Reagan became President. Reagan offered Americans a different approach to government. He believed that government should be less involved in business and public life.

One of Reagan's first acts was to cut taxes. The tax cuts helped the nation's economy grow. They also created a shortage in the government's budget. A _budget_ is a plan for spending money.

President Reagan believed that to win the Cold War, the nation needed a stronger military. He soon increased military spending to help fight the spread of communism. He said that the Cold War was a struggle between "good and evil." He called the Soviet Union an "evil empire."

Ronald Reagan also experienced a scandal while he was President. In 1985, Reagan's staff was accused of giving money illegally to the Contras in Nicaragua. The Contras were fighting against the spread of communism in Central America. People criticized Reagan's staff for covering up the scandal.

▶ **A NEW PRESIDENT** The inauguration of Ronald Reagan on January 20, 1981

❯ THE GULF WAR Soldiers had to adapt to hot, dry weather during Operation Desert Storm.

The Gulf War

In 1988, George H. W. Bush was elected President. In 1990, Iraq took control of the small country of Kuwait (ku•WAYT). Iraq's leader was a dictator named Saddam Hussein (hoo•SAYN).

Kuwait, a major producer of oil, was an ally of the United States. Bush worked to build a coalition to force the Iraqis out of Kuwait. A **coalition** is a group united around the same goal. Thirty-three nations, including Canada and Honduras, joined the coalition against Iraq.

The United States led the attack. It was called Operation Desert Storm, or the Gulf War. After seven months, the allied forces had returned Kuwait's leaders to power. Saddam Hussein stayed in power in Iraq.

During the Gulf War, many Americans kept track of the war by watching 24-hour news channels. For the first time, journalists traveled with soldiers and reported live from battle zones.

❯ THE GULF WAR Soldiers had to adapt to hot, dry weather during Operation Desert Storm.

 **TextWork**

❸ Write down the event that is missing from the sequence below.

• **In 1990, Iraq took control of the small country of Kuwait.**

• _____

_____

_____

• **After seven months, the allied forces had returned Kuwait's leaders to power.**

❹ Underline the sentences that describe how the Gulf War was different from other wars.

 **TextWork**

5 Underline the sentence that describes why President George H. W. Bush did not win reelection in 1992.

6 How did Congress and President Clinton work together?

_____

_____

_____

_____

The 1990s

President Bush led the country to victory in the Gulf War. However, unemployment and a weak economy at home worried people. In 1992, Bill Clinton was elected President.

President Bill Clinton

President Clinton and Congress began working together to end the government's budget shortage. They also worked to balance the national budget.

While Clinton was President, the country had one of the greatest periods of growth in American history. Businesses created millions of jobs. Unemployment dropped to the lowest level in years. During this time, Congress and President Clinton balanced the national budget.

President Clinton also experienced controversy. In 1999, he became only the second President to be impeached, or accused of a crime. The Senate did not convict him, and he finished his term.

▶ **BALANCING THE BUDGET** President Clinton and Congress worked together to balance the national budget.

A Balanced Budget
That Protects Our Families, Invests in Our People and Cuts Taxes for Middle Class Families

▶ THE OKLAHOMA CITY NATIONAL MEMORIAL honors those killed in the terrorist attack.

Facing New Dangers

In the 1990s, the United States faced new dangers. These dangers came in the form of terrorism.

In 1993, terrorists attacked the World Trade Center in New York City. They exploded a powerful bomb that was hidden in a truck. The bomb killed 6 people and wounded about 1,000 more.

In 1995, an American who was angry with the government set off a bomb at a government building in Oklahoma City, Oklahoma. The attack killed 168 people and wounded many more.

The terrorist attacks at the World Trade Center and Oklahoma City worried Americans. The attacks showed that terrorists would plan attacks on American soil. People also attacked the United States outside its borders.

In 1998, bombs exploded at two United States embassies in the African countries of Kenya and Tanzania. Terrorists also exploded a bomb next to the USS *Cole*. The *Cole* was a United States Navy ship that was docked near the country of Yemen.

7 Scan the text. Circle the names of the two places in the United States that suffered terrorist attacks.

8 Where did terrorists attack Americans outside of the United States?

_____

_____

_____

_____

1. SUMMARIZE What problems did the United States face in the 1980s and 1990s?

_____

_____

_____

2. Use the word **terrorism** in a sentence about the 1990s.

_____

_____

3. What happened after the Gulf War?

_____

_____

Circle the letter of the correct answer.

4. What did President Ronald Reagan believe about government?

  A It should be more involved in business and public life.

  B It should be less involved in business and public life.

  C It should have a balanced budget.

  D It should cut military spending.

5. Who was President during the Gulf War?

  A Ronald Reagan

  B George H. W. Bush

  C Bill Clinton

  D George W. Bush

6. What did President Clinton and Congress do?

  A win the Gulf War

  B defeat terrorism

  C end welfare

  D balance the budget

FILL IN THE BLANK Use the words in the box to complete the sentences.

> terrorism p. 167   coalition p. 169

7. President Bush built a _____ to help fight the Gulf War.

8. In an act of _____, United States embassies in Africa were attacked in 1998.

writing

Write an Editorial Imagine that you are a newspaper editor. Write an editorial explaining why the President and Congress should work together.

New Challenges

Over time, the countries of North America have come to depend on one another. Today, the countries and people of North America are connected by trade. More trade has caused businesses to grow. Many people have moved to cities in North America to find jobs and new opportunities. In some cases, companies have moved to get workers to fill jobs. **What do you think you will read about in this lesson?**

_____

_____

_____

A CROWDED STREET in Mexico City

NORTH CAROLINA STANDARD COURSE OF STUDY

4.07 Compare and contrast changes in rural and urban settlement patterns in the United States, Canada, Mexico, and selected countries of Central America.

4.08 Trace the development of the United States as a world leader and analyze the impact of its relationships with Canada, Mexico, and selected countries of Central America.

1 What was the result of the 2000 presidential election?

_____

_____

_____

2 How did terrorists attack the United States on September 11?

_____

_____

_____

_____

▶ **SEPTEMBER 11, 2001** After the attacks on the World Trade Center, President Bush flew to New York City to speak with rescue workers.

Events Shape the Nation

The presidential election of 2000 showed how important every person's vote is. Republican George W. Bush ran against Democrat Al Gore. The winner would be decided by votes in Florida.

The election was too close to call. Florida officials began to count the votes again. Supporters of each candidate went to court. The Supreme Court ruled in George W. Bush's favor. On January 20, 2001, he became the forty-third President. As President, George W. Bush soon faced new challenges.

On September 11, 2001, the nation suffered the worst terrorist attacks in its history. Terrorists hijacked four American airplanes. To **hijack** is to take control of a vehicle illegally.

The terrorists flew two airplanes into the twin towers of the World Trade Center in New York City. A third plane hit the Pentagon building near Washington, D.C. The fourth plane crashed into a field in Pennsylvania on its way to Washington, D.C. About 3,000 people were killed in the attacks.

Fighting Terrorism

The United States responded quickly to the September 11 attacks. Leaders learned that many of the terrorists were connected to the Taliban. The Taliban controlled the government of Afghanistan.

In October 2001, the United States and its allies defeated the Taliban government. Since then, the United States has kept troops in Afghanistan to help rebuild the country and fight terrorism.

The United States believed that other countries also threatened peace. President Bush said that Saddam Hussein was a danger as long as he ruled Iraq. The United Nations said that Iraq had to list all its weapons. Hussein failed to do so.

In 2003, the United States and its allies attacked Iraq. The government fell, but the fighting in Iraq continued. The United States and its allies continue to work for democracy and peace in Iraq.

At home, the United States government made changes to guard against terrorism. To help protect the country, it set up the Department of Homeland Security and made other changes.

TextWork

❸ What happened after the attacks of September 11?

_____

_____

_____

_____

❹ Scan the text. What changes did the United States government make to guard against future terrorist attacks? Circle the sentence that gives this information.

⑤ Define the vocabulary word *interdependence* in your own words.

_____

_____

_____

_____

⑥ How can countries increase international trade?

_____

_____

_____

▶ **PORT VANCOUVER in British Columbia, Canada, handles large amounts of trade goods.**

Economic Challenges

The United States depends on other countries for some resources, goods, and services. Depending on one another for resources, goods, and services is called **interdependence**. The United States and many other countries are interdependent.

International Trade

Modern transportation has made it easier for people in one country to trade with people in other countries. Goods from the United States are sent all over the world. The United States also brings in goods.

To add to *international trade*, or trade among different countries, many countries have signed free-trade agreements. In a *free-trade agreement*, countries agree not to charge taxes on goods they buy and sell to each other.

In 1994, Mexico, Canada, and the United States signed the North American Free Trade Agreement, or NAFTA. NAFTA requires these countries to cooperate on issues of trade. Trade has grown, and the prices of some goods have fallen.

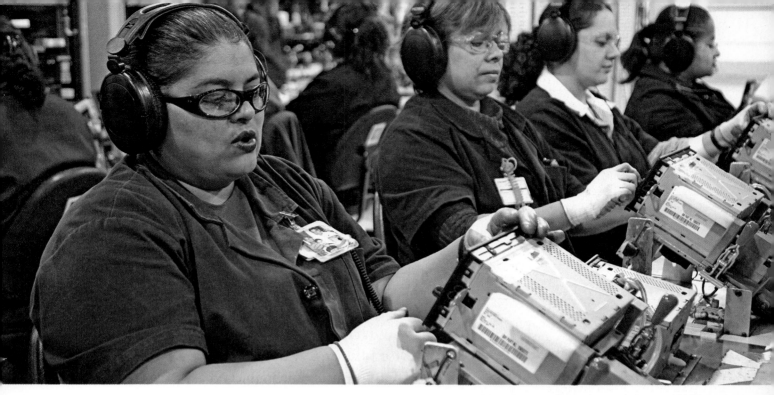

▶ **MAQUILADORAS** Workers in Mexican factories build electronics and other goods.

NAFTA has also caused problems. Some companies have moved jobs to countries where workers are paid less. Moving jobs to other countries is called *outsourcing*. Also, workers from other countries, especially Mexico, have entered the United States illegally to get jobs. Illegal immigration has led to problems in both nations.

Globalization

The nations of the world have gone through **globalization**, or the growth of a world market. Companies from different countries buy and sell goods and services on the world market.

Many companies in the United States have offices and factories in other parts of the world. Many companies from other countries also have offices and factories in the United States.

Many factories in Mexico have been built along the border with the United States. These factories are called *maquiladoras* (mah•kee•lah•DOH•rahs). In the maquiladoras, people put together goods from parts that are brought into Mexico. The finished products are sent mainly to the United States.

TextWork

7 Study the graph below. To which two countries does the United States export the most goods?

_____

United States Top Export Markets	
COUNTRY	**DOLLAR AMOUNT**
Canada	💵💵💵💵💵 💵💵💵💵
Mexico	💵💵💵💵💵
Japan	💵💵💵
China	💵💵
United Kingdom	💵💵

 = 25 billion dollars

The Effects of Growth

The United States is a huge country. In some places, there are few people or none at all. The urban, or city, regions in some parts of the United States are among the most densely settled areas in the world.

Since 1980, more than 10 million acres of what was open land and forest have been used for new houses, apartment buildings, roads, and businesses. That is more than twice the size of four of the largest national parks put together. This spread of urban areas is sometimes called **urban sprawl**.

Growth changes the environment as people clear land for building. More people in an area means more cars, traffic, garbage, and air pollution. Many communities work hard to balance growth and protect the environment.

Mexico's cities also have grown quickly. Many people have moved to these urban regions from Mexico's rural areas to find jobs. This large migration to the cities has caused many problems. Houses in some cities do not have electricity and running water. Automobiles cause large traffic jams and add to air pollution.

8 Use the term *urban sprawl* in a sentence about the environment.

_____

_____

_____

9 Study the graphs below. Which country had the largest change in rural and urban population between 1960 and 2000?

_____

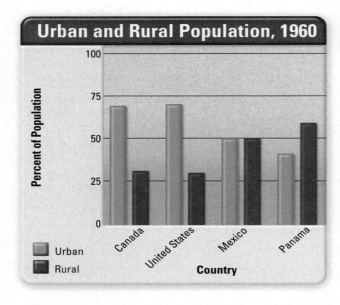

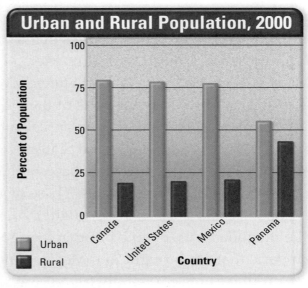

▶ THE RIO GRANDE is used by people in the United States and in Mexico.

Changing the Environment

People change the environment in many ways. They build bridges and highways. They build dams across rivers and bring water to new places. All these actions help make life easier for people. They can also change the environment.

Highways, for example, let people travel and transport goods. But highways are sometimes built through forests or other types of natural land. This affects the plants and animals that live there.

Today, many farmers in the United States and Mexico use the Rio Grande to bring water to their crops. People in Colorado and New Mexico use a lot of the Rio Grande's water. Sometimes, people downstream, in Mexico, do not have enough water. To protect Mexico's use of the river, the United States has agreed that a certain amount of water must reach Mexico.

The United States and other countries around the world often work together to use resources. They also work to protect nonrenewable resources. At the same time, scientists are coming up with new ways to produce energy from renewable resources.

 **TextWork**

10 Scan the text. Circle the sentence that describes the benefits of highways. Underline the sentences that describe how highways affect the environment.

11 What is the effect if people in Colorado and New Mexico use too much of the Rio Grande's water?

_____

_____

_____

_____

_____

1. SUMMARIZE What challenges did the United States face in the new century?

_____

_____

_____

2. What is **globalization**?

_____

_____

3. List three effects of urban sprawl.

_____

_____

Circle the letter of the correct answer.

4. Who was declared the winner of the 2000 presidential election?

   A George W. Bush

   B Al Gore

   C Ronald Reagan

   D Bill Clinton

5. What country did the United States go to war against in 2003?

   A Afghanistan

   B Iran

   C Iraq

   D Kuwait

6. What are factories along Mexico's border called?

   A outsources

   B maquiladoras

   C NAFTA

   D urban sprawl

FILL IN THE BLANK Use the words in the box to complete the sentences.

> hijack p. 174   interdependence p. 176   globalization p. 177

7. The growth of international trade has led to _____ and _____.

8. To _____ is to take control of a vehicle illegally.

activity

Draw a Picture Draw a picture that shows how growth has changed the environment in your community. Be sure to add a caption that describes your picture.

Review and Test Prep

💡 The Big Idea

Wars, inventions, and population growth have had an impact on the people and land of North America.

Summarize the Unit

🌟 **Sequence** Complete the organizer below to show that you understand the order in which some key events happened.

First	Next	Last
During the 1920s, many Americans put money in the stock market.	On October 29, 1929, the stock market crashed.	_____ _____ _____

Use Vocabulary

Fill in the missing term in each sentence, using the correct vocabulary term from the Word Bank.

1. The contest between the United States and the Soviet Union to build new weapons resulted in an _____ .

2. Escape routes that were part of the _____ led enslaved people to freedom.

3. The United States formed a _____ to help fight the Gulf War.

4. United States Navy ships used a _____ to keep other ships from entering or leaving Cuba.

5. Many immigrants lived in _____ , or poorly built apartment buildings.

Word Bank

Underground Railroad p. 116
tenements p. 131
blockade p. 134
arms race p. 156
coalition p. 169

Think About It

6. How was President Johnson's plan for Reconstruction different from Congress's plan?

_____

_____

7. How did the Panama Canal change North America?

_____

_____

8. How did the Cuban Missile Crisis affect people living in the United States?

_____

_____

Circle the letter of the correct answer.

9. Who became the leader of Germany in the 1930s?

   A Benito Mussolini

   B Adolf Hitler

   C Joseph Stalin

   D Franklin D. Roosevelt

10. What is the name of the trade agreement signed by the United States, Canada, and Mexico in 1994?

   A the International Trade Agreement

   B the Interdependence Treaty

   C NAFTA

   D the Globalization

Show What You Know

Writing Write a Speech
Imagine that you are a historian. Write a speech about an important event in North America's history since 1850. Describe the event, and tell why it was important.

Activity Publish a Newspaper
Publish a newspaper that describes events, people, and places in North America's history since 1850. You can include news articles, an editorial, a cartoon, and classified advertisements. Be sure to include headlines for all articles.

GO online
To play a game that reviews the unit, join Eco in the North Carolina Adventures online or on CD.

Government and Society

 THE WASHINGTON MONUMENT, IN WASHINGTON, D.C.

Spotlight on Goals and Objectives

North Carolina Interactive Presentations

NORTH CAROLINA STANDARD COURSE OF STUDY

COMPETENCY GOAL 2 The learner will analyze political and social institutions in North America and examine how these institutions respond to human needs, structure society, and influence behavior.

183

# The Big Idea

What kinds of groups do people form in order to help them meet their needs and live together?

All societies have political and social *institutions,* or organizations, that help people meet their needs. A **society** is a group of people living together in a community who have shared customs, laws, and institutions.

Government is a type of political institution. Government makes laws to help keep people safe and to protect their rights and property. Government also offers services, such as police and fire protection, to people. Some people in government are elected or appointed to office. Other people are hired to work in the government.

Social institutions are groups such as families, religious groups, and community groups. These institutions bring people together. They also offer services for the community and help people in need.

Complete the web organizer. List three examples of political institutions and three examples of social institutions in your community.

Political Institutions	Society	Social Institutions

Political Institutions:
- _____
  _____
- _____
  _____
- _____
  _____

Social Institutions:
- _____
  _____
- _____
  _____
- _____
  _____

Reading Social Studies

Main Idea and Details

> ## LEARN

The **main idea** is the most important idea of what you read. **Details** give more information about the main idea. Each piece of writing has a main idea and details. The main idea is often found at the beginning of a piece of writing. In long pieces of writing, each paragraph has a main idea and details.

Main Idea

The most important idea of a paragraph or piece of writing

Details

| Fact about the main idea | Fact about the main idea | Fact about the main idea |

> ## PRACTICE

Circle each paragraph's main idea, and underline its details. The first paragraph has been done for you.

In early 1776, Thomas Paine wrote a pamphlet called *Common Sense.* In it, he wrote that the colonists should no longer be ruled by Britain. They should rule themselves. People in the colonies began to talk about Paine's ideas. Many of them began to call for independence. In July 1776, the colonists declared their independence and formed a new country—the United States of America.

Main Idea

Details

The leaders of the new United States knew that the country needed a government to make laws, keep order, and protect the people. To form this government, they wrote the Articles of Confederation. However, the Articles of Confederation did not give the national government much power. Each state had its own laws, money, and militia. The United States did not run well under the Articles of Confederation.

Read the article. Then complete the activities below.

Washington, D.C.

In 1789, Congress chose George Washington to be the first President of the United States. Congress wanted President Washington to choose a place for the United States capital. He finally chose land that was located between Maryland and Virginia. The new city would be called Washington, D.C. In 1800, the federal government moved from Philadelphia to the new and permanent United States capital.

Two people had important jobs in building the city. Benjamin Banneker, a free African American, helped Pierre Charles L'Enfant plan Washington, D.C. Banneker figured out the size of the city. L'Enfant decided to use a grid of numbered and lettered streets to plan the city. This way, the city would be very organized. L'Enfant also wanted to have many small parks all over the city.

Over the years, large, beautiful buildings were built for the government workers. The President lives in the White House. Congress works in the United States Capitol building. The Supreme Court building is located near the Capitol building. Many government agencies, including the Treasury, work in buildings in Washington, D.C.

There are also many museums, memorials, and monuments in Washington, D.C. People travel from around the country and the world to visit them. Some of the most popular places include the Lincoln Memorial, the Washington Monument, and the museums of the Smithsonian Institution. The Smithsonian Institution runs many museums in Washington, D.C., such as the National Museum of Natural History and the National Air and Space Museum.

1. **In the second paragraph, circle the main idea and underline the details.**

2. **What is the main idea of the fourth paragraph?**

_____

_____

Foundations of United States Government

In 1776, the 13 colonies declared their independence. After the first government proved to be too weak, leaders of the United States began to plan a new government for the nation. They studied many documents. These documents helped form the *foundation*, or base, for the plan of government that the leaders finally approved. The plan made the United States a republic. In a **republic**, people elect representatives to run the government and to make laws for them. **How will this lesson improve your understanding of United States government?**

_____

_____

THE CONSTITUTIONAL CONVENTION

**NORTH CAROLINA
STANDARD COURSE OF STUDY**

2.01 Analyze major documents that formed the foundations of the American idea of constitutional government.

TextWork

1 Reread the first sentence of the second paragraph on this page. Look for context clues that help you understand the meaning of *self-government*. Underline the clue words.

2 Number the four parts of the Declaration of Independence below in the order in which they appear in the document.

___ Statement of independence

___ Grievances

___ Preamble

___ Statement of rights

3 The photograph on page 189 shows a primary source—one of the original copies of the Declaration of Independence. Use what you have read about the Declaration, and the terms from the box below, to add labels to the photograph.

> **date**
> **preamble**
> **signers**
> **grievances**

The Mayflower Compact

The Pilgrims came to North America in 1620. They arrived in a place that had no government. They needed to keep order. To do this, all the men aboard the *Mayflower* signed an agreement. It became known as the Mayflower Compact.

The Mayflower Compact gave those who signed it the right to rule themselves. At this time, **self-government** was a new idea. The Mayflower Compact also included the idea of **majority rule**. If more than half the people agreed to a law, everyone had to follow it.

The Declaration of Independence

In 1776, leaders of the 13 American colonies voted to become independent from Britain. They decided to write a *declaration*, or statement, about independence. Thomas Jefferson, a 33-year-old lawyer from Virginia, was the main author.

Jefferson had studied government. He used his knowledge to carefully plan the Declaration of Independence. Jefferson started by writing the **preamble**, or introduction. He explained why the colonies had the right to break away from Britain.

The next part of the Declaration states the colonists' rights and their ideas about government. It says that people have rights that cannot be taken away: "We hold these truths to be self-evident, that all men are created equal, that they are endowed [provided] by their Creator with certain unalienable Rights, that among these are Life, Liberty, and the pursuit of Happiness."

The longest part of the Declaration lists the colonists' *grievances*, or things they did not like about the British government. The last part says that the 13 colonies are free and independent states.

The Declaration of Independence

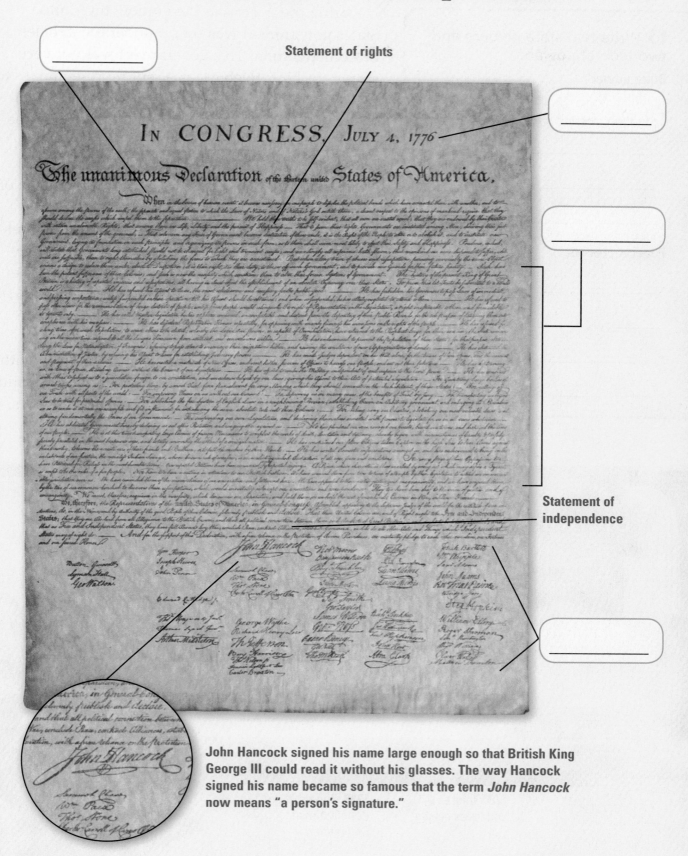

Statement of rights

_____

_____

_____

Statement of independence

_____

John Hancock signed his name large enough so that British King George III could read it without his glasses. The way Hancock signed his name became so famous that the term *John Hancock* now means "a person's signature."

 **TextWork**

4 Write two state powers and two federal powers.

State powers:

- _____
  _____
- _____
  _____

Federal powers:

- _____
  _____
- _____
  _____

The United States Constitution

During the American Revolution, the United States government was set up under the Articles of Confederation. This government was not very strong. In 1787, twelve states sent representatives to a meeting called the Constitutional Convention in Philadelphia. The representatives decided that the United States needed a new constitution, or plan of government. The plan they wrote is called the United States Constitution. It is the supreme law of the land. Everyone in the nation has to follow it.

The United States Constitution sets up a **federal system** of government for the United States. The national and state governments share power. The states keep some powers. They have the power to set up public schools, set up local governments, and conduct elections. The national, or federal, government has power over matters that deal with the nation as a whole. It has the power to form and keep up a military, print money, let in new states, and declare war and make peace.

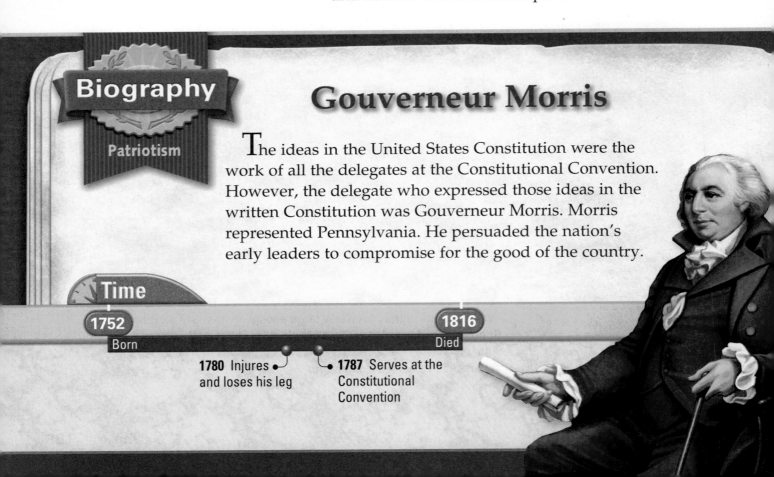

Biography

Patriotism

Gouverneur Morris

The ideas in the United States Constitution were the work of all the delegates at the Constitutional Convention. However, the delegate who expressed those ideas in the written Constitution was Gouverneur Morris. Morris represented Pennsylvania. He persuaded the nation's early leaders to compromise for the good of the country.

Time

1752 Born

1816 Died

1780 Injures and loses his leg

1787 Serves at the Constitutional Convention

The Bill of Rights

Some state leaders called for a *bill*, or list, of rights to be added to the Constitution. In 1791, ten **amendments**, or changes, were added to the Constitution. These ten amendments are called the Bill of Rights. They protect people's freedoms.

The First Amendment gives people the freedom to follow any religion or none at all. It also protects freedom of speech, freedom of the press, freedom to petition the government, and the right to *assemble*, or gather together, peacefully.

The Second Amendment protects people's right to have weapons. The Third Amendment says the government cannot make people house soldiers during times of peace. The Fourth Amendment protects people against unfair searches.

The Fifth through the Eighth Amendments deal with **due process of law**. This means that people have the right to a fair trial and a lawyer. They also do not have to speak against themselves in court or other legal matters. The Ninth Amendment says that people have other rights not listed in the Constitution. The Tenth Amendment says that the government can do only the things listed in the Constitution.

▶ VISITORS look at original copies of the Declaration of Independence, the Constitution, and the Bill of Rights at the National Archives in Washington, D.C.

 TextWork

❺ Circle the main idea sentence in the first paragraph. Underline the sentences that give supporting details.

❻ Scan the text. What freedoms does the First Amendment protect? Underline the sentences that give this information.

1. **SUMMARIZE** What documents helped form the foundation of the United States government?

_____

_____

_____

2. Use the two terms **self-government** and **majority rule** to describe the Mayflower Compact.

_____

_____

_____

3. What two important ideas were included in the Mayflower Compact?

_____

_____

_____

Circle the letter of the correct answer.

4. Which of these documents is the supreme law of the land in the United States?

   A the Mayflower Compact

   B the Declaration of Independence

   C the United States Constitution

   D the Fifth Amendment

5. Which power does the Constitution give to the national government?

   A the power to set up local governments

   B the power to print money

   C the power to conduct elections

   D the power to set up public schools

6. Which of the following does the First Amendment protect?

   A freedom of speech and religion

   B the right to a trial by jury

   C the right to have weapons

   D freedom from unfair searches

writing

Write a Letter Imagine that you are living at the time one of the documents described in this lesson was written. Write a letter to a friend telling why you think that document is important to people and to the government.

> UNITED STATES CAPITOL
BUILDING in Washington, D.C.

In the United States, the power to rule is shared among the national, state, and local governments. Local governments serve all the citizens in a community, town, or city. State governments serve all the citizens in a state. The national government serves all the citizens in the United States. **What will you learn about United States government as you read this lesson?**

_____

_____

_____

**NORTH CAROLINA
STANDARD COURSE OF STUDY**

2.02 Describe the similarities and differences among the local, state, and national levels of government in the United States and explain their legislative, executive, and judicial functions.

National Government

TextWork

❶ Define the term *separation of powers* in your own words.

_____

_____

_____

_____

❷ Underline the sentence in the text that describes the main function of Congress.

The Constitution divides the powers of the federal government among three branches—the legislative branch, the executive branch, and the judicial branch. Each branch has its own job and powers. This **separation of powers** keeps any one branch from controlling the government.

The Legislative Branch

Congress is the **legislative branch** of the federal government, or the branch that makes laws. Congress makes laws for the whole country.

Congress is made up of two houses, or parts—the House of Representatives and the Senate. The 435 seats in the House of Representatives are divided among the states based on each state's population. North Carolina has 13 representatives in the House of Representatives. Members of the House of Representatives serve two-year terms. In the Senate, each state has two senators. Senators serve six-year terms.

Members of either house can introduce a *bill*, or idea for a law. For a bill to become law, more than half of the members in each house must vote for it.

How a Bill Becomes a Law

❶ A member of the House or Senate introduces a bill.

❷ The bill is reviewed and approved by House and Senate committees.

❸ The House and Senate vote to approve the bill.

❹ The bill goes to the President.

The Executive and Judicial Branches

The Constitution gives the **executive branch** the power to enforce laws passed by Congress. The President leads the executive branch. The President is elected to a four-year term.

The President has many duties. The President is commander in chief of the military and speaks for the United States in its dealings with other countries. The President must also come up with a *budget*, or plan for spending tax money.

The President can suggest a budget and other bills but cannot vote for them. The President can **veto**, or reject, any bill passed by Congress. A vetoed bill can still become a law if two-thirds of both houses of Congress vote for it again.

The **judicial branch** of the federal government is the federal court system. These courts hear the cases of people accused of federal crimes. They also decide if laws are being applied fairly and equally.

The United States Supreme Court is the highest court. It can strike down any law that goes against the Constitution. Nine *justices*, or judges, serve on the Supreme Court. The President nominates justices, but the Senate must approve them. Justices serve in their positions for life.

TextWork

❸ What are some duties of the President?

_____

_____

_____

_____

❹ Scan the text on this page. Underline the sentence that describes one key power of the Supreme Court.

❺ Study the flowchart below. What happens when a bill reaches the President?

_____

_____

_____

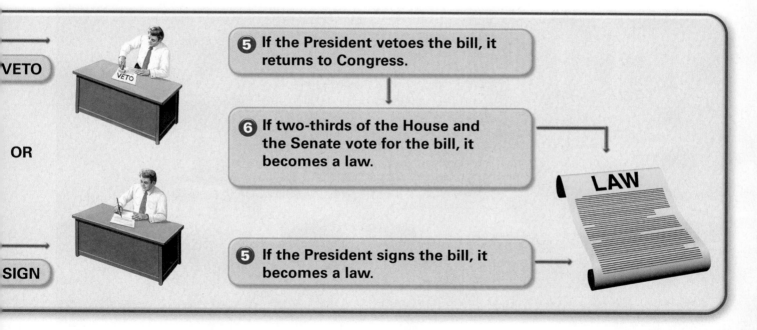

VETO

OR

SIGN

❺ If the President vetoes the bill, it returns to Congress.

❻ If two-thirds of the House and the Senate vote for the bill, it becomes a law.

❺ If the President signs the bill, it becomes a law.

LAW

State Governments

Each of the 50 states in the United States has a state constitution. A state constitution is a written plan for state government. All state constitutions are based on the United States Constitution.

Like the national government, all state governments have three branches—the legislative branch, executive branch, and judicial branch. The function, or job, of each branch of state government is similar to that of each branch of the national government.

The State Legislative Branch

The legislative branch of state government makes the state's laws. It also approves the state's budget. Like the United States Congress, most state legislatures are divided into two houses. Nebraska is the only state with a one-house legislature.

In state legislatures with two houses, members of either house can introduce a bill. As in the United States Congress, a majority of the members in each house must vote to approve a bill in order for it to become a law.

6 List two ways that a state legislature is similar to the United States Congress.

- _____
  _____
- _____
  _____

7 Underline the sentence that describes how Nebraska's legislative branch is different from that of other states and the United States Congress.

▶ **THE LEGISLATIVE BRANCH in North Carolina is called the General Assembly. Members of the General Assembly meet in this room (below).**

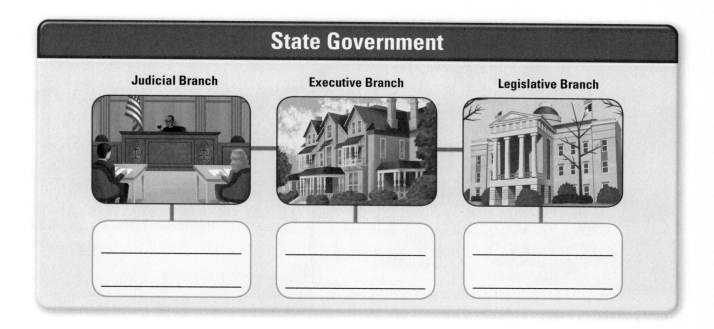

State Government

Judicial Branch   **Executive Branch**   **Legislative Branch**

The State Executive Branch

The governor leads the executive branch of state government. In most states, including North Carolina, voters elect a governor to a four-year term. Many states do not allow a governor to serve more than two terms in a row.

The governor's main job is to enforce laws passed by the legislature and to oversee the state government. The governor can suggest new laws to the legislature. The governor also has to prepare a state budget.

Like the President, the governor has the power to veto a bill. However, the legislature can over-ride a veto if enough of its members vote again to approve the bill.

The State Judicial Branch

The judicial branch of state government is made up of courts and judges that decide legal cases. In most states, the state supreme court is the highest state court. It makes sure that state laws follow that state's constitution. Most states have other courts that hear cases of people charged with a crime. Many cases are tried by a *jury*. This group of citizens decides if a person is guilty or innocent.

 **TextWork**

8 Study the diagram above. Place the labels from the box below under the correct branch of government on the diagram.

> governor
>
> state legislature
>
> state supreme court

9 Underline the sentence that describes a power that both the governor and the President have.

▷ **THE CABARRUS COUNTY GOVERNMENT**
offices are in Concord, North Carolina.

Local Governments

Almost every state is divided into smaller parts called counties. Each county has its own leaders and government.

In many counties, voters elect commissioners to run the county's government. County commissioners often act as the legislative and executive branches. They make laws for the county and see that people follow the laws. They also decide the county's budget.

Voters in most counties elect other county officials as well. These include judges for the county courts and a sheriff, who makes sure that the laws are obeyed.

Counties may have several cities. Cities also have their own government. The legislative branch of city government is often the city council. Members of the city council make laws for a city.

Many cities have a mayor, who heads the executive branch. Like the President or a governor, the mayor often prepares a city's budget. In some cities, the mayor can veto bills.

Some larger cities have their own courts. These courts hear cases about traffic, parking, and other matters that are important to the city.

TextWork

10 What group often acts as the legislative branch of city government?

_____

_____

11 List two details related to the main idea below.

Main Idea: Many city governments have a mayor.

Detail: _____

_____

Detail: _____

_____

Sharing Powers

The federal government has the power to take care of matters that affect the whole country. The federal government controls trade between states and with other countries. It has the power to print and coin money. It can declare war and make peace. It also has the power to collect taxes.

Like the federal government, the state and local governments have certain powers and responsibilities. States can set up public schools, conduct elections, and set up local governments. States can also collect taxes. Local governments make laws for their communities and collect taxes. They use tax money to provide services, such as trash collection, police and fire protection, and medical care. They also run local schools, libraries, museums, and parks.

TextWork

12 Use what you have read in the text to complete the diagram below. Fill in the missing power of the national government, the missing power of the state governments, and the missing shared power.

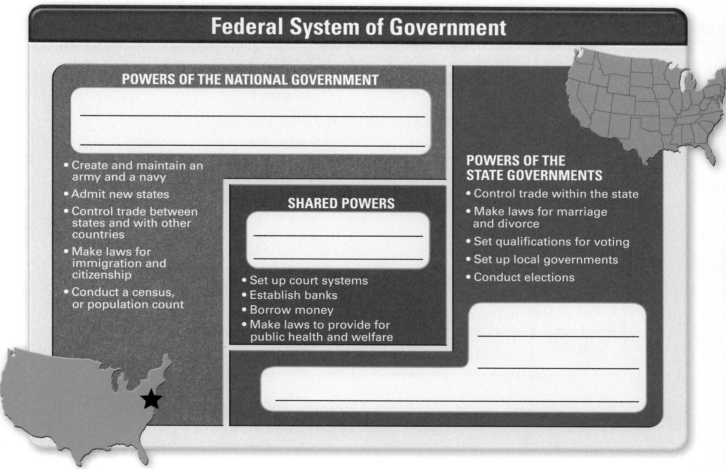

Federal System of Government

POWERS OF THE NATIONAL GOVERNMENT

_____
_____

- Create and maintain an army and a navy
- Admit new states
- Control trade between states and with other countries
- Make laws for immigration and citizenship
- Conduct a census, or population count

SHARED POWERS

_____
_____

- Set up court systems
- Establish banks
- Borrow money
- Make laws to provide for public health and welfare

POWERS OF THE STATE GOVERNMENTS

- Control trade within the state
- Make laws for marriage and divorce
- Set qualifications for voting
- Set up local governments
- Conduct elections

_____
_____

1. **SUMMARIZE** What are the three levels of government in the United States? What is the main function of each level?

_____

_____

_____

2. Use the word **veto** in a sentence about the **executive branch**.

_____

_____

_____

Circle the letter of the correct answer.

3. What is the main job of the United States Congress?

   A to strike down laws that go against the Constitution

   B to veto bills

   C to make laws for the United States

   D to serve in their positions for life

4. Which group or person has the power to make laws for a county?

   A city council

   B county commissioners

   C mayor

   D sheriff

MATCHING Draw a line connecting the level of government on the left to the official who belongs to that level on the right.

5. national government   governor

6. state government   President

7. local government   sheriff

writing

✏ **Write a Report** Write a report about government in the United States. In your report, describe at least one way that local, state, and national governments are alike and at least one way that they are different.

A Changing Government

   The writers of the United States Constitution knew that as time passed, the Constitution might need to be changed. Since the Constitution was written, there have been many changes in government. There have also been important changes in the ways voters elect government officials. **How will reading this lesson help you learn more about changes in the United States government?**

_____

_____

_____

▷ THE PRESIDENT speaks to Congress.

**NORTH CAROLINA
STANDARD COURSE OF STUDY**

2.03 Recognize how the United States government has changed over time.

2.05 Assess the role of political parties in society.

TextWork

❶ Circle the main idea in the second paragraph. Then underline the details that support the main idea.

❷ Study the flowchart below. How can an amendment to the Constitution be proposed?

_____

_____

_____

_____

_____

_____

Changing the Constitution

The Constitution can be changed only through amendments. The Bill of Rights was added in 1791. Since then, 17 more amendments have been added.

Expanded Rights

Some amendments extended freedoms to more people. The Thirteenth Amendment ended slavery in the United States. The Fourteenth Amendment says that all persons born or naturalized in the United States are citizens. A **naturalized citizen** is someone who has followed the legal steps needed to become a United States citizen.

Other amendments changed laws about voting. The Fifteenth Amendment says that no citizen can be denied the right to vote because of race. In 1920, the Nineteenth Amendment gave women the right to vote in all elections. In 1971, the Twenty-sixth Amendment changed the voting age from 21 to 18.

Other amendments deal with the way that the United States government works. In 1913, the Sixteenth Amendment gave Congress the power to collect taxes on people's *incomes*, or earnings.

Amending the Constitution

PROPOSING AN AMENDMENT

A proposal for a new amendment is voted on by both houses of Congress. It must pass by a two-thirds majority. This is how most amendments are proposed.

Two-thirds of the state legislatures can call for a Constitutional Convention to propose amendments. This method has never been used.

APPROVING AN AMENDMENT

The proposed amendment goes to the state legislatures or state conventions. The state legislatures or state conventions then vote to ratify, or approve, the proposed amendment.

AMENDMENT ADDED TO THE CONSTITUTION

If two-thirds of the state legislatures or state conventions vote to ratify the amendment, it becomes part of the Constitution.

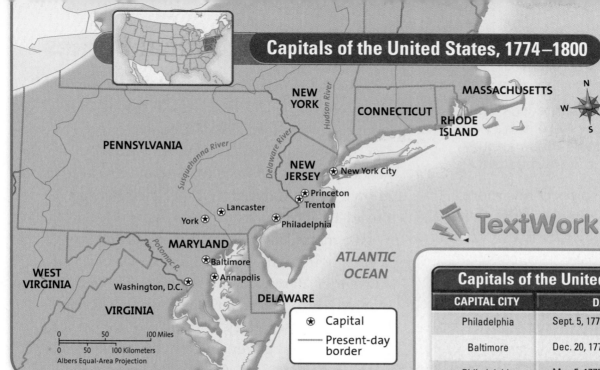

Capitals of the United States, 1774–1800

Capitals of the United States	
CAPITAL CITY	**DATE**
Philadelphia	Sept. 5, 1774–Dec. 12, 1776
Baltimore	Dec. 20, 1776–Feb. 27, 1777
Philadelphia	Mar. 5, 1777–Sept. 18, 1777
Lancaster	Sept. 27, 1777
York	Sept. 30, 1777–June 27, 1778
Philadelphia	July 2, 1778–June 21, 1783
Princeton	June 30, 1783–Nov. 4, 1783
Annapolis	Nov. 26, 1783–Aug. 19, 1784
Trenton	Nov. 1, 1784–Dec. 24, 1784
New York City	Jan. 11, 1785–Aug. 12, 1790
Philadelphia	Dec. 6, 1790–May 14, 1800
Washington, D.C.	Nov. 17, 1800–present

That same year, the Seventeenth Amendment became law. It lets voters directly elect United States senators. Before that time, senators were elected by state legislatures. The Twenty-second Amendment set a two-term limit for Presidents.

Differences in Government

Before 1800, the United States government had no permanent capital. Congress met at different times in eight different cities. In 1791, Congress voted to build a new capital—Washington, D.C. It remains the nation's capital today.

Over the years, Congress has started many new government agencies to help solve problems or to provide services. For example, the Social Security Administration pays money to people who are retired or disabled. In 2002, Congress created the Department of Homeland Security to help the nation guard against terrorist attacks.

Acts of Congress have given the federal government more power and made it larger. Today, about 2 million people work for the federal government.

3 PLACE Refer to the map and the table above. Which city served as the United States capital for only one day? Circle it on the map. Then write that date on the line below.

_____

4 Scan the text on this page. How have acts of Congress changed the United States government? Underline the sentence that gives this information.

TextWork

5 Circle the sentences that describe how Hamilton's and Jefferson's ideas about government were different.

6 The word *party* has more than one meaning. What does *party* mean in the term *political party*?

_____

_____

_____

_____

▷ **ALEXANDER HAMILTON**

▷ **THOMAS JEFFERSON**

The First Political Parties

In 1789, George Washington became the first President of the United States. Working with Congress, he set up a State Department, a Treasury Department, and a War Department. Together, the heads of these departments and others came to be known as the **Cabinet**. Cabinet members advise the President about important issues.

Two members of Washington's Cabinet began to argue about what was best for the United States. Alexander Hamilton, the secretary of the treasury, wanted a stronger federal government. Thomas Jefferson, the secretary of state, did not want to give the federal government more power.

Their different beliefs led to the rise of the nation's first political parties. A **political party** is a group that tries to elect officials who will support its beliefs and policies. Members of political parties often give money to their party's candidates. They also often work in their election campaigns.

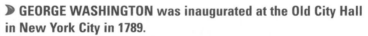

▷ **GEORGE WASHINGTON** was inaugurated at the Old City Hall in New York City in 1789.

▶ **DEBATE** President George W. Bush (right) and Senator John Kerry (left) participate in a presidential debate in 2004.

Political Parties Today

Today, the United States has a mainly two-party system. While there are many smaller political parties, the Democratic party and the Republican party are the two major parties. Between them, they hold almost all the offices in the local, state, and national governments. Most voters in the United States are members of a political party.

In the United States, government gets its power from the people. Elected leaders use the power given to them by citizens who vote them into office. In turn, political parties use their power to help set the public agenda. The **public agenda** is what most people want from government. If voters do not like certain laws, they can elect or support people from other political parties who they think will make changes.

In **primary elections**, voters choose the leaders who will represent their party in an election. In states with closed primaries, only voters who are part of a political party can vote for their party's leaders in the primaries. In states with open primaries, anyone can vote for leaders from any party.

 **TextWork**

7 Scan the text on this page. Circle the names of the two major political parties in the United States today.

8 Why is it important for voters in states with closed primaries to be members of a political party?

_____

_____

_____

_____

_____

▶ **POLITICAL PARTIES** Party members show support for their candidates by wearing political buttons.

The Role of Political Parties

Political parties play an important role in society. A **society** is an organized group of people living and working under a set of rules and traditions. Political parties help organize people who think alike. Members of political parties help to get voters to support the parties' candidates for office.

Another important role of political parties is to raise money. It takes a lot of money to run for an office such as President or governor. Members of a political party give money to help candidates pay for commercials on television and radio. The money is also used for travel expenses and for salaries for each candidate's staff.

Political parties play an important role in helping get their candidates elected. They also give people a way to support candidates who share their point of view.

Lesson 3 Review

1. **SUMMARIZE** How has the United States government changed over time?

_____

_____

2. Tell how the terms **political party** and **public agenda** are related.

_____

_____

3. What is the only way to change the United States Constitution?

_____

_____

4. How is the role of political parties important in society?

_____

_____

activity

✏ **Make a Poster** At the library or on the Internet, learn more about one of the amendments to the Constitution. Then design a poster to highlight this amendment. Use drawings and photographs to illustrate your poster.

Governments in North America

   Almost every country in North America is a democracy. These countries have free elections, majority rule, and a guarantee of individual rights. Even so, there are differences among the governments. Canada's government is similar to that of the United States in some ways. In other ways, it is more like the government of Britain. Mexico, like the United States, is a country made up of states. All seven countries of Central America are democracies. **How will this lesson help you compare and contrast the governments of North American countries?**

_____

_____

➤ SOME FLAGS OF NORTH AMERICA

 NORTH CAROLINA STANDARD COURSE OF STUDY

2.04 Compare and contrast the government of the United States with the governments of Canada, Mexico, and selected countries of Central America.

Canada's Government

① Underline the sentence that tells how Canada's legislative branch is similar to that of the United States.

② Compare and contrast Canada's Senate with the United States Senate.

_____

_____

_____

_____

_____

_____

Canada is a **parliamentary democracy**. In this kind of government, voters elect members of the national legislature, called a *parliament*. Then the parliament chooses the **prime minister**, or chief executive of the government.

Canada's prime minister leads both the executive and the legislative branches of government. In contrast, the chief executive of the United States—the President—leads only the executive branch.

Like that of the United States, Canada's legislative branch is made up of two houses. The two houses of Canada's Parliament are the House of Commons and the Senate. However, Canada's Senate has little say in passing laws. It studies issues and suggests ideas for laws. Unlike United States senators, its members are appointed rather than elected.

The House of Commons makes laws for Canada. Citizens vote directly for the members of the House of Commons. Its members serve terms of up to five years, depending on when elections are held. Members of the United States House of Representatives are elected every two years.

▶ A SESSION of the Canadian Parliament

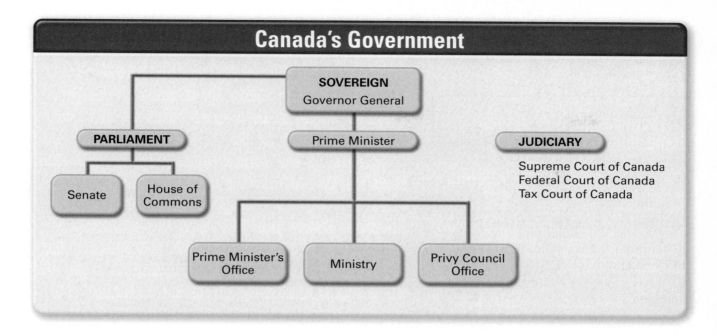

Canada's Government

SOVEREIGN
Governor General

PARLIAMENT

Prime Minister

JUDICIARY

Supreme Court of Canada
Federal Court of Canada
Tax Court of Canada

Senate

House of Commons

Prime Minister's Office

Ministry

Privy Council Office

As in the United States Congress, members of the Canadian House of Commons represent different political parties. The United States has only two major parties, while Canada has more. The party that controls the majority of seats in the House of Commons is known as the majority party. The majority party chooses the prime minister.

Canada's national government also has a judicial branch. As in the United States, the judicial branch consists of a national court system. The highest court in Canada is the Supreme Court of Canada.

The Canadian Supreme Court has nine justices. One serves as the chief justice. The justices decide if laws are fair. The prime minister chooses the justices for the Supreme Court. In the United States, the President nominates justices and the Senate must approve them.

Canada belongs to the British Commonwealth of Nations. This group is made up of former British colonies. Members recognize the British monarch as the head of state. However, the British monarch does not take part in governing Canada or other Commonwealth countries.

TextWork

❸ Study the diagram above. Circle the label for Parliament. What are the two branches of Canada's Parliament?

_____

_____

_____

_____

_____

❹ Circle the main idea of the first paragraph on this page. Then underline the sentences that provide supporting details for the main idea.

5 Write a main idea for the details listed below.

- **The Mexican president sets policies, influences lawmaking, and plans the budget.**

- **The Mexican president appoints government officials, military officers, and judges.**

Main Idea: _____

_____

_____

6 Scan the text. Circle the names of the two houses of Mexico's General Congress.

▶ **A POLITICAL RALLY in Mexico City**

Mexico's Government

The United States is not the only North American country made up of states working together. South of the United States are the *Estados Unidos Mexicanos*, or the "United States of Mexico."

Like that of the United States, Mexico's government has an executive, a legislative, and a judicial branch. In Mexico, though, the executive branch has more power than the other two branches.

Mexico, like the United States, is a presidential democracy. A **presidential democracy** is a government that is headed by an elected president. The Mexican president sets policies, influences lawmaking, and plans the budget. The president also appoints government officials, military officers, and judges. Unlike in the United States, Mexico's president has more power in government than the other two branches.

Even though Mexico has a strong executive branch, its legislative branch is still important to the government. Mexico's legislative branch is called the General Congress. This lawmaking body is made up of two houses—the Chamber of the Senate and the Chamber of Deputies.

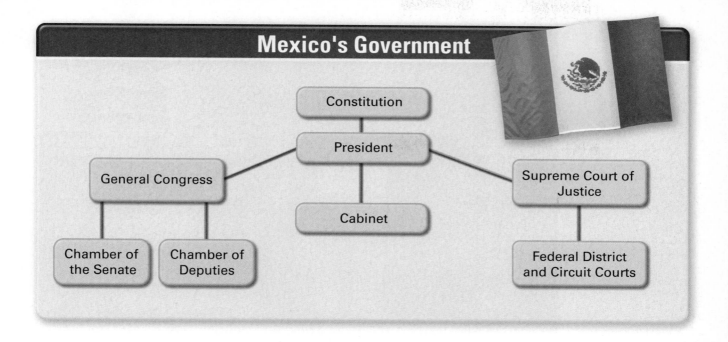

Mexico's Government

Constitution

President

General Congress

Supreme Court of Justice

Cabinet

Chamber of the Senate

Chamber of Deputies

Federal District and Circuit Courts

The Chamber of the Senate is made up of 128 members. Citizens in each of Mexico's 31 states and its Federal District elect 3 senators. The remaining senators come from Mexico's different political parties. The number of senators from each political party is based on the percentage of the total vote won by the party. This is called **proportional representation**. It gives all political parties a chance to take part in government.

The Chamber of Deputies has 500 members. Of these, 300 are directly elected by voters. Each elected deputy represents the people of a different part of Mexico. The rest are selected through proportional representation.

The General Congress has less power than the United States Congress. In the past, it often just approved the president's actions. Since the 2000 election, however, the General Congress has gained a greater voice in Mexico's government.

Mexico's national government has a two-level judicial branch. The top level is the Supreme Court of Justice. Under this are the federal district and circuit courts. As in the United States, each state has its own court system.

 TextWork

7 Study the diagram above. Who is the highest-ranking official in the Mexican government?

_____

8 Write a definition of the term *proportional representation* in your own words.

_____

_____

_____

_____

▶ A VOTER casts his ballot in an election in Managua, Nicaragua.

9 Which Central American countries have governments similar to those of the United States and Mexico?

_____

_____

_____

10 What is required of citizens in Guatemala that is not required of citizens in the United States?

_____

_____

_____

The Governments of Central America

Today, all seven Central American countries are democracies. The citizens of each country have the right to take part in their country's government. Costa Rica, El Salvador, Guatemala, Honduras, Nicaragua, and Panama have systems of government similar to those of the United States and Mexico. Belize has a parliamentary system, like Canada.

Central American Republics

In the past, the military has taken over the government of Honduras. For the past 20 years, though, citizens have elected their president. Unlike in the United States, the president, rather than the legislature, suggests most new laws.

The citizens of Guatemala elect both a president and a vice president. Each serves a single term of five years. Citizens also elect lawmakers. By law, all citizens 18 years or older are required to register to vote. This is not required in the United States.

The presidents of El Salvador and Nicaragua serve five-year terms. Unlike the United States, both countries have a one-house legislature. The members of El Salvador's legislature serve three-year terms. The members of Nicaragua's legislature serve five-year terms.

Like the United States government, Panama's national government has three branches. Panama's president leads the executive branch. Unlike other countries in North America, Panama has two vice presidents. Panama's National Assembly is the legislative branch of government. The nine-member supreme court of Panama forms the highest level of the judicial branch.

Costa Rica has free elections, majority rule, multiple political parties, and a guarantee of individual rights. Election Day in Costa Rica is a national holiday. Everyone over 18 years old must register to vote and get a voter-identification card.

TextWork

11 Underline the sentence that describes how Panama's government is different from that of other countries in North America, including the United States.

12 Scan the text. Circle the sentence that describes Costa Rica's system of government.

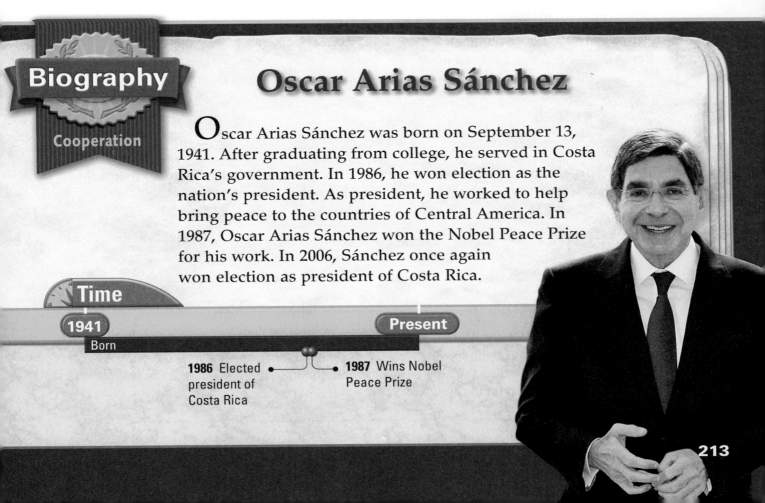

Biography

Cooperation

Oscar Arias Sánchez

Oscar Arias Sánchez was born on September 13, 1941. After graduating from college, he served in Costa Rica's government. In 1986, he won election as the nation's president. As president, he worked to help bring peace to the countries of Central America. In 1987, Oscar Arias Sánchez won the Nobel Peace Prize for his work. In 2006, Sánchez once again won election as president of Costa Rica.

Time

| 1941 | Present |

Born

1986 Elected president of Costa Rica

1987 Wins Nobel Peace Prize

213

SAID MUSA, the prime minister of Belize, gives a speech.

Belize's Parliamentary Democracy

Belize was once a British colony. It became independent in 1981. Today, Belize is the only English-speaking country in Central America.

Belize is part of the Commonwealth of Nations, which is made up of former British colonies. Other North American countries in the Commonwealth are Canada and Jamaica.

Like Canada, Belize is a parliamentary democracy. The British monarch is the head of Belize's government but has little say in governing. The prime minister carries out the day-to-day governing of the country. Belize also has a two-house National Assembly. It consists of a House of Representatives and a Senate.

Lesson 4 Review

1. **SUMMARIZE** What kind of government do most of the countries in North America have?

_____

_____

2. How is Mexico's **presidential democracy** different from that in the United States?

_____

_____

3. How is Canada's government similar to that of the United States? How is it different?

_____

_____

4. Which two countries in Central America have one-house legislatures?

_____

_____

activity

Make a Chart With a classmate, make a chart to compare and contrast three different kinds of governments in North America. List each country's name, the kind of government the country has, and the way the government of the country is organized.

Education in North America

Education plays an important part in the United States and in the other countries of North America. Today, every country in North America has a system of free public education. Some countries are able to offer excellent, free public education to all young people. Other countries find it hard to offer a basic education to their citizens. **What might you learn about education in North America as you read this lesson?**

_____

_____

_____

STUDENTS IN WINSTON-SALEM, NORTH CAROLINA

NORTH CAROLINA STANDARD COURSE OF STUDY

2.06 Explain the role of public education in the United States.

2.07 Compare and contrast the educational structure of the United States to those of Canada, Mexico, and selected countries of Central America.

▶ **STUDENTS in Wake County, North Carolina, in 1949**

 **TextWork**

❶ Skim the text in this lesson. Write a question you have about education in North America.

_____

_____

How could you find the answer to this question?

_____

_____

❷ Use the parts of the term *secondary education* to write a definition in your own words.

_____

_____

_____

Education in the United States

In the United States today, all children have the opportunity to receive a free public education. This education usually begins in kindergarten and ends at grade 12. In most states, students must attend school until the age of 16.

Elementary education is the first level of schooling in the United States. It usually includes kindergarten through grade 5 and sometimes goes through grade 8. Many young students also attend preschool before attending kindergarten.

Secondary education, the second level of schooling, usually includes grades 7 through 12 and sometimes grade 6. Students often attend a middle school or junior high school and then a senior high school. In senior high school, students can either prepare for college or get job training.

Today, about 75 percent of students in the United States graduate from senior high school. Many students go on to attend a college or university. In the United States, most students have to pay to attend a college or university.

Education in Canada

Some Canadian students attend preschool or kindergarten. All students in Canada attend free public elementary school for six years. They then attend middle school or junior high school, followed by senior high school. Depending on where they live, students must attend school until the age of 16, 17, or 18. About 72 percent of students in Canada graduate from senior high school.

Canada has two official languages—English and French. English is the main language for about three-fourths of the population. French is the main language for people in Quebec Province. Quebec has both English and French schools.

Education in Quebec is different from the United States in other ways. Students in Quebec attend secondary school through grade 11 only. They then attend special schools for three years. There, they prepare either to go to a university or to get jobs. These special schools are free to students. Because of this, Quebec offers more years of free schooling than the United States or other Canadian provinces.

TextWork

3 Complete the table below to compare and contrast education in Canada and the United States. List the percentage of students who graduate from senior high school in Canada and the percentage who graduate in the United States.

Percent of High School Graduates	
Country	Percent
United States	
Canada	

4 Scan the text on this page. Underline the sentences that describe how the education system in Quebec Province is different from that of the United States and of the rest of Canada.

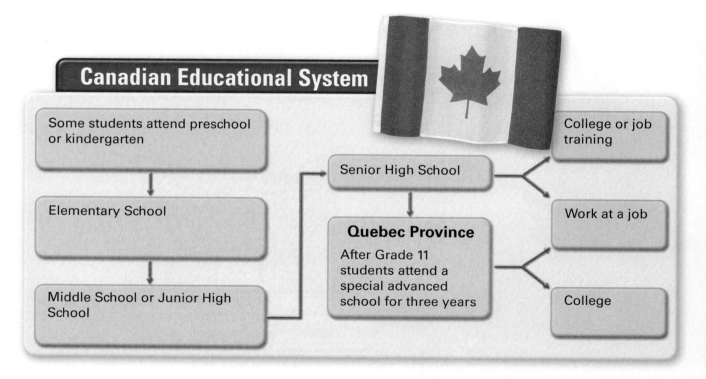

5 Circle the main idea of the first paragraph. Underline the supporting details.

6 Why do you think fewer Mexican students graduate from senior high school compared to students in the United States and Canada?

_____

_____

_____

_____

Education in Mexico

Mexico has less money to spend on education than either the United States or Canada. Leaders in Mexico are working hard to improve education. They are aware that people with better educations often get better-paying jobs. In turn, educated workers help the economy grow.

By law, all students in Mexico must complete ten grades. They must attend preschool. Then there are six grades of elementary school, followed by three years of junior high school. Students then take a test to enter senior high school. Senior high school students can prepare for college or learn how to do different jobs. After senior high school, Mexican students can attend a college or university.

Today, far more students attend Mexican schools than 15 years ago. Still, only about 68 percent of students complete the ninth grade. About 35 percent of students complete senior high school, and only 9 percent complete college. Children of poor families often must leave school to go to work.

▶ **THE CENTRAL LIBRARY** at the University of Mexico

> COSTA RICA
Students attend an outdoor assembly at a school in Costa Rica.

Education in Central America

Like Mexico, the countries of Central America are working to improve their schools and to educate their people. In Guatemala and Honduras, students must complete six years of elementary school. About 70 percent of Guatemalan children and 79 percent of Honduran children complete elementary school. However, only about 48 percent of Guatemalan children and 65 percent of Honduran children go to secondary school. Outside of the cities, there are few schools. Many schools don't have enough teaching tools or money to pay teachers.

Costa Rica has one of the best school systems in Central America. In 1869, it became one of the first nations in the world to set up free public education. In the past few years, Costa Rica has spent 28 percent of its national budget on education.

Students in Costa Rica must attend school for at least nine grades. Six years of elementary school are followed by three years of junior high school. Senior high school lasts two or three years. To finish high school, students must pass a test to show that they are ready for college. In Costa Rica, 92 percent of students complete elementary school. About 74 percent of students go on to secondary school.

TextWork

7 Scan the text to find the data that tells how many students finish elementary school in Guatemala, Honduras, and Costa Rica. Circle each of these figures.

8 Complete the graph below. Draw a bar on the graph to show the percentage of students who finish elementary school in Costa Rica.

Education in Central America

Percent of Students

100 90 80 70 60 50 40 30 20 10 0

Costa Rica   Guatemala   Honduras

Country

1. **SUMMARIZE** Why do all of the countries in North America offer a free public education?

_____

_____

_____

2. Use the term **elementary education** to describe preschool.

_____

_____

_____

3. How do you think the level of education of workers in a country helps or hurts that country's economy?

_____

_____

_____

Circle the letter of the correct answer.

4. In which Central American country do 92 percent of students finish elementary school?

   A Panama

   B Guatemala

   C Honduras

   D Costa Rica

MATCHING Draw a line connecting each country on the left with the correct description of its education system on the right.

5. Canada   Preschool is required.

6. Mexico   All students must attend school until the age of 16.

7. United States   There are both English and French schools.

activity

Make a Flowchart Make a flowchart that shows the school system of the United States. Add labels for elementary and secondary education to show which grades are usually included in each.

Families in North America

Families play an important role in every society. Families have children and teach them right from wrong. Families also pass on traditions and religious beliefs. **How will reading this lesson improve your understanding of families?**

_____

_____

_____

▶ A FAMILY PICNIC

NORTH CAROLINA
STANDARD COURSE OF STUDY

2.08 Describe the different types of families and compare and contrast the role the family plays in the societal structures of the United States, Canada, Mexico, and selected countries of Central America.

TextWork

❶ The word *nuclear* can mean a "central group." Use this information to write a sentence using the term *nuclear family*.

_____

_____

_____

_____

❷ Place an *X* on the photograph below that shows an extended family.

▶ **FAMILIES** There are many different kinds of families in North America.

Families in the United States

Families have always played an important role in the United States. Today, some children live with their nuclear family. A **nuclear family** is made up of a mother, father, and children. Some children live with members of their **extended family**—their grandparents, aunts, or uncles. Other children live in **single-parent families**. These are families with a mother or a father in the household, but not both. Children may see the other parent on weekends or vacations. Sometimes, single parents from two families marry and form a **blended family**.

Today, many Americans move to different parts of the country to find jobs or new opportunities. This means that families often move away from their extended family. Today, many children see grandparents, aunts, uncles, and cousins only once or twice a year. People today often live much longer than people did in the past. Instead of living with their grown children, many grandparents live by themselves or in retirement homes.

Families in Canada

Families in Canada are like families in the United States in many ways. Both fathers and mothers often work. In Canada, the average family has only one child. In the United States, the average family has two children.

People in Canada move often. But many families in Canada do not move as far from their extended families as people in the United States do. Of those who move each year, only about 3 percent move to a different province. Of all the people who move in the United States, 19 percent move to a new state.

Families in Mexico

Families in Mexico are very different from those in Canada and the United States. The extended family lies at the heart of Mexican life and culture. Families spend a lot of time with their grandparents, aunts, uncles, and cousins.

Many mothers in Mexico do not work outside the home. Many adult children live with their parents until they get married. Fathers often make most of the choices for the family. Grandparents often live with their adult children.

TextWork

3 Circle the main idea of the first paragraph. Then underline the supporting details.

4 What kind of family is especially important in Mexico?

_____

_____

Families in Central America

▶ A MAYAN FAMILY in Antigua, Guatemala

Family life in Central America is a lot like family life in Mexico. In Guatemala and Honduras, for example, the extended family is very important to society. Grandparents, aunts, uncles, and cousins often live in the same house with parents and children. More women work in Central America than in Mexico. Still, not as many women work as in the United States and Canada.

In countries such as Guatemala, there are also many American Indian families. They continue to live traditional lives and work in traditional jobs. Most American Indians live in small villages with their extended families.

Lesson 6 Review

1. **SUMMARIZE** How is the role of the family in Mexico and Central America different from that in the United States and Canada?

_____

_____

2. What is a **blended family**?

_____

_____

3. In which country are mothers least likely to work outside the home?

_____

_____

4. How is family life in Central America like family life in Mexico?

_____

_____

activity

🖍 **Draw a Picture** Draw a picture of your family, and draw labels to name each person in your picture. Then write a caption that describes the role each member of your family plays in your life.

Review and Test Prep

🔆 The Big Idea

People form political institutions, such as government, and social institutions, such as families and religious groups, to meet their needs and live together.

Summarize the Unit

Focus Skill Main Idea and Details Complete the graphic organizer below to show that you know how to identify a main idea and details about government in the United States.

Main Idea

_____

_____

Details

| The federal government prints money. | State governments set up local governments. | Local governments run local schools. |

Use Vocabulary

Fill in the missing term in each sentence, using the correct vocabulary term from the Word Bank.

1. People who advise the President are members of the _____.

2. In parliamentary democracies, the _____ leads both the executive and legislative branches of government.

3. What most people want from government is called the _____.

4. The _____ of government makes laws.

5. A change to the Constitution is called an _____.

Word Bank

amendment
 p. 191
legislative
 branch p. 194
Cabinet p. 204
public agenda
 p. 205
prime minister
 p. 208

Unit 4 ■ 225

Think About It

6. What is one power given to the state governments in the Constitution?

_____

_____

7. Describe one difference between Canada's government and the government of the United States.

_____

_____

8. Why do you think every North American country has a system of free public education?

_____

_____

Circle the letter of the correct answer.

9. Which branch of government makes sure laws are being applied fairly and equally?

   A the local branch

   B the legislative branch

   C the executive branch

   D the judicial branch

10. Which country in Central America is a parliamentary democracy?

   A Panama

   B Belize

   C Costa Rica

   D El Salvador

Show What You Know

Writing Write an Article
Write an article explaining how one of the governments of North America works. Describe two similarities and two differences between that government and the government of the United States.

Activity Create a Bulletin Board
Create a bulletin board to showcase different governments of North America. Prepare an organizational diagram, a biography, an illustration, a map, a chart, or a graph for your bulletin board display.

GO online
To play a game that reviews the unit, join Eco in the North Carolina Adventures online or on CD.

A Land of Many People

THE NEW YORK CITY MARATHON

Spotlight on Goals and Objectives

North Carolina Interactive Presentations

NORTH CAROLINA STANDARD COURSE OF STUDY

COMPETENCY GOAL 3 The learner will examine the roles various ethnic groups have played in the development of the United States and its neighboring countries.

# The Big Idea

How have different groups of people affected the cultures of the United States and its neighboring countries?

People of many different ethnic groups live in the United States and the other countries of North America. An **ethnic group** is a group of people from the same country, of the same race, or with a shared culture.

The many different ethnic groups in the United States add to the country's diversity. People from different ethnic groups often have different cultures. Many things, such as music, art, food, religion, and language, help shape culture.

Complete the table below. Give an example from your community of the things that shape culture.

Cultures Around Me	
Music	
Art	
Food	
Religion	
Language	

Reading Social Studies

Summarize

Why It Matters Summarizing can help you understand and remember the most important information in a paragraph or passage.

▶ LEARN

When you **summarize**, you state in your own words a short version of what you read. A summary is made up of only the most important ideas.

Key Facts		Summary
Important idea from the reading	▶	A shortened version of what you read
Important idea from the reading	▶	

▶ PRACTICE

Write a sentence to summarize each paragraph. The first paragraph has been done for you.

People from many different cultures live in the United States. Many Americans have ancestors who came from other countries. Some Americans were born in other countries and later moved to the United States. These people brought their cultures with them to the United States.   **Facts**

Summary: Today, the United States is a country full of many cultures.   **Summary**

One important part of culture is food. People who come to the United States often eat traditional foods from their home countries. As a result, many people in the United States eat Italian food, Chinese food, and other kinds of food. Many regions of the United States have their own ways of preparing food.

Summary: _____

Read the article. Then complete the activities below.

A Changing Nation

Millions of Europeans came to the United States in the late 1800s and early 1900s. They came to find new opportunities and to make better lives for themselves. Most of these people settled in large cities, such as New York City, Boston, and Chicago.

Many of the people who came to the United States at this time did not have a lot of money. Starting a farm was more difficult for them than it had been for American pioneers. There was not as much cheap land, and new farm equipment cost a lot of money. For these reasons, immigrants mostly moved to cities, where there were a lot of factory jobs.

During this time period, the number of factories grew. This growth led to many new jobs that immigrants could get. Workers were also needed to build large buildings, bridges, tunnels, highways, and railways.

Immigrant workers were often not paid enough money and were not treated fairly. Still, many of them began making money. Some bought their own homes. Others started their own businesses.

Today, in many cities in the United States, people can see the influence of immigrants who arrived during the late 1800s and early 1900s. They created communities in many cities. Their hard work helped the nation grow.

1. **Underline the key facts that explain why most European immigrants settled in large cities.**

2. **Write a sentence that summarizes the information in the third paragraph.**

_____

_____

_____

3. **Circle the key facts that explain how immigrants helped the United States grow.**

Cultures Past and Present

Cultural differences help explain why people in the United States often seem different from one another in so many ways. Over the years, people have come to the United States from countries all over the world. Having people from so many different places has made the United States a more diverse country. At the same time, it has made the United States a more interesting place in which to live. **What might you learn about culture in the United States as you read this lesson?**

_____

_____

A NATURALIZATION CEREMONY
on Ellis Island in New York Harbor

**NORTH CAROLINA
STANDARD COURSE OF STUDY**

3.01 Locate and describe people of diverse ethnic and religious cultures, past and present, in the United States.

3.04 Hypothesize how the differences and similarities among people have produced diverse American cultures.

Cultures Shaped the Past

The first groups of people to live in North America were American Indians. Their ways of life were shaped mainly by the land.

Newcomers from Europe and Africa

Some of the first European settlers to arrive in what is now the United States came from England. The culture of these people changed as they adapted to life in a new land.

Among the early English settlers were the Pilgrims and Puritans. They wanted to build communities where everyone shared the same Christian beliefs. The Pilgrims and Puritans first founded small villages in what is today Massachusetts.

People from England also settled in other places along the Atlantic Coast. There they started plantations, small farms, and villages. Over time, as the need for workers grew, enslaved people were brought from Africa against their will. Most were made to work mainly in the Southern colonies.

These Africans brought their cultures with them. Their traditions have become a part of the American culture. Musical styles such as jazz, blues, and gospel have their roots in African music.

![pencil icon] **TextWork**

❶ Where did some of the early English settlers in what is now the United States settle?

_____

_____

_____

_____

❷ Underline the sentences that describe how African culture influenced American culture.

▶ **ENGLISH SETTLERS** land in North America.

▶ **TRADITIONAL BASKETMAKING** is still done in the Appalachian Mountains.

Cultures Spread Out

Over time, people moved west to settle in the Appalachian Mountains. Their culture was shaped by life in the mountains. They lived far from towns and cities and had to make the things they needed. Many activities, such as furniture making, are still done by the people who live in this area.

Spanish settlers traveled north from Mexico to settle in what is today the southwestern and western United States. There they built large *ranchos*, or ranches, where they raised cattle. Most of the work on ranchos was done by vaqueros (vah•KAY•rohs). They were the first cowhands in North America. Cowhands still work on ranches in the Southwest and West.

In 1848, gold was discovered in California. The following year, thousands of people from around the world began arriving there. Most people did not find gold, but they still stayed in the area.

Some of these people came from China. They came to find gold and to make a better life for their families. Today, several cities in the West have neighborhoods that were started by Chinese immigrants.

TextWork

❸ Summarize the paragraph about the culture of people living in the Appalachian Mountains.

_____

_____

_____

_____

❹ Scan the text on this page. Underline the reason that immigrants from China first came to what is now the United States.

Cultures Shape the Present

Between 1860 and 1910, about 23 million immigrants arrived in New York City and San Francisco. They settled in cities and towns across the United States.

In the past, most immigrants came to the United States from Europe. Today, most immigrants come from countries in Asia and Latin America. Like immigrants in the past, they come seeking freedom and new opportunities for a better life. Many seek refuge from war, weak economies, and poor living conditions in their homelands.

Diverse American Cultures

The people of the United States are very diverse. Today, about 210 million Americans are of European background. Almost 35 million are African Americans, and more than 10 million Americans are of Asian background. About 2 million people in the country are American Indians.

Hispanic Americans are the fastest-growing ethnic group in the nation. An **ethnic group** is a group of people from the same country, of the same race, or with a shared culture.

TextWork

5 Write a sentence using the term *ethnic group*.

_____

_____

_____

_____

6 The circle graph below shows where immigrants have come from and the percentage of immigrants who have come from that region. A *percent*, shown by the symbol %, is given to each part of the graph. One percent is one-hundredth of something. Use the information in the circle graph to complete the bar graph below.

Foreign-born People in the United States, 2003

- South America, 6%
- Other Regions, 8%
- Caribbean, 10%
- Asia, 25%
- Europe, 14%
- Mexico and Central America, 37%

Foreign-born People in the United States, 2003

Percentage of People (0–100)

Region: Asia, Caribbean, Europe, Mexico and Central America, South America, Other Regions

More than three-fourths of Hispanic Americans live in the Southeast, Southwest, and West. California and Texas have the largest number of Hispanic people. But the state with the highest percentage of Hispanic American citizens is New Mexico.

Customs, Celebrations, and Traditions

Some Americans still speak the language of the country in which they were born, and so do some of their children. In fact, about one-fifth of all students in the United States today speak a language other than English at home.

Some Americans continue to dress in the styles of their home country. They also take part in the customs, celebrations, or traditions of their cultures. Cultural differences among Americans can be seen in the kinds of music people listen to, the foods they eat, and the religions they belong to. For example, Dearborn, Michigan, has one of the largest Arab American communities in the United States today. Many people there are Muslims, or people who follow the Islamic religion.

▶ HISPANIC AMERICANS celebrate Cinco de Mayo. The holiday honors the Mexican victory at the Battle of Puebla.

TextWork

7 Which state has the highest percentage of Hispanic American citizens?

_____

8 Underline a sentence that gives a fact about languages in the United States.

9 How do Americans continue the cultures of their home countries?

_____

_____

_____

Religion in the United States

▶ **A BUDDHIST TEMPLE** This Buddhist temple is located in Hawaii.

Immigrants have brought the many different religions of their home countries to the United States. The United States Constitution gives people in this country freedom of religion. People who live in the United States are free to follow any religion they choose, such as Christianity, Islam, Judaism, Buddhism, Sikhism, or Hinduism. People in the United States can also choose not to follow any religion at all.

Having so many different religions and cultures has given Americans a richer life. Over the years, people from each culture have added to the American culture. People borrow traits from cultures other than their own. Cultures in the United States have mixed to make new ways of life.

Lesson 1 Review

1. **SUMMARIZE** Why are there so many cultural differences in the United States?

_____

_____

2. Define the term **ethnic group** in your own words.

_____

_____

3. What is one way that African culture has added to the American culture?

_____

_____

4. How have different religions and cultures given Americans a richer life?

_____

_____

activity

Make a Poster Make a poster that shows the different cultures in your community. Use photographs and drawings to illustrate your poster.

On the Move

Lesson 2

Throughout history, people have moved from place to place. Early people likely moved on foot. They followed herds of animals, which they hunted for food. This *migration*, or movement, took place very slowly, with groups traveling only a few miles during their lives.

Over time, people developed new ways to travel. Machines allowed people to travel faster and over longer distances. As people traveled, they often traded goods and shared ideas. This movement of people, goods, and ideas has affected ways of living in the United States and around the world. **What will you read about the movement of people, goods, and ideas in this lesson?**

_____

_____

To Wilshire / Western

▶ **A SUBWAY STATION in Los Angeles, California**

NORTH CAROLINA STANDARD COURSE OF STUDY

3.02 Examine how changes in the movement of people, goods, and ideas have affected ways of living in the United States.

Changes in Transportation

① The diagram shows how a dugout was made. Study the drawings. Then match each drawing with the description below by placing the correct number on the line provided.

Steps in Making a Dugout:

___ The log is shaped, and the sides are chipped away.

___ The end pieces are attached, and the dugout is ready for sanding and painting.

___ The wood is removed from the inside.

___ A log is split lengthwise and placed round-side up.

___ Water is placed in the dugout and heated by rocks to soften the wood and make the dugout wider.

Many American Indian groups living near rivers, lakes, and oceans made boats for travel and trade. In the Northwest, the Columbia River became a "highway." American Indians in that region traveled on the river by using wooden **dugouts**, or boats made from logs. These dugouts held goods that could be traded.

The people who lived on the Great Plains were **nomads**, or people who moved from place to place. To carry things, they built travois (truh•VOYZ). These carriers were made of two poles fastened to a harness on a dog. Goods were carried on an animal skin that was tied between the poles.

The Spanish brought horses to North America. In time, the Plains people began to use horses to pull their travois, making travel faster and easier. Using horses also helped them hunt buffalo.

European colonists built roads between towns and villages. They used wagons pulled by horses or oxen to travel and to carry goods. European colonists also had large sailing ships that could carry people and goods long distances.

Making a Dugout

> STEAMBOATS were a faster way to travel and to ship goods.

Transportation Speeds Up

In the 1800s, steam power changed transportation even more. Steamboats could carry people and goods against the flow of a river. Cities such as St. Louis and Cincinnati grew up along rivers.

Steam railroads changed the way people and goods moved on land. By 1900, railroad tracks stretched across the United States. Railroads made it easier for people to move goods from place to place. They also let people travel to and settle in new parts of the country.

In the early 1900s, the automobile changed the way people lived. People drove to work and to stores. They took long car trips with their families.

In time, the government built a series of highways to connect cities and towns. Highways let people live farther from their jobs. Communities began to spread out from cities. In their new automobiles, people could travel to more places.

Today, airplanes give people even more freedom. Airplanes can carry people and goods almost anywhere in the world. A trip that in the past might have taken days or months can now be completed in just a few hours.

 TextWork

❷ Scan the text on this page. Underline the sentences that describe how steam power changed the movement of goods and people.

❸ How did automobiles and highways change ways of life for people in the United States?

_____

_____

_____

_____

_____

4 Use the vocabulary word *communication* to write a sentence about the early colonies.

_____

_____

_____

_____

5 Study the time line below. In which year did Thomas Paine publish *Common Sense*? Circle this date on the time line.

Changes in Communication

At first, most American Indian groups did not have a written language. They shared ideas mostly by talking. At the time, trade helped ideas spread among different groups.

In the early colonies, **communication**, or the exchange of information or news, was difficult. Messages traveled slowly. It took months for ships to cross the Atlantic Ocean. Also, few roads connected towns and villages.

In time, some people opened print shops. They printed newspapers and pamphlets that spread news and ideas. In 1732, Benjamin Franklin began printing *Poor Richard's Almanack*. This **almanac**, or book of facts, had information and ideas for farmers. It also had interesting stories and jokes.

Before the American Revolution began, people in the 13 colonies spread ideas about independence through pamphlets. In his pamphlet *Common Sense*, Thomas Paine questioned the right of kings to rule. From Georgia to New Hampshire, people read and talked about Paine's pamphlet.

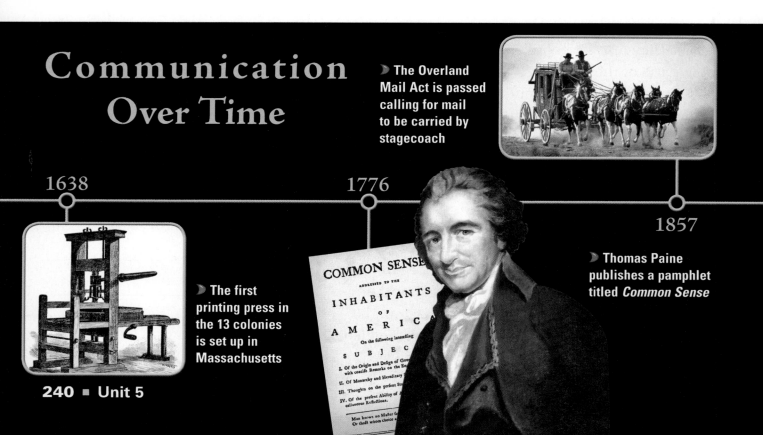

Communication Over Time

1638

▷ The first printing press in the 13 colonies is set up in Massachusetts

1776

▷ The Overland Mail Act is passed calling for mail to be carried by stagecoach

COMMON SENSE
ADDRESSED TO THE
INHABITANTS
OF
AMERICA

1857

▷ Thomas Paine publishes a pamphlet titled *Common Sense*

Communication Gets Faster

As the United States grew, communication needed to improve. It could take months for news from one side of the country to reach the other side. One way to improve communication was to improve the mail service.

It was decided that the quickest way to deliver mail was by enclosed wagons called stagecoaches. A stagecoach could bring news and mail from Missouri to San Francisco in as few as 24 days. Soon people came up with an even faster way to deliver mail. A large number of riders on horseback, called the Pony Express, could make the trip in as few as 9 days.

However, the telegraph was even faster. It used electricity to send messages over wires. The telegraph could send messages across the country in just minutes. In 1876, a new telephone was designed. People could use the telephone to speak with someone who was far away.

Today, people can send mail by using the United States Postal Service. It delivers letters and packages anywhere in the United States.

TextWork

6 Circle the sentences that compare and contrast stagecoaches and the Pony Express.

7 How did the telegraph change communication?

_____

_____

_____

_____

_____

Telegraph lines connect the East and West coasts of the United States

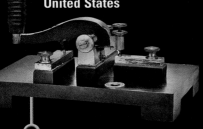

1861

Alexander Graham Bell designs a new telephone

1876

Most American homes have a television

1960

1991

The World Wide Web (www) begins to connect people around the world through the Internet

Communication Today

In the 1900s, radio and television gave people a way to spread new ideas quickly to many people at once. Radio and television did not need wires. Instead, they received signals that were sent through the air. Without leaving their homes, people could now learn about other people, events, and new ideas from around the country and around the world.

With the growth of computers and the Internet, people today are even more connected than they were in the past. Instead of going to a store, people can shop for and buy goods on the Internet. They can communicate through e-mails with family and friends. They can even make their own websites to share ideas.

▶ INTERNET CAFÉS are popular places throughout North America.

Lesson 2 Review

1. **SUMMARIZE** How have communication and transportation affected life in the United States?

   _____

   _____

2. How has **communication** changed as a result of the Internet?

   _____

   _____

3. How did the airplane change transportation?

   _____

   _____

   _____

4. What ideas did *Common Sense* spread to people in the 13 colonies?

   _____

   _____

writing

✎ **Write a Diary Entry** Pretend you are living during the 1920s. Your family has just bought its first automobile. Explain how the automobile has changed your life.

Cultures Coast to Coast

The United States has many cultural regions. In a **cultural region**, many people share similar ways of life, traditions, and customs. A cultural region can be as small as a neighborhood or as large as one of the five regions of the United States. In the United States, people in different cultural regions interact with one another. This cultural interaction makes the United States more diverse. **What will you learn about cultures in the United States?**

_____

_____

HULA DANCERS at Volcanoes National Park in Hawaii

NORTH CAROLINA STANDARD COURSE OF STUDY

3.03 Identify examples of cultural interaction within and among the regions of the United States.

3.05 Describe the religious and ethnic impact of settlement on different regions of the United States.

TextWork

1 Underline the sentences in the text that describe the holidays that help unite Americans.

2 What does the word *plural* mean? How does this help you understand the word *pluralistic*?

_____

_____

_____

_____

_____

_____

National Culture

The United States is a country made up of people from many different cultures. Still, Americans share many things that help unite them.

One thing that helps bring Americans together is patriotism. Americans celebrate holidays that mark important events in the nation's history. On July 4, Americans gather to celebrate Independence Day. On Veterans Day, they honor and remember all soldiers who have fought for the country. American leaders, such as Dr. Martin Luther King, Jr., and George Washington, are also remembered and honored with holidays.

Americans also share a deep belief in freedom. They believe in freedom of religion, freedom to choose their work, freedom of speech, freedom to go where they like, and freedom to meet with other people.

The United States can be described as being **pluralistic**. That is, the people of the United States share a culture while also keeping many of the traditional ways of their ancestors.

▶ **A VETERANS DAY ceremony held in Washington, D.C.**

▶ **A SAINT PATRICK'S DAY PARADE** The Boston Gaelic Fire Brigade marches in the South Boston Saint Patrick's Day Parade.

The Northeast

Each region of the United States has its own culture. A region's culture is shaped by the people who settled there, by its geography, and by its history.

Many small towns in the Northeast were founded long ago, in the colonial period. People there take care of historic sites so that important events, people, and places will not be forgotten.

The Northeast is also a region of very large cities. People from different countries around the world have come to live in New York City, Boston, and many other cities in the Northeast.

Immigrant communities in the Northeast often hold festivals to celebrate their heritage and traditions. Chinese Americans celebrate Chinese New Year. Irish Americans hold parades to celebrate Saint Patrick's Day. Columbus Day is an important holiday for Italian Americans. They celebrate this day with parades and festivals.

The fishing industry is very important in the Northeast. People there eat a lot of seafood. Clam chowder is a popular seafood dish there.

 **TextWork**

❸ Underline the sentences that describe how history is a part of the culture of the Northeast.

❹ List three facts about cultures in the Northeast.

- _____

_____

_____

- _____

_____

_____

- _____

_____

_____

▶ MUSICIANS at a music festival in North Carolina

The Southeast

Some of the first settlers in the Southeast were from Europe. Later, farmers in the Southeast brought enslaved people from Africa to work on plantations. Over time, the cultures from Africa and from Europe began to mix.

This cultural mix can be seen in the music that developed in the Southeast. For example, banjos came from Africa and were later used in country and bluegrass music. Gospel music developed from a mix of traditional African work songs and Christian beliefs brought by Europeans. Today, people from all regions listen to music from the Southeast. Music festivals across the Southeast celebrate the region's musical styles.

The traditional foods of the Southeast have also come from many cultures. American Indians grew corn, pumpkins, squash, and beans. Europeans brought pigs, cattle, chickens, and rice. Okra, eggplant, peanuts, and yams all came from Africa. Many of these foods can be found in Southern dishes today. For example, gumbo is a stew that combines European, African, and American Indian kinds of food.

TextWork

5 How has the mix of different cultures affected music in the Southeast?

_____

_____

_____

_____

_____

6 Gumbo is a food that

combines _____,

_____, and

_____ influences.

The Midwest

As in all of the regions of the United States, many years of immigration and migration have brought a strong **cultural diversity**, or variety, to the Midwest. In the late 1800s, factories in the Midwest provided many jobs. Those jobs attracted many immigrants to the area. Most came from Ireland, Poland, Italy, Greece, and other European countries.

In the early 1900s, many African Americans moved from the South to cities in the North for work. So many African Americans moved that their travels became known as the Great Migration.

More recently, immigrants have come to the Midwest from Mexico, Africa, and Asia. Michigan has one of the nation's largest Arab American communities. Many people from Somalia, in Africa, have settled in Minnesota.

All of these groups have shaped life in the region. African Americans shaped Detroit's "Motown sound" and Chicago's blues and jazz music. Irish immigrants in Chicago started the Saint Patrick's Day parade there. In Milwaukee, Wisconsin, many people celebrate their Polish heritage at Polish Fest.

 **TextWork**

7 The information in the box below shows the percentage of the population in the Midwest from each cultural group. Use the information to fill in the circle graph.

Midwest Cultural Groups

Group	Percent of Population
European	82%
African American	11%
Hispanic	5%
Asian	1.5%
American Indian	Less than 1%

Midwest Cultural Groups

African American 11%

American Indian less than 1%

▶ **SMOKEY ROBINSON AND THE MIRACLES** were a popular Motown singing group in the 1960s.

The Southwest

Long ago, many groups of American Indians lived in what is today the Southwest. The first Europeans in the area were Spanish. They came to spread the Catholic religion and to find gold.

In 1821, the Southwest came under the control of the new country of Mexico. Soon many people from Mexico, Europe, and the United States went to live in the Southwest. Today, the Southwest has a mix of cultures, yet many buildings and place-names reflect the region's Spanish heritage.

American Indian culture is also a large part of the region's heritage today. More than 800,000 American Indians live in the Southwest. Many live in cities, while others live on *reservations*. On reservations, American Indians govern themselves.

American Indians on reservations try to keep their heritage alive. They make traditional goods and hold cultural celebrations. Their children learn to read and speak American Indian languages.

TextWork

8 Circle the sentence that gives a reason why the Spanish first came to North America.

9 How do American Indians on reservations work to keep their heritage alive?

_____

_____

_____

Biography

Citizenship

Luci Tapahonso

Luci Tapahonso is a Navajo poet. She helps spread the Navajo culture through her writings. She writes in both English and the Navajo language.

Today, Tapahonso is a professor at the University of Arizona. She was also part of a group that helped plan and organize the National Museum of the American Indian in Washington, D.C.

Time

1953
Born

PRESENT

1981 Tapahonso publishes her first collection of poems

The West

Many different American Indian groups lived in the West. Each group had its own culture. Through trade, American Indians shared goods and ideas.

The first Europeans in the West came from Spain. Later, people from Mexico moved there. In the 1800s, people from the United States began to move west. One religious group, the Mormons, settled in present-day Utah.

In 1848, gold was discovered in California. The gold rush that followed brought many new cultural groups to the West. People from around the world came to California in the 1850s.

Today, California's population is one of the most diverse in the country. People of many different cultures and religions live there, including many Buddhists, Muslims, Sikhs, and Hindus.

Alaska and Hawaii are also diverse states. About one in seven Alaskans is an American Indian. Many American Indians follow both old and new ways of life. Hawaii is the only state that has two official languages—English and Hawaiian.

▶ THE MORMON TEMPLE in Logan, Utah, stands out against the Wellsville Mountains.

 TextWork

10 What does the temple shown in the photograph above tell you about the importance of religion to the people of Logan, Utah?

_____

_____

_____

_____

11 Scan the text on this page. Where did the Mormons settle? Circle the name of this place in the text.

1. **SUMMARIZE** What makes the cultural regions in the United States different from one another?

_____

_____

_____

2. Use the word **pluralistic** to describe culture in the United States.

_____

_____

_____

Circle the letter of the correct answer.

3. What part of culture in the Southeast has spread across the country?

    A language

    B music

    C holidays

    D art

4. Which region most reflects a mix of Spanish, Mexican, and American Indian cultures?

    A the Northeast

    B the Midwest

    C the Southeast

    D the Southwest

MATCHING Draw a line connecting each region on the left with a cultural characteristic on the right.

5. the Southwest   seafood

6. the Midwest   reservations

7. the Northeast   Polish Fest

writing

✎ **Write a Poem** Write a poem that celebrates the diversity of people in the United States. In your poem, also describe how people of such diverse cultures are brought together as Americans.

Cultural Groups

Most people living in North America today, or their ancestors, have come from somewhere else. When all these different groups came to North America, they brought with them their languages, customs, religions, and traditions. Over time, these ethnic and religious groups have shaped cultures in North America. **What do you think you will learn about the roles different cultural groups have played in the development of countries in North America?**

_____

_____

_____

A CHINESE NEW YEAR PARADE in New York City

NORTH CAROLINA STANDARD COURSE OF STUDY

3.06 Compare and contrast the roles various religious and ethnic groups have played in the development of the United States with those of Canada, Mexico, and selected countries of Central America.

❶ Underline the sentences that tell why many of the first Spanish settlers came to North America.

❷ Write an effect for the cause listed below.

Cause: Spanish missionaries came to North America to convert American Indians to the Catholic Church.

Effect: _____

_____

_____

_____

▶ **A SPANISH MISSION** This mission in northern Mexico was built by Spanish missionaries in the 1700s.

Religious Groups

American Indian groups had their own religious beliefs and practices. When Europeans came to North America, they brought with them their religious beliefs.

Spanish Missionaries

Many of the first Spanish settlers who came to North America were missionaries. These religious teachers came to convert American Indians to the Catholic Church. They built missions in what are today the Southwest and West regions of the United States. Spanish settlements also stretched south into Mexico and Central America.

Today, most of the people in Mexico and in the countries of Central America belong to the Catholic Church. In the United States and Canada, fewer people are Catholic. However, many places there have names that reflect an area's Catholic heritage. For example, San Francisco, California, was named for Saint Francis, a Catholic religious figure. *San Francisco* means "Saint Francis" in Spanish.

▷ THE GREAT PURITAN MIGRATION
Between 1630 and 1643, more than 20,000
Puritans, a Protestant group, left Europe to
settle in New England.

Early Protestant Groups

Other early European settlers in what is now the United States came from England. Many were Protestants, or members of churches that formed because of protests against the Catholic Church. Today, many Americans belong to a Protestant church.

Other religious groups also settled in the English colonies. Maryland was founded as a *refuge*, or safe place, for Catholics. At that time, Catholics in England could not worship freely. Jewish groups also settled in the colonies. *Religious toleration*, or the acceptance of religious differences, grew in the colonies. Today, freedom of religion is an important right for all Americans.

More Recent Groups

In the 1800s and 1900s, new waves of immigrants from Europe and Asia came to the United States and Canada. They brought with them their religious beliefs and customs. Many people follow Buddhism, Hinduism, or Sikhism. Other people follow Islam or Judaism. Many people whose families came from eastern Europe practice the Eastern Orthodox or Greek Orthodox religions.

3 Which religious group is shown in the painting above? Where did they settle?

_____

_____

4 In your own words, explain the term *religious toleration*.

_____

_____

_____

_____

_____

▶ **MEXICO CITY was the capital of New Spain. Today, it is the capital of Mexico.**

 TextWork

5 Circle the names of the regions in the United States that were claimed by Spanish settlers.

6 What is the official language of Mexico and of most countries of Central America?

_____

Ethnic Groups Shape Regions

Over the years, people from many different ethnic groups have come to live in North America. Each group has brought its own culture and beliefs from its home country.

Mexico and Central America

The Spanish were the first Europeans to control much of the land that is now Mexico and Central America. Today, these areas still show their Spanish background. Spanish is the official language of Mexico and of most countries of Central America. Many place-names and buildings in these areas reflect a Spanish heritage. Most people who live there still follow the Catholic religion.

The Spanish also claimed land in what is now the Caribbean and the United States. Many places there also show their Spanish background. The Spanish started colonies in Florida and the Southwest and West regions. Cities founded by Spain in these areas include San Diego, California; Santa Fe, New Mexico; and St. Augustine, Florida.

The United States

The English founded Jamestown, Virginia, in 1607. In time, they founded 13 colonies. After the American Revolution, these colonies would become the first states. Even though the United States has no official language, most people living there today speak English. Many holidays and customs can be traced back to England. The system of government is also influenced by English laws.

Even though many places in the United States have an English heritage, the country is very diverse. People from many cultures around the world have come to the United States. As a result, the United States has a more diverse population than the other countries of North America.

However, not all groups who came to what is now the United States came freely. Traders and plantation owners brought enslaved people from Africa. These people continued to practice the traditions and customs of their African cultures. Over time, the traditions and customs of enslaved people and their ancestors have had a great influence on culture in the United States.

TextWork

7 Circle the year in which Jamestown was founded. What country founded this place?

_____

8 Why do you think that the United States today reflects many English traditions?

_____

_____

_____

_____

_____

▶ **IMMIGRANTS** who came to Ellis Island had to give their information in the Registration Room.

▶ **CANADIAN SIGNS** have both English and French writing.

Canada

In 1630, the first French settlers arrived in Canada. In 1718, they founded the city of New Orleans, in what is now the state of Louisiana. Today, that city's French background can still be seen in the buildings, food, and festivals there.

In 1763, Britain won control of Canada from France. As a result, most of Canada today speaks English and reflects a British heritage. However, to keep control of the people living in French-speaking Quebec, the British let the French colonists there keep their language and their Catholic religion.

Even today, people in Canada work hard to protect Quebec's French culture and language. In 1969, the Canadian government passed a law called the Official Languages Act. This law made Canada a **bilingual**, or two-language, country. The federal government requires that services be offered in both English and French all across Canada.

Lesson 4 Review

1. **SUMMARIZE** How have religious and ethnic groups affected North America?

_____

_____

2. Describe Canada's Official Languages Act, using the term **bilingual**.

_____

_____

3. Why do most people in Mexico and Central America belong to the Catholic Church today?

_____

_____

4. Why do you think that Canada protects the French culture?

_____

_____

activity

Make a Word Web Label the center cultural groups. Out from the center add labels for Canada, the United States, Mexico, and Central America. Name cultural groups who settled in each region.

The Arts in North America

Lesson 5

People create their own forms of art, music, and crafts based on their history and culture. **Crafts** are items that are both beautiful and useful.

American Indians were the first to make art, music, and crafts in North America. As people from other areas of the world came to North America, they brought their arts with them. By the late 1800s and early 1900s, new forms of art, music, and crafts began to mix American Indian, African, Asian, and European styles. **How will this lesson help you understand the arts in North America?**

_____

_____

ALFOMBRAS, or art made of flower petals or sawdust, in Antigua, Guatemala

NORTH CAROLINA STANDARD COURSE OF STUDY

3.07 Describe art, music, and craft forms in the United States and compare them to various art forms in Canada, Mexico, and selected countries of Central America.

Arts

American Indians created some of the first art in North America. They made petroglyphs on rock walls. **Petroglyphs** are pictures cut into rock.

European explorers and settlers brought their art forms to North America. Some of the earliest European art was religious art, such as paintings in Spanish missions. European artists also painted *landscapes*, or pictures of the land, and *portraits*, or pictures of people. In the early 1900s, Diego Rivera and other Mexican artists made **murals**, or huge paintings that spread across the walls of public buildings.

People also began to accept photography as an art form in the early 1900s. Ansel Adams was an American photographer who was well known for photographing landscapes.

The major art forms in North America today are painting, sculpture, and photography. Many artists work in North America. Some make art that is influenced by their cultures.

① The word *glyph* means "a carved symbol." How does knowing the meaning of this word help you understand the word *petroglyph*?

_____

_____

_____

_____

② Scan the text on this page. What kind of art form did people make in Mexico in the early 1900s? Underline the sentence that gives this information.

▶ **AN ANCIENT PUEBLOAN PETROGLYPH** in the Rinconada Canyon in New Mexico

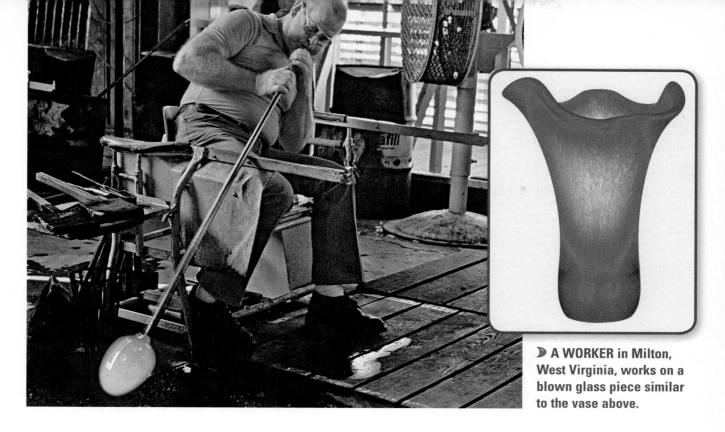

▶ A WORKER in Milton, West Virginia, works on a blown glass piece similar to the vase above.

Crafts

The people of North America have a tradition of making crafts. Crafts are generally made by hand to be both useful and beautiful.

Crafts in the United States

Before there were factories, people made goods by hand. Today, people choose to continue making certain crafts by hand to keep the tradition alive. Older family members often teach younger people in the family how to make crafts.

Early American Indians made crafts such as baskets and pottery. Today, many American Indians still make crafts just as their ancestors did. The Seminole and Cherokee make baskets from pine needles and river canes. The Navajo, Hopi, and Pueblo peoples make pottery from clay.

Many other people in the United States make crafts that reflect their culture. People in the Appalachian Mountains make wooden furniture, toys, quilts, and blown glass in much the same way as their ancestors did.

🖊 **TextWork**

❸ How is a craft different from other forms of art?

_____

_____

_____

_____

_____

❹ Circle the main idea of the fourth paragraph. Then underline the sentence that supports this main idea.

5 What kinds of crafts are made by the Zapotec in Mexico?

_____

_____

_____

_____

6 Underline the sentence that describes crafts made by people in Jamaica.

▶ **AMERICAN INDIANS** in the Northwest Coast region made totem poles, like the ones below in Stanley Park in Canada, to tell stories or record notable events.

Crafts in Canada and Mexico

People in Canada also make crafts. They make quilts, pottery, wood carvings, baskets, and hand-blown glass, among many other goods. Inuit artists carve animals from stone, bone, and walrus ivory.

People in Mexico make pottery, baskets, silver jewelry, and belts. Native people in Mexico, such as the Zapotec, make fine woven rugs, blankets, and cloth. In southern Mexico, artists carve animals from wood and paint them with bright colors.

Crafts in Central America and the Caribbean

Each country in Central America has unique crafts. Guatemala is famous for its colorful woven cloth. The Emberá and Wounaan people, who live in Panama's rain forest, weave fine, colorful baskets.

People in Jamaica make clothing dyed with bright colors, goods from shells, and carvings from native woods. In Haiti, people make bright painted objects from used pieces of metal. All across North America, people continue to mix old crafts with new materials and new ideas.

▷ A MARIACHI BAND performs on the streets of Zacatecas, Mexico.

Music in North America

American Indians made music and instruments, such as flutes and drums. When Europeans and Africans came to North America, they brought with them new music and new instruments.

Music from Africa has influenced much of the music in the United States. It has also influenced much of the music of the Caribbean. Reggae, salsa, calypso, and merengue are all musical styles from the Caribbean. All of these styles of music have their roots in African music.

Country music is popular in the United States. It is made up of simple tunes and songs played on traditional instruments, such as guitars and fiddles. Country music came from the music of settlers and immigrants from Ireland, England, and Scotland. It was also influenced by blues music played by African Americans.

One popular form of music in Mexico is the music played by *mariachis*, or musicians who walk from place to place as they play and sing. Mariachis often play violins, trumpets, and several types of guitars.

TextWork

7 Describe the instruments being played by the mariachis in the photograph above.

_____

_____

_____

_____

8 Describe how music in North America is a mix of musical styles.

_____

_____

_____

_____

Lesson **5** Review

1. SUMMARIZE How are art, music, and craft forms in the United States like those in other North American countries?

_____

_____

_____

2. Use the word **mural** in a sentence.

_____

_____

3. Why do you think art is important to people in North America?

_____

_____

Circle the letter of the correct answer.

4. What art form became accepted in the early 1900s?

  A sculpture

  B landscapes

  C portraits

  D photography

5. Which of the following is a kind of Caribbean music?

  A country

  B calypso

  C blues

  D mariachi

MATCHING Draw a line connecting each country on the left with the correct kind of art, craft, or music made there on the right.

6. United States   brightly dyed clothing

7. Jamaica   country music

8. Mexico   silver jewelry

writing

Write a Paragraph Write a paragraph describing the art, music, and crafts you have seen in your community.

Review and Test Prep

The Big Idea

Ethnic groups add to a country's diversity. They influence culture, including music, art, food, religion, and languages.

Summarize the Unit

Summarize Complete the graphic organizer to show that you know how to summarize information about cultures in the United States.

Key Facts

People from many different ethnic groups live in the United States.

People from different ethnic groups continue to practice their traditions.

Summary

_____

_____

_____

Use Vocabulary

Fill in the missing term in each sentence, using the correct vocabulary term from the Word Bank.

1. A person who moves often and has no permanent home is called a
    _____.

2. A person who speaks two languages is _____.

3. An _____ is a group of people from the same country, of the same race, or with a shared culture.

4. A _____ is a good that is both useful and beautiful.

5. _____ describes a person who shares in the common culture while also keeping traditional ways.

> *Word Bank*
>
> **ethnic group**
> p. 234
> **nomad** p. 238
> **pluralistic**
> p. 244
> **bilingual** p. 256
> **craft** p. 257

6. How have different ethnic groups influenced your community?

   _____

   _____

7. How have radio and television changed life in the United States?

   _____

   _____

8. Why do you think arts and crafts are important to people in North America?

   _____

   _____

Circle the letter of the correct answer.

9. Which of the following is a part of the culture of the Southeast?

   A clam chowder

   B bluegrass music

   C Polish Fest

   D Hawaiian language

10. In which languages does the Canadian government offer services?

   A Spanish and English

   B Spanish and French

   C French and English

   D French and Dutch

Show What You Know

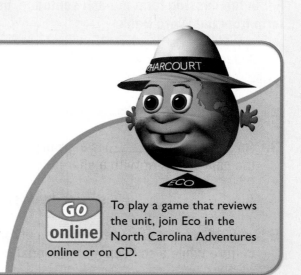

✏️ **Writing** Write a Poem

Write a poem that celebrates your culture. This poem can be about traditional food, music, language, or other parts of culture.

🖌️ **Activity** Make a Scrapbook

Design a scrapbook about the cultures of North America. You might include pictures and illustrations, poems and other writings, or charts and diagrams in your scrapbook.

GO online To play a game that reviews the unit, join Eco in the North Carolina Adventures online or on CD.

Economic
Neighbors

▶ A MARKET IN GUATEMALA

Spotlight on Goals and Objectives

North Carolina Interactive Presentations

NORTH CAROLINA STANDARD COURSE OF STUDY

COMPETENCY GOAL 5 The learner will evaluate ways the United States and other countries of North America make decisions about the allocation and use of economic resources.

 # The Big Idea

How do people in North America decide how to allocate and use economic resources?

Not every economic resource can be found in every part of North America. **Economic resources** are the people, materials, and natural resources used to make goods and to offer services to people. No country has enough economic resources to make every kind of good and offer every kind of service.

Each day, people in North America have to make economic decisions. They decide how to *allocate*, or divide, available economic resources. They also decide how to use economic resources.

Study the flowchart, and answer the questions.

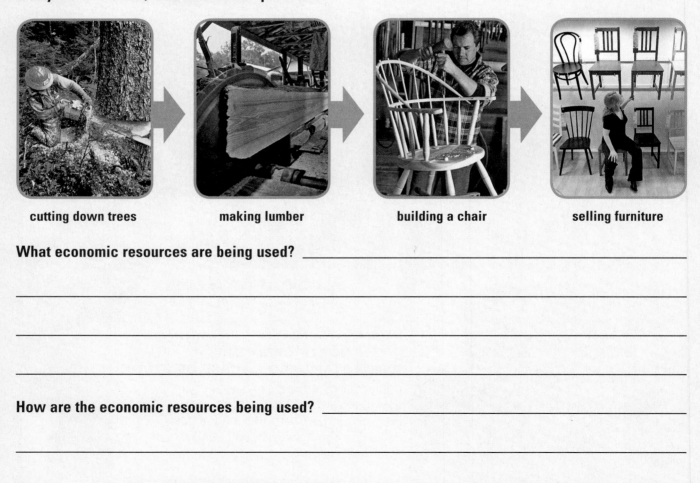

cutting down trees   making lumber   building a chair   selling furniture

What economic resources are being used? _____

_____

_____

_____

How are the economic resources being used? _____

_____

_____

Reading Social Studies

 **Generalize**

▶ LEARN

When you **generalize**, you make a statement that shows how different facts in a piece of writing are related. Being able to generalize can help you better understand and remember what you read. Words such as *most, many, some, generally*, and *usually* are hints to help you find generalizations.

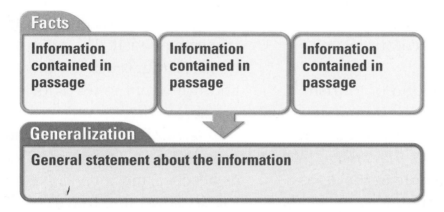

Facts

| Information contained in passage | Information contained in passage | Information contained in passage |

Generalization

General statement about the information

▶ PRACTICE

Write a generalization about each paragraph. The first one has been done for you.

> Many people go on vacations in the United States. They go to cities such **Facts** as New York City and Orlando. Other people visit national parks, such as the Grand Canyon and Yellowstone. People spend a lot of money while they are on vacation. People on vacation help the economy in the areas they visit.

Generalization: Tourism is an important industry in the United States. **Generalization**

After the Industrial Revolution, people could make goods by machine. These machines made a large amount of goods in a short period of time. Today, factories make most of the goods in the United States.

Generalization: _____

_____

Read the article. Then complete the activities below.

Ecotourism

Costa Rica is one of the richest nations in Central America. One reason is the country's tourism industry. Many people visit Costa Rica because of its natural beauty. The land makes Costa Rica a popular place for ecotourists to visit.

Ecotourism is a kind of tourism that deals with the environment of an area. Ecotourists learn about cultures in the areas they visit. They also help people in the areas they visit and learn new ways to live on the planet. Some ecotourists visit rain forests. They can stay in tree houses in the top of the rain forest, called the canopy.

Many ecotourists also take part in outdoor activities, such as hiking, bike riding, swimming, and other water sports.

Many ecotourists try not to change the environment of the places they visit. They do this by recycling, reusing water, and trying not to use a lot of energy.

In Costa Rica, ecotourism is centered on tropical areas, such as beaches and forests. National forests cover one-fourth of Costa Rica's land. Ecotourists often visit these areas so that they can experience the natural beauty of the land.

1. **Circle the sentences that support the generalization that ecotourism is the most popular way for visitors to see Costa Rica.**

2. **From the second paragraph, what generalization can you make about ecotourists?**

_____

_____

3. **Underline the sentences that support the generalization that ecotourists are generally concerned about the environments they visit.**

Economic Resources

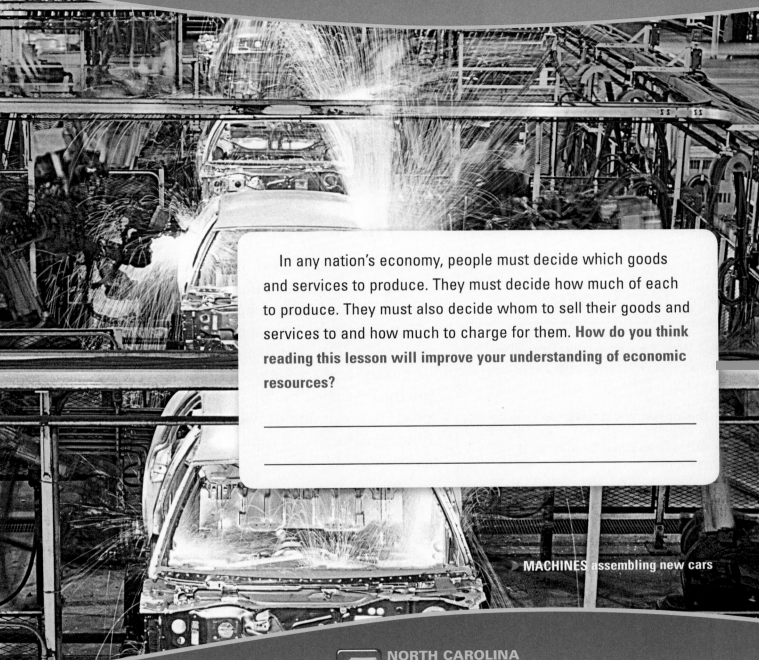

In any nation's economy, people must decide which goods and services to produce. They must decide how much of each to produce. They must also decide whom to sell their goods and services to and how much to charge for them. **How do you think reading this lesson will improve your understanding of economic resources?**

_____

_____

MACHINES assembling new cars

**NORTH CAROLINA
STANDARD COURSE OF STUDY**

5.01 Categorize economic resources found in the United States and neighboring countries as human, natural, or capital and assess their long-term availability.

5.08 Cite examples of surplus and scarcity in the American market and explain the economic effects.

▶ **HUMAN RESOURCES** Workers in a factory produce electronic equipment.

Three Types of Resources

To produce any good or provide any service, a business uses different kinds of economic resources. It must have **human resources**, or workers. It must have natural resources, such as soil, water, minerals, and fuel. It must also have *capital*, or money, and capital resources. **Capital resources** are the machines, buildings, and tools needed to produce goods and provide services. Together, human, natural, and capital resources are called the *factors of production*.

Human Resources

Each day, millions of people around the world go to work. They bring important ideas and skills to their jobs. Some workers run machines in factories. Businesses also depend on workers, such as teachers and doctors, to provide services. To succeed in the long term, businesses must continue to have skilled, educated workers.

Without human resources, businesses could not produce the goods that allow people to meet their wants. A *want* is something that people would like to have. Some wants, such as food, clothing, and shelter, are needs.

TextWork

❶ Write a generalization about businesses, using the facts below.

- **Businesses must have workers.**

- **Businesses must have natural resources.**

- **Businesses must have buildings and tools.**

Generalization: _____

_____

_____

❷ Scan the text. Circle the term *human resources* each time it appears on this page. Then underline the context clues that help you understand the meaning of this term.

Natural Resources

Natural resources are an important kind of economic resource. Businesses use different natural resources to produce goods and provide services. Some businesses begin with a raw material. A **raw material** is a natural resource that can be used to make a product.

In North America, businesses use many natural resources to make goods. Wood is an important natural resource. From wood, businesses make paper, furniture, and other goods. Oil is another important natural resource. People use oil to make fuels to power cars and heat homes.

In Central America, some people work on plantations that grow coffee and bananas. The natural resources of this region—rich soil and plentiful rainfall—allow these crops to grow well.

Not all resources occur in large amounts. Nonrenewable resources will not be available in the long term. Throughout North America, many countries work to *conserve,* or protect, natural resources. By using natural resources wisely, countries make sure that people will have resources to meet their needs.

TextWork

3 In your own words, write a definition for the term *raw material.*

_____

_____

_____

_____

4 Study the photograph below. Put an *X* on the natural resource shown. Draw a box around the human resources, and circle an example of capital resources.

NATURAL RESOURCES Rivers are sometimes used to move logs to mills, where they are cut into boards.

▶ **CAPITAL RESOURCES** Tools in a steel plant are used to produce steel.

![TextWork]

5 Study the photograph above. Circle the capital resources in the photograph. Place a box around the human resources.

6 Identify the heading of this section. What does this heading tell you about the subject of this section of the text?

_____

_____

_____

_____

Capital Resources

Businesses use capital resources, too. Without capital resources, workers could not make goods or offer services. Machines, tools, and buildings are all different kinds of capital resources.

Over time, the kinds of capital resources that businesses depend on have changed. Long ago, goods were made by hand. Today, machines in factories make most goods. Other machines, such as computers and telephones, make it easier for people to do work.

Buildings are another important capital resource. All businesses need a place in which to operate. Some places in which businesses operate are office buildings, factories, or shopping malls.

Many businesspeople get money from selling stocks to people called *stockholders*. These stock-holders then share in the profits that the business makes. *Profit* is money left over after businesses pay their costs. Part of the profit businesses earn is used to improve existing capital resources and buy new ones. This allows businesses to succeed in the long term.

Surplus and Scarcity

When there is a **surplus**, or extra amount, of economic resources, economies run well and most people's wants are met. However, the resources needed to produce goods and services are limited. The money needed to buy goods and services is also limited. This **scarcity** means that people can never have all the things that they might want. People must make choices about how to use resources, what to produce, and what to buy.

Some goods are scarce and plentiful at different times of year. Fruits and vegetables are harvested at certain times of year, in different seasons. When fruits and vegetables are in season, they are more available at stores and markets and often cost less. When fruits and vegetables are not in season, they are less available in stores and markets and are often more expensive.

In some industries, such as nursing, there is a scarcity of workers. Not enough people have the skills needed to work in those jobs. When there is a scarcity of human resources, industries sometimes raise pay so more people will want to work in that industry. Some industries encourage people to get the education needed for those jobs.

TextWork

7 The word *scarce* means that there is a small amount of something. Use this information to write a definition of *scarcity* in your own words.

_____

_____

_____

_____

_____

8 Circle the main idea sentence in the third paragraph. Then underline the sentences that provide supporting details.

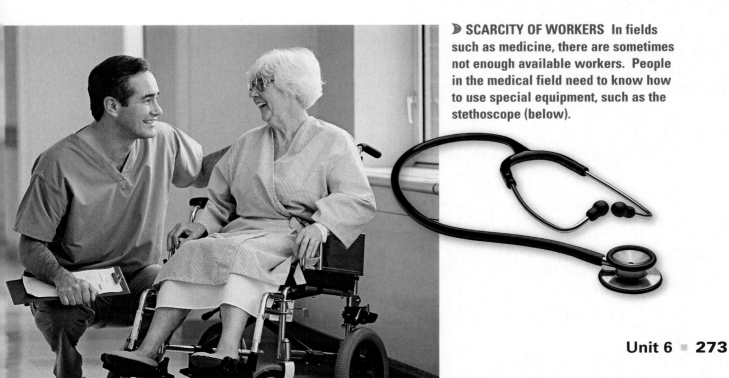

▶ **SCARCITY OF WORKERS** In fields such as medicine, there are sometimes not enough available workers. People in the medical field need to know how to use special equipment, such as the stethoscope (below).

1. SUMMARIZE What three kinds of economic resources must businesses have to produce goods and services?

_____

_____

2. What is a **raw material**?

_____

_____

3. How does having a surplus of a good or a service affect the economy?

_____

_____

Circle the letter of the correct answer.

4. What kind of economic resource is land?

  A human resource

  B capital resource

  C natural resource

  D renewable resource

5. How does scarcity affect the economy?

  A Goods are easier to find, and prices go down.

  B Goods are easier to find, and prices go up.

  C Good are harder to find, and prices go down.

  D Goods are harder to find, and prices go up.

MATCHING Draw a line connecting each kind of economic resource on the left with the correct resource on the right.

6. capital resource   soil

7. human resource   tractor

8. natural resource   farmer

activity

Make a Poster Make a poster showing the three kinds of economic resources. Add a caption to your poster to describe each kind of economic resource. Use drawings and photographs to illustrate your poster.

Natural resources are not distributed, or spread out, evenly across Earth's surface. Some countries have many natural resources. Others have few. Countries with a lot of natural resources can use those resources or trade them with other countries. Having unequal amounts of resources makes countries **interdependent**. They depend on one another for natural resources, finished products, and services. **What do you think you will learn about the economies of the United States and its neighbors in this lesson?**

_____

_____

> **FREIGHTERS ship goods to other countries.**

**NORTH CAROLINA
STANDARD COURSE OF STUDY**

5.02 Analyze the economic effects of the unequal distribution of natural resources on the United States and its neighbors.

5.04 Describe the ways in which the economies of the United States and its neighbors are interdependent and assess the impact of increasing international economic interdependence.

TextWork

① Write a sentence about the use of natural resources in Haiti, using the word *deforestation*.

_____

_____

_____

② Why do countries trade with one another?

_____

_____

_____

_____

_____

Natural Resources

The strength of a nation's economy often depends on its natural resources. Countries with many natural resources, such as the United States and Canada, often have strong economies. Countries with fewer natural resources, such as those in Central America, generally have weaker economies.

Countries with few natural resources usually depend heavily on the resources they do have. As a result, some countries have used too much of their natural resources. For example, in Haiti, too many trees were cut down to use or to send to other countries. Clearing an area of forests is called **deforestation**. Because of deforestation, few forests are left in Haiti today.

Some natural resources are more valuable than others. How valuable a resource is usually depends on how much of it there is and how many people want it. For example, gold is more valuable than iron. Gold is rare, but iron is not. Gold is also used to make valuable goods, such as jewelry.

No country has every natural resource. Through trade with one another, countries can better meet the wants of their people.

▶ **NATURAL RESOURCES** In Haiti, people cut down forests, leading to deforestation.

> CANADA'S RESOURCES In Canada, farmers harvest wheat in the Interior Plains (left). A worker marks a mine for mineral drilling in the Canadian Shield (right). Fishing is a big industry in Canada's bodies of water (center).

The United States and Canada

The United States has a large amount of many natural resources. Among these plentiful resources are fresh water, rich soil, and fuels, such as coal. Fuel resources help the country make the energy needed to power schools, homes, and factories.

The rich agricultural resources of the United States usually allow its farmers to grow more food than its people can use. Surplus crops grown in the United States are sold to other countries.

Much of Canada's wealth comes from its wide range of natural resources. The Canadian Shield is rich in minerals, such as copper, gold, iron, and nickel. Fuels such as coal, oil, and natural gas are found in the Interior Plains. Large amounts of fish are found along the Atlantic and Pacific coasts and in Canada's rivers and lakes.

Across much of southern Canada, farmers grow large amounts of many different kinds of crops. In much of the rest of Canada, which is not suited to farming, trees grow very well.

TextWork

❸ Place an X on the photo above that shows a worker searching for minerals. List two types of minerals found in Canada.

Minerals: _____

_____

❹ Why does the United States have a food surplus?

_____

_____

▶ ECOTOURISM brings many people to Costa Rica. People can participate in outdoor activities (right) and view animals (above).

 **TextWork**

5 Scan the text. Underline the sentences that tell where farming occurs in Central America.

6 Write a generalization about tourism in Central America and the Caribbean based on the facts below.

• **Many cruise ships stop at Caribbean islands.**

• **Ecotourism is important to Costa Rica's economy.**

Generalization: _____

_____

_____

_____

Mexico, Central America, and the Caribbean

Some of Mexico's natural resources include rich soil, minerals, and oil. Mexico sells much of its oil to the United States. Money from oil, which the Mexican government controls, helps Mexico's economy. The government has used this money to build factories and start new businesses.

Ash from volcanic eruptions has given much of Central America rich soil. Because much of this soil is along the sides of mountains, most people in Central America live in the highlands. There they earn a living on small farms. Commercial farming also takes place in Central America. Plantations in the region's mountains and hills grow most of the world's coffee crop. Plantations in lower areas grow most of the world's banana crop.

The Bahamas has only small areas of rich soil. As a result, little farming is done there. The most important natural resource in the Bahamas and other parts of the Caribbean is natural beauty. Tourism is a large industry in the Caribbean. Many cruise ships stop at Caribbean islands.

Tourism is also important to Central America. Many people travel to Costa Rica for *ecotourism*, which is tourism centered on enjoying the land.

Exchanging Resources

Each day, people in different countries exchange natural resources, finished goods, and services. Because no one country has all the natural resources that people and businesses may need, no one country can make all the goods and services that people want.

Many goods from the United States are **exported**, or sent, to places all over the world. Some of these goods are crops, computers, and cars. At the same time, many goods are **imported**, or brought into the United States, from other countries. Some of these goods are oil from Mexico and bananas from Central America. This international trade lets people in the United States and in other countries buy goods that their own countries do not have enough of or do not make or grow.

International trade has increased economic interdependence among the nations of the world. The world has seen the growth of a global economy, or *globalization*. Many countries are now part of free-trade agreements, such as NAFTA. These free-trade agreements allow countries to trade without charging tariffs, or taxes, on goods. This helps trade and adds to globalization and interdependence.

TextWork

7 List two examples each of goods the United States exports and imports.

Exports: _____

_____

Imports: _____

_____

8 How has globalization affected world economies?

_____

_____

_____

_____

❯ **NAFTA** President Bill Clinton signs the North American Free Trade Agreement.

1. SUMMARIZE How are the economies of the United States and its neighbors interdependent?

_____

_____

2. Explain economic interdependence, using the terms **exported** and **imported**.

_____

_____

3. Why do countries trade natural resources?

_____

_____

Circle the letter of the correct answer.

4. Which is a natural resource in Mexico?

    A hardwood trees

    B uranium

    C oil

    D limestone

5. Where are many of Canada's mineral resources found?

    A the Canadian Shield

    B the Interior Plains

    C the Atlantic coast

    D the Pacific coast

6. Where does most farming happen in Central America?

    A near rivers

    B in valleys

    C near the coast

    D in the highlands

FILL IN THE BLANK Use the words in the box to complete the sentences.

> deforestation p. 276   ecotourism p. 278   globalization p. 279

7. Many people travel to Costa Rica to enjoy _____.

8. The growth of a global economy is called _____.

9. _____ is the clearing of an area's trees.

writing

✎ **Make a List** Make a list of North America's imports and exports mentioned in the lesson. In a brief paragraph, describe how these imports and exports make countries interdependent.

Economic Systems

The world has three major kinds of economic systems. An **economic system** is the way that people in a country decide how to use resources to produce goods and services. Economic systems have different ways of meeting people's needs. Each economic system has different *economic institutions*, such as banks and governments, that help people meet their basic needs. **What do you think you will learn about economic systems and institutions in this lesson?**

_____

_____

▷ **ECONOMIC SYSTEMS help countries meet their needs.**

**NORTH CAROLINA
STANDARD COURSE OF STUDY**

5.03 Assess economic institutions in terms of how well they enable people to meet their needs.

5.06 Examine the different economic systems such as traditional, command, and market developed in selected countries of North America and assess their effectiveness in meeting basic needs.

Economic Systems

Every country has to make decisions about how to allocate, or distribute, its resources and how to produce the goods and services that its citizens want. Most countries use one of three main kinds of economic systems—a traditional economy, a command economy, or a market economy.

Traditional Economy

A **traditional economy** shows little change from earlier times. Most people do the same kinds of work as they have always done. Economic choices are usually based on custom or habit.

Most people in a traditional economy make their living by **subsistence farming**, or raising just enough food for themselves and their families and very little more. They are not able to earn enough to buy better tools to improve their way of farming. They must work mostly as they always have.

No country in North America has a fully traditional economy. However, many people living in mountainous areas of Central America still follow the traditional farming ways of life of their American Indian ancestors.

TextWork

1 Underline the three main kinds of economic systems.

2 Define *subsistence farming* in your own words.

_____

_____

_____

_____

▶ **AN AMISH FARMER** prepares a field by using traditional equipment.

 **A DRUM FACTORY IN CUBA** Most factories in Cuba are owned by the government.

In the United States and Canada, some groups also follow traditional ways of life. The Inuit in Canada make a living by fishing and hunting animals. In the United States, the Amish people follow a simple way of life. They do not use electricity, automobiles, or modern machines.

Command Economy

In a **command economy**, the government or some central power makes most of the economic choices. It controls both farms and factories.

People and businesses in a command economy are not free to make their own decisions. The government decides what goods will be made and in what amounts. The government decides how much the workers will earn and how much the goods and services will cost. The government also tells *consumers*, or buyers, what and how much they can purchase. As a result, a command economy often leads to a shortage of some goods and a surplus of other goods.

Cuba has one of the world's few remaining command economies. All major industries in Cuba are owned and run by the government.

TextWork

❸ Write a generalization about the Amish people.

_____

_____

_____

_____

❹ Scan the text. Circle the name of the country that has one of the few remaining command economies.

▶ **A MARKET ECONOMY** In a market economy, consumers decide which goods are most important to purchase.

Market Economy

In a **market economy**, like the United States, businesses are owned and run by individuals or groups. People and businesses decide which goods and services they will buy or make. They decide how they will spend their money and what kind of work they will do. This freedom of people to own and run their own business with only limited control of the government is called **free enterprise**.

In a market economy, people base their economic choices in part on prices. They must decide if the benefit of having a good or service is equal to its price.

Prices are affected by consumers' *demand* for a good or service. If the demand increases, prices usually rise. If there are only a few copies of a popular video game, its price is likely to be high. If the demand decreases, prices will fall.

Prices are also affected by the *supply* of a good or service. If businesses increase the amount of a good they produce, then prices usually fall. If businesses decrease the amount of a good they produce, then prices tend to rise.

TextWork

❺ Study the diagram below. What happens to prices as supply and demand change?

_____

_____

_____

_____

How Supply and Demand Can Affect Prices

Prices Usually Rise
• high demand
• low supply

• low demand
• high supply
Prices Usually Fall

Economic Institutions

Economic institutions, such as banks and the stock market, also help people meet their needs. Many people borrow money from banks to buy homes or start businesses. Many people also use banks to save money.

A savings account in a bank earns interest. Banks loan to other people some of the money deposited in savings accounts. These people often borrow money to buy houses or cars or to start businesses. They pay interest to the bank until the loan is paid back.

People also invest money in the stock market. Depending on whether stocks that people buy go up or down in value, people can gain or lose money by buying stocks.

In some democracies, the government acts as an economic institution. It runs some parts of the economy to meet people's needs. The government may run an industry because private businesses do not have the money or the interest to take part in that industry. In other cases, the government runs an industry for the good of the people.

TextWork

6 Underline the sentences that explain how people use banks and the stock market.

7 How can the government be an economic institution?

_____

_____

_____

_____

▶ **THE NEW YORK STOCK EXCHANGE**
At the New York Stock Exchange, people buy and sell stocks, hoping to make money.

Crown Corporations

Canada has many Crown Corporations, which are businesses run by the government. The government directly controls the budget and appointment of leaders of Crown Corporations. Some Crown Corporations are power companies, broadcasting companies, insurance companies, and research agencies. Canada's government runs these businesses for the good of its people.

Air Canada, Canada's largest airline, was once a Crown Corporation. In 1989, the airline was privatized. To **privatize** means to move ownership of a business or industry from the government to a private business. Today, many former Crown Corporations are owned by private businesses. Some of the businesses include Nova Scotia Power and Petro-Canada.

▶ **AIR CANADA** was previously run by the Canadian government. Today, it is a private company.

Lesson 3 Review

1. **SUMMARIZE** What are the three different kinds of economic systems?

_____

_____

2. Explain the term **free enterprise** in your own words.

_____

_____

3. How do economic institutions help people meet their needs?

_____

_____

4. Why do you think a market economy is more effective in meeting peoples' needs than a command economy?

_____

_____

✎ *writing*

Write a Report Write a report describing the three main kinds of economic systems. Explain what the government does in each system and the rights that people have in each system.

Specialization and Interdependence

Over the years, the countries of the world have become more and more interdependent. New discoveries, inventions, and innovations have helped interdependence grow by making it easier for people to trade goods and talk to one another. The increase in trade has also led to an increase in **specialization**, or becoming good at one kind of job. Because of specialization, workers and businesses have become even more dependent on one another. **How will this lesson improve your understanding of economic interdependence?**

_____

_____

▷ **A TECHNICIAN** using a pill coating machine

NORTH CAROLINA STANDARD COURSE OF STUDY

5.05 Evaluate the influence of discoveries, inventions, and innovations on economic interdependence.

TextWork

1 Underline the sentences that explain why specialization grew.

2 Use the parts of the term *high-tech* to write a definition of the term in your own words.

_____

_____

_____

_____

_____

Becoming Specialized

In the past, people had to grow or make almost everything they needed. As trade grew, people were able to specialize in certain jobs. For example, some people could become bakers. They did not have to grow their own wheat and grind their own flour. Instead, they could buy flour or trade for it to bake bread to sell. Other people did not have to bake at all.

New discoveries, inventions, and innovations have led to even more specialization. Many of the changes in the kinds of jobs that people do have come about because of changes in technology. **Technology** is the use of scientific knowledge or tools to make or do something.

In recent years, high-technology, or high-tech, industries have made fast advances. **High-tech** industries are those that invent, build, or use computers and other kinds of electronic tools. High-tech industries have made interdependence work better among the nations of the world. The industries aid interdependence by making it easier to communicate, travel, trade goods and services, and organize information.

▶ SKILLED WORKERS help increase the amount of goods and services that a business can make or offer.

The Information Age

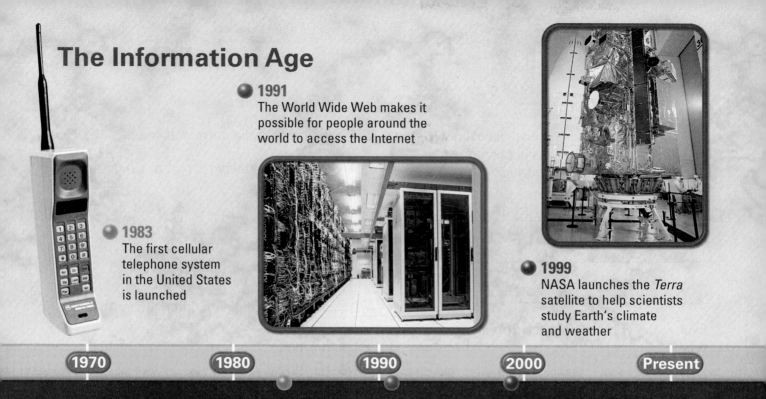

1991
The World Wide Web makes it possible for people around the world to access the Internet

1983
The first cellular telephone system in the United States is launched

1999
NASA launches the *Terra* satellite to help scientists study Earth's climate and weather

1970   1980   1990   2000   Present

The Information Age

The early 1970s marked the beginning of the **Information Age**. Since then, people have been able to receive a growing amount of information.

Today, storing information and getting the information to people when they need it are parts of a major industry. Much of this type of work is done through computer networks and websites. Computer networks and websites let people and businesses store and share information.

New technologies are also changing the way people buy and sell goods and services. Electronic commerce, or **e-commerce**, lets people and businesses buy and sell goods and services all over the world. E-commerce has increased interdependence.

New technologies have also let people share ideas and knowledge. People around the world can add to scientific discoveries. Today, for example, the United States and other countries are working together to explore space. They are also working together to build the International Space Station.

 **TextWork**

❸ In what year was the World Wide Web launched? Circle this entry on the time line.

❹ Write two facts that support the generalization below.

Generalization: Technology is changing the way many people buy and sell goods and services.

Fact: _____

_____

_____

Fact: _____

_____

_____

1. **SUMMARIZE** How have new discoveries, inventions, and innovations led to more interdependence between countries?

_____

_____

_____

2. Explain the word **specialization** in your own words.

_____

_____

Circle the letter of the correct answer.

3. Which of the following is part of a high-tech industry?

   A computers

   B education

   C service jobs

   D agriculture

4. In which decade did the Information Age begin?

   A the 1960s

   B the 1970s

   C the 1980s

   D the 1990s

FILL IN THE BLANK Use the terms in the box to complete the sentences.

> specialization p. 287   Information Age p. 289   e-commerce p. 289

5. Because of _____, workers and businesses have become even more dependent on one another.

6. Since the beginning of the _____, people have been able to receive a growing amount of information.

7. _____ lets people and businesses buy and sell goods all over the world.

writing

✎ **Write a Letter to the Editor** Identify a worker in your community who specializes in a job. Write a letter to the editor of a newspaper explaining what is good or bad about specialization.

Economic Activities

5

The United States and other countries in North America sometimes specialize in certain economic activities. Economic activities often depend on a country's economic resources. Countries that have more of certain economic resources often have an economy that is based on producing goods and providing services that require these resources. **What will you read about economic activities of the United States and its neighbors in this lesson?**

_____

_____

▶ A SUPERMARKET in Mexico

NORTH CAROLINA
STANDARD COURSE OF STUDY

5.07 Describe the ways the United States and its neighbors specialize in economic activities, and relate these to increased production and consumption.

⟩ **AEROSPACE INDUSTRY** Seattle, Washington, is a center for the nation's aerospace industry. Workers there build airplanes in large buildings.

Economies in the United States and Canada

The United States has a lot of rich soil, mineral resources, and forests, as well as a large, skilled workforce. As a result, the United States has a **diverse economy**, or an economy based on many industries rather than just a few. Most Americans work in service industries, but the United States remains a leading agricultural and industrial power in the world.

Many cities in the United States are centers for trade and business. New York City, for example, is a leading center for banking and trade. The city of Los Angeles, California, is the center of the entertainment industry.

Much of Canada's wealth comes from its natural resources. Canada has two major kinds of manufacturing. One kind of manufacturing processes natural resources—for example, turning trees into lumber, pulp, and paper goods. The other makes goods for use by Canadians and for selling to other countries.

TextWork

1 What does the word *diverse* mean? Use the meaning of this word to define the term *diverse economy* in your own words.

_____

_____

_____

2 List two kinds of products that are made from trees in Canada.

_____

_____

Economies in Mexico and Central America

For much of its history, Mexico's economy specialized in farming and mining. It did not have a lot of other businesses. Then, beginning in the 1940s, the Mexican government started to promote the growth of manufacturing. Factories began to make goods. Mexico now makes many of the goods its people buy and use.

The rich soil of Central America is farmed to grow crops such as bananas, sugarcane, coffee, corn, cotton, and beans. Other important industries are fishing and mining. Fishing is an important industry in Belize. Some countries, such as Guatemala and Panama, have mineral resources.

People who live in the Caribbean grow many of the same crops as people in Central America. They also make a living in many of the same ways. Many people who live in the Caribbean are farmers or work in service jobs related to tourism.

 **TextWork**

❸ How has Mexico's economy changed over the years?

_____

_____

_____

_____

_____

❹ Study the photo below. Of which industry in the Caribbean and Central America are cruise ships a part?

_____

▶ **CRUISE SHIPS** bring tourists to Central America and the Caribbean.

5 Write a sentence using the words *production* and *consumption*.

_____

_____

_____

_____

_____

6 Scan the text. How does specialization help production? Circle the sentence that gives this information.

Production and Consumption

In a market economy, businesses are free to decide what goods to make and what to charge for them. Often **production**—the making of goods and services—is based on supply and demand. When the demand for a good or service is high, usually more of it will be produced or offered. The **consumption**, or use, of that good or service will also increase because more of it is available. When the demand for a good or service is low, production and consumption will usually go down.

Specialization also affects production and consumption. It allows businesses and nations to produce more goods and provide more services faster and for less money. As a result, the consumption of those goods or services usually rises.

Specialization allows for the **division of labor**, or dividing work so that each worker does only one part of a larger job. The division of labor lets companies use assembly lines to produce goods. Goods are assembled, or put together, as they move past a line of workers.

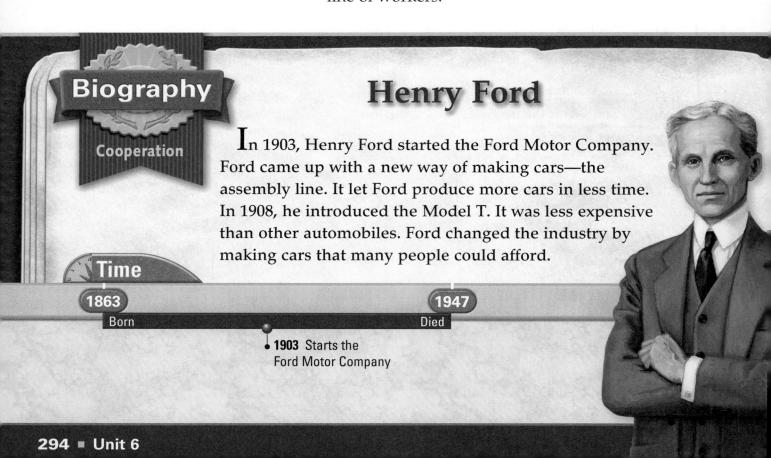

Biography

Cooperation

Henry Ford

In 1903, Henry Ford started the Ford Motor Company. Ford came up with a new way of making cars—the assembly line. It let Ford produce more cars in less time. In 1908, he introduced the Model T. It was less expensive than other automobiles. Ford changed the industry by making cars that many people could afford.

Time

1863 Born

1947 Died

1903 Starts the Ford Motor Company

➤ **LARGE FARMING BUSINESSES can afford to purchase or hire crop dusters to spray pesticides on crops.**

Economic Wealth

Natural resources, human resources, and capital resources are the factors of production. They are the resources necessary to produce a good or provide a service. Countries with high levels of all three factors of production often have strong economies. These countries have more and higher-paying jobs. People in these countries make more money. In turn, they are able to buy and consume more goods and services.

Workers with more skills and knowledge are often able to develop better ways of working. They can also adapt more easily to new jobs. They are able to produce more goods and services than workers with fewer skills.

Without the latest and best capital resources, companies usually produce fewer goods and provide fewer services. For example, large farming businesses in the United States and Canada have a lot of capital resources. New farm machinery, fertilizers, and pesticides help farming businesses grow a lot of crops.

Small farms across North America may not have enough money to buy the best machinery, fertilizers, and pesticides. They cannot grow as many crops as large farming businesses.

TextWork

7 Scan the text. Underline the sentence that gives a generalization about countries that have all three factors of production.

8 Write a main idea based on the following details.

• **Large farming businesses have a lot of capital resources.**

• **New farm machinery, fertilizers, and pesticides help farmers grow a lot of crops.**

Main Idea: _____

_____

_____

_____

_____

1. **SUMMARIZE** Describe the specialized economic activities of the United States, Canada, and Mexico.

_____

_____

_____

2. Define the term **division of labor** in your own words.

_____

_____

3. What are Canada's two major kinds of manufacturing activities?

_____

_____

_____

4. How are production and consumption related to economic activities?

_____

_____

_____

FILL IN THE BLANK Use the terms in the box to complete the sentences.

> diverse economy p. 292   production p. 294   consumption p. 294

5. The use of a good or service is called _____.

6. _____ is making goods and offering services.

7. A _____ has many industries rather than just a few.

activity

Make a Diagram Make a diagram that shows how production and consumption are related. Using arrows, show what happens when production and consumption go up and down.

Review and Test Prep

The Big Idea

People decide how to allocate and use economic resources based on several things, including production, consumption, surplus, and scarcity.

Summarize the Unit

Focus Skill **Generalize** Complete the graphic organizer to show that you know how to generalize information about economics in North America.

Facts

| Countries do not have every economic resource. | Countries exchange economic resources. | Countries exchange goods and services. |

Generalization

_____

_____

Use Vocabulary

Fill in the missing term in each sentence, using the correct vocabulary term from the Word Bank.

1. _____ is the freedom of businesses to run as they choose.

2. The use of a good or service is called _____.

3. To _____ is to bring goods in from another country.

4. _____ is becoming good at one kind of job.

5. A country that gets natural resources from another country is _____ with that country.

Word Bank

interdependent p. 275

import p. 279

free enterprise p. 284

specialization p. 287

consumption p. 294

6. How do surplus and scarcity affect the economy?

_____

_____

7. How has specialization led to more interdependence?

_____

_____

8. How does learning new skills in school make you more prepared for work in the future?

_____

_____

Circle the letter of the correct answer.

9. Where does much of Canada's wealth come from?

A its human resources

B its capital resources

C Crown Corporations

D its natural resources

10. For most of its history, what was Mexico's economy based on?

A businesses

B manufacturing

C farming and mining

D fishing

Show What You Know

Writing **Write a Speech**
Choose one kind of economic system. Write a speech that describes the economic system.

Activity **Give an Economic Presentation**
Create and give a presentation about the economy of a country in North America. Include charts, graphs, maps, or pictures to describe the country's economic system. You might also include information about the country's natural resources, industries, and workers.

GO online
To play a game that reviews the unit, join Eco in the North Carolina Adventures online or on CD.

Technology Leads the Way

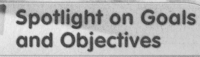

Spotlight on Goals and Objectives

North Carolina Interactive Presentations

NORTH CAROLINA STANDARD COURSE OF STUDY

COMPETENCY GOAL 6 The learner will recognize how technology has influenced change within the United States and other countries in North America.

▷ A SPACEWALK FROM THE
INTERNATIONAL SPACE STATION

299

The Big Idea

How has technology affected the United States and other countries?

Technology is the use of scientific knowledge or tools to make or do something. People invent new kinds of technology to meet certain needs. For example, people began making cars to improve transportation. Many times, new kinds of technology give rise to more new kinds of technology. For example, after companies began making computers, other companies then began to write software programs.

Technology can improve people's lives. It can make people healthier. It can also make people's lives more comfortable and more interesting through entertainment, communication, and transportation. Technology can also cause new challenges for people.

On the lines provided, compare the technology of long ago to the technology of today.

Long Ago   **Today**

Transportation

Wagon: _____

_____

_____

Car: _____

_____

_____

Communication

Telegraph: _____

_____

_____

Internet: _____

_____

_____

Entertainment

Theater: _____

_____

_____

Television: _____

_____

_____

Reading Social Studies

 Draw Conclusions

▶ LEARN

A **conclusion** is a broad statement about an idea or event. You reach a conclusion by using what you learn from reading, along with what you already know. Being able to draw a conclusion can help you better understand what you read. Keep in mind what you already know about the subject and the new facts you learn. Look for hints, and try to figure out what they mean.

Evidence	Knowledge
What you learn	What you already know

Conclusion

A broad statement about an idea or event

▶ PRACTICE

Draw a conclusion from the following paragraphs. The first one has been done for you.

On December 17, 1903, Orville and Wilbur Wright made the world's first airplane flight. They flew their airplane in Kitty Hawk, North Carolina. Their plane could fly only a short distance. (Later, people began making airplanes that could fly longer distances.)   **Evidence**   **Knowledge**

Conclusion: The flight helped start the airplane industry.   **Conclusion**

Today, millions of people fly on airplanes every day. People fly for business, to visit family and friends, and to go on vacation. There are many different airline companies around the world. Most big cities have an airport.

Conclusion: _____

_____

Read the article. Then complete the activities below.

The Aerospace Industry

During World War II, many scientists and engineers in different countries began drawing plans for new airplanes, such as fighter jets. Businesspeople in the United States started factories to make the new planes. The government set up military training bases so that they could test the new planes.

Some engineers also helped build rockets. Wernher von Braun worked for the Nazis during World War II. He helped make the V-2, one of the most powerful missiles at the time. After the war, von Braun and other German scientists came to the United States. Their work helped the aerospace industry grow in the United States. The aerospace industry builds and tests equipment for air and space travel.

In the 1950s, the aerospace industry helped form the United States space program, known as the National Aeronautics and Space Administration (NASA). NASA has offices and bases in many parts of the United States. Thousands of Americans work for NASA and for companies whose work helps NASA. NASA research has led to many inventions, such as cell phones and certain kinds of medicines.

Other countries are also involved in space flight. The Russian Space Agency has launched two space stations and is now helping build the International Space Station. The European Space Agency has sent many satellites and research probes into space. Several NASA astronauts have come from other countries, including Canada and Mexico. The Canadian Space Agency built the robot arm for NASA's space shuttle.

---

1. **What conclusion can you draw about NASA from the third paragraph?**

_____

_____

2. **Underline the evidence from the article that supports the conclusion that space flight is important to many countries.**

Technology Through the Ages

Throughout history, people have come up with new kinds of technology to meet different needs. New technology has had both positive and negative effects.

Early people made tools such as spears to hunt animals. They also made tools to store food and to farm. Over time, people invented new tools, such as the automobile and the computer. **How will this lesson improve your knowledge of technology?**

_____

_____

▷ **VERY LARGE ARRAY radio telescopes in New Mexico**

NORTH CAROLINA STANDARD COURSE OF STUDY

6.01 Explore the meaning of technology as it encompasses discoveries from the first primitive tools to today's personal computer.

6.02 Relate how certain technological discoveries have changed the course of history and reflect on the broader social and environmental changes that can occur from the discovery of such technologies.

▶ **EARLY PEOPLE used technology to improve agriculture.**

![TextWork]

1 Why did farming lead to the building of permanent villages?

_____

_____

_____

_____

2 Scan the text about agriculture. Underline the sentences that explain the factors that allowed people to start doing arts and crafts.

Early Technology

Early people in North America developed tools to help make it easier to farm, hunt, and travel. Over the years, several major advances have helped change life in North America.

Agriculture

Agriculture, or farming, was one of the earliest major advances. The earliest form of agriculture was *subsistence farming*, or raising just enough food to meet a group's needs. People had to stay in one place to tend their crops. In time, farming led to the building of permanent villages.

Some farmers raised more food than they needed to live. They traded the *surplus*, or extra, food for goods that they did not have. In time, people learned how to store surplus food by drying or smoking it. They stored surplus food in pottery made from clay and in baskets made from grass and straw.

People used the stored food when harvests were bad. People did not have to spend as much time looking for food. They could spend more time on other things, such as arts and crafts.

Navigation

People in Europe had been building boats for thousands of years. They used boats to travel on rivers, lakes, and oceans. However, people did not often sail far from the shore. They needed to stay close to the land so that they would not get lost.

Then, in the 1400s, navigation began to improve. *Navigation* is the use of technology to sail to different places. Sailors developed new tools, such as the compass, the chronometer, and the astrolabe. Sailors could use these new tools to explore the oceans. They were able to travel far away from the shore.

Soon Europeans began looking for sea routes to Asia. After the voyages of Christopher Columbus, other Europeans began exploring and settling in North America. Europeans brought new foods, plants, and animals to North America.

Europeans also unknowingly brought diseases to the Americas. At the time, most American Indians had never been exposed to these diseases. Many American Indians died because their bodies were not able to fight off the new diseases.

TextWork

3 How was technology used to bring new people, plants, and animals to North America?

_____

_____

_____

_____

4 List one way European exploration affected American Indians.

_____

_____

_____

_____

▶ **CARAVELS** were a new kind of ship that could sail quickly over long distances.

TextWork

5 Where did more people work after the Industrial Revolution?

_____

_____

6 Skim the text. What is the main title of this section? What period of history does this title refer to?

_____

_____

_____

_____

Technology Changes Rapidly

In the late 1700s, the Industrial Revolution came to the United States. This period of time saw the invention of many new kinds of technology.

New technology, such as machines that spun thread and wove cloth, changed the way many people lived. More people began to work outside the home. They worked mostly in factories. Many of these workers were women and children. More people moved from rural areas to towns and cities.

After the Industrial Revolution began, new inventions helped people make large amounts of goods. Goods could also be made faster and at less cost. Factories began to produce more goods.

Electricity Brings Change

In 1882, the first central electric power station opened in New York City. People could now have electricity in their homes and businesses. Electricity provided people with light and power.

Biography

Perseverance

Thomas Alva Edison

Thomas Edison produced 1,093 inventions in his lifetime. He is credited with inventing the incandescent lightbulb, the motion picture camera, and the phonograph. Edison was also a wise businessperson. He started several companies, including the Edison Electric Light Company.

Time

1847 Born

1931 Died

1882 Builds the first permanent electric power station at Pearl Street in New York City

> **CONSUMER GOODS, such as electric vacuum cleaners, were popular after World War I.**

Electricity changed people's lives in many ways. It was easier for people to use electricity than to burn oil lamps or use wood fires. Electricity also provided more power. Factories could make more goods with electricity than with steam power.

To make electricity, most power plants have to burn fossil fuels, such as coal. Fossil fuels are non-renewable resources. Also, burning fossil fuels can be harmful to the environment. Today, people are inventing cleaner ways to make electricity, such as by using wind power and power from the sun.

Consumer Goods

After World War I, many people began buying *consumer goods*, such as vacuum cleaners, toasters, and washing machines. More people could use these goods because more people had electricity in their homes.

Of all the consumer goods people bought, the one people wanted most was the automobile. The automobile changed people's lives in many ways. People could live farther from their jobs. Many people began moving to the suburbs. Businesses also began to spread out from cities.

 **TextWork**

7 Scan the text. How did electricity change people's lives? Underline the sentences that give this information.

8 What consumer good is shown in the photograph above? Use the term *consumer good* to describe an item in your home.

_____

_____

_____

_____

_____

Service Industries

▶ **HAIR CUTTING** is one example of a service job.

Factories in the United States still make many products, such as cars and computers. However, service industries now make up the largest part of the United States economy. **Service industries** are industries that provide services for people, such as cooking food in restaurants or serving customers in stores.

Today, more Americans work in service industry jobs than in any other kinds of jobs. They may be doctors, lawyers, or teachers. They may repair cars, cut hair, or work in banks.

Today, some people in service industries work in high-tech jobs. These are jobs that are related to computers and other kinds of technology. People in high-tech service jobs help repair computers, sell communication tools, or work on the Internet.

Lesson 1 Review

1. **SUMMARIZE** How has technology affected the history of North America?

_____

_____

2. Define the term **service industry** in your own words.

_____

_____

3. List three kinds of technology that you use every day.

_____

_____

4. List one way in which technology has changed ways of life in North America.

_____

_____

writing

✏ **Write a Diary Entry** Imagine that you are living without technology. Write a diary entry explaining how your life is different from the way it would be with technology.

People and Technology

New technology benefits people in many ways. Some kinds of technology help people live longer. Others help people live more comfortable lives. Still others help people work better or faster. To get the most out of technology, people must know how to manage it. This makes sure that it is safe and that it is used in ways that benefit the most people. **What might you learn about technology as you read this lesson?**

_____

_____

A CAR MECHANIC using technology

**NORTH CAROLINA
STANDARD COURSE OF STUDY**

6.03 Forecast how technology can be managed to have the greatest number of people enjoy the benefits.

6.06 Predict future trends in technology management that will benefit the greatest number of people.

1 Look at the two parts of the term *national security*. Use the meaning of each part to write a definition for the term in your own words.

_____

_____

_____

_____

2 Who do you think manages the technology shown in the photo below? Explain.

_____

_____

_____

Managing Technology

In the United States, the economy often determines what kinds of technology are developed and how they are used. People and businesses make and improve technology based on demand. For example, as fuel prices rise, car companies are building cars that use less fuel.

Some kinds of technology are too large, cost too much, or are too complex for people or businesses to manage. In these cases, the government steps in to manage the technology. For example, the National Aeronautics and Space Administration (NASA) is part of the United States government. NASA develops technology to explore space.

Governments in North America often manage technology that is dangerous. Mexico, Canada, and the United States all use nuclear power to produce electricity. Each of these countries has government agencies and officials to oversee nuclear power production and the removal of nuclear waste.

Governments in North America also manage technology that threatens national security. **National security** refers to all of the actions taken by the government to protect a country. For example, each North American country, except Costa Rica, has its own military to manage weapons technology.

❱ **THE MILITARY** uses technology, such as airplanes, for the purpose of national security.

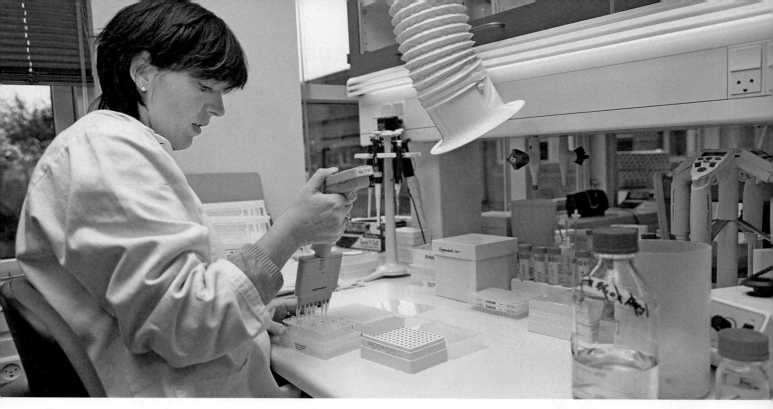

New Trends in Technology

Governments often manage expensive kinds of technology that may not show a benefit right away. One example is the Human Genome Project.

The goal of the Human Genome Project is to identify all of the different kinds of genes that make up humans. A *gene* is a part of a cell that has the code for certain human traits. All human traits—such as eye color—are controlled by genes.

By knowing this information, doctors and other medical workers can better understand the human body. In turn, these workers might be able to find new cures for diseases or better ways to help people who are ill.

Unlike governments, businesses often manage technology that has a benefit for people right away. These kinds of technology can usually be sold. For example, drug companies make new medicines to help people fight pain and illnesses. Car companies research how to make cars safer with airbags and better brakes.

 **TextWork**

❸ Write a conclusion based on the following evidence and knowledge.

Evidence: Knowing information about genes will allow doctors to better understand the human body.

Knowledge: Medicine helps people live healthier and longer lives.

Conclusion: _____

_____

_____

_____

❹ Scan the text. Underline the kinds of technology that businesses develop.

Managing Resources

> WIND is a clean, renewable energy source.

Governments and businesses also manage technology related to natural resources. These kinds of technology often help save limited resources.

Many new kinds of technology help reduce people's dependence on nonrenewable fuels, such as coal, oil, and natural gas. Governments and businesses in North America have spent money to develop and manage renewable sources of energy, such as solar power, wind power, and tidal, or wave, power.

Governments have also studied and developed new fuels, such as hydrogen fuel and ethanol. Hydrogen fuel is made from the hydrogen atom. Ethanol is made from corn. People hope that one day these new fuels can take the place of gasoline in cars and trucks.

Lesson 2 Review

1. **SUMMARIZE** How do people manage technology?

_____

_____

2. Use the term **national security** to explain why governments often control dangerous kinds of technology.

_____

_____

3. What changes could be made to technology management to benefit more people?

_____

_____

4. What might happen if people do not come up with new kinds of energy sources?

_____

_____

writing

✎ **Write a Persuasive Letter** Write a letter to a government official to persuade him or her to develop new ways to manage future technology. Explain why this is important.

Technology and Culture

Technology has changed the world in many ways. It has helped people share and spread new ideas. Technology has become a necessary part of people's everyday lives. However, technology can also pose a threat to people's privacy and rights. People of the United States and other countries of North America are working to preserve their fundamental, or basic, values and beliefs in an ever-changing world. **How will this lesson add to what you know about technology?**

_____

_____

MEN'S
NCAA
FINAL FOUR
APPEARANCES

1940 1976 1992
1953 1981 2002
1973 1987

TECHNOLOGY is used at sporting events.

**NORTH CAROLINA
STANDARD COURSE OF STUDY**

6.04 Determine how citizens in the United States and the other countries of North America can preserve fundamental values and beliefs in a world that is rapidly becoming more technologically oriented.

 **TextWork**

❶ What is meant by the term *cultural borrowing*?

_____

_____

_____

_____

❷ Study the photo below. How does it show *cultural diffusion*?

_____

_____

_____

_____

⏵ **CULTURAL DIFFUSION** With the help of technology, people all around the world can read the news to learn about other countries.

Technology Spreads Culture

When groups of people interact, they sometimes take cultural traits from one another to use as their own. This is called **cultural borrowing**. Cultural borrowing can be seen in clothing, music, and sports. For example, many people in the Caribbean play baseball, which is a sport invented in the United States.

The spread of cultural traits from one society to another society is called **cultural diffusion**. All through history, many things have made cultural diffusion possible. Today, one important factor is communication technology. People with access to newspapers, television, and the Internet, even in remote areas, can learn about other cultures.

The movement of people also adds to cultural diffusion. Transportation technology, such as cars, trains, and airplanes, has made it easier for people to travel to and move to new places. When people move to another country, they may give up their own traditional ways and take on the cultural traits of their new homeland. They may also spread cultural traits from their home country to their new country.

❯ TRADITIONS One way people keep their traditions and cultures alive is by eating traditional foods.

Preserving Values and Beliefs

Even in today's modern world, people continue to preserve their fundamental values and beliefs in many ways. Some people eat traditional foods. Others attend cultural festivals.

Eating traditional foods helps people connect with their cultures. These foods might remind people of their homeland. They might also help parents teach children about their family's heritage and background.

Many people attend cultural festivals. Some festivals celebrate many cultures. Others honor only one culture. At the Grandfather Mountain Highland Games and Gathering of Scottish Clans, people take part in sports from Scotland, sample Scottish food, and learn about Scottish traditions.

Technology can also help people preserve their cultures. People can use the Internet to learn about traditions from their cultures. Many organizations have websites that teach people about their values and beliefs. People can also use the Internet to do research on *genealogy*, or their family tree. They can learn about their ancestors and where they came from.

TextWork

❸ Write a conclusion based on the following evidence and knowledge.

Evidence: People eat traditional foods, attend cultural festivals, and practice traditional ways of life.

Knowledge: People preserve their values and beliefs in many ways.

Conclusion: _____

_____

_____

❹ List one way that technology can help preserve culture.

_____

_____

1. **SUMMARIZE** How does technology affect culture?

_____

_____

_____

_____

2. Explain the term **cultural diffusion** in a sentence.

_____

_____

_____

3. List an example of cultural borrowing in your community.

_____

_____

_____

Circle the letter of the correct answer.

4. How can people preserve their culture?
   A by visiting new places
   B by eating traditional foods
   C by watching TV
   D by moving to a new country

MATCHING Draw a line connecting each activity on the left with the correct example on the right.

5. cultural borrowing

6. cultural diffusion

7. preserving culture

a school cafeteria menu listing tacos, egg rolls, and pizza

dressing in your culture's traditional clothing

cooking food from another culture

writing

Write a Letter Write a letter to a friend. In your letter, explain some of the traditions and customs your family takes part in to help preserve your culture.

Technology in North America

Technology has brought many changes to the countries of North America. Many of these changes have been for the good of the people. However, technology can also have harmful effects, especially on the environment.

In developed countries, such as the United States, Canada, and Mexico, many people use technology. In countries that are not very developed, such as some areas in Central America, people do not use as much modern technology. The levels of technology are different in those places. **How will this lesson improve your understanding of technology?**

_____

_____

A NASA ROVER is tested on Earth.

NORTH CAROLINA STANDARD COURSE OF STUDY

6.05 Compare and contrast the changes that technology has brought to the United States to its impact in Canada, Mexico, and Central America.

TextWork

❶ Write evidence and knowledge for the conclusion below.

Conclusion: In some undeveloped areas, people use less technology.

Evidence: _____

_____

Knowledge: _____

_____

❷ Underline the sentence that describes how the development of technology in other countries has affected Central America.

Technology in North America

In the United States, Canada, and Mexico, most people use technology. People depend on technology, such as different kinds of transportation and communication, every day. In some undeveloped areas, people use less technology. This is especially true in parts of Mexico, where some people still earn a living as subsistence farmers.

Most people in Central American countries use modern technology less than people in Canada, Mexico, and the United States do. Many of the countries in Central America do not have a lot of money to spend on new kinds of technology. Some of their people do not have money to buy goods such as electronics, cars, or communication tools.

In Central America, many people live as subsistence farmers. In recent years, more people have started to work in factories and in the tourist industry. New types of transportation in other countries have brought tourists to some Central American countries. Many people travel there on cruise ships and in airplanes to see the natural beauty of the land.

▶ **DONKEYS** are used in some places to carry crops to markets.

▶ **MOBILE TELEPHONES** can be used to help hikers keep in touch with the outside world.

The Effects of Technology

The use of technology changes people and the world in many ways. The effects of technology can be intended or unintended. *Intended effects* are known before the new technology is used. *Unintended effects* are unknown before the new technology is used.

An intended effect of the development of a new medicine would be to cure an illness. An intended effect of mobile telephone technology would be to allow people to communicate more easily.

Unintended effects may be social changes, such as how individuals, groups, institutions, and even entire societies act. For example, mobile telephones let people talk to one another from almost any-where. However, they can be dangerous when used by someone while driving a car.

Sharing the benefits of technology is a major challenge. Today, in developed nations such as the United States, most people benefit from new kinds of technology. Even in those nations, how-ever, some families benefit little. They still have problems meeting their basic needs for food, water, clothing, and shelter.

TextWork

❸ Circle the communication technology being used in the photograph above. What are the two kinds of effects that technology can have?

_____

_____

❹ Circle the sentence that describes an unintended effect of mobile telephones.

▶ **MEDICAL TECHNOLOGY** has allowed some people with physical disabilities to use prosthetic limbs to have active lives.

![TextWork icon] **TextWork**

5 Scan the text. Underline the sentences that describe how technology has changed transportation.

6 List two ways in which technology has improved your life.

_____

_____

_____

_____

_____

Improving Lives

Technology improves people's lives in many ways. Computers have changed the way people buy goods and services, store information, and talk with others. Thanks to the Internet, people can search for and receive news and entertainment from all over the world.

At one time, most people did not travel more than a few miles from where they were born. Now, trains, cars, and airplanes let people travel great distances. They can visit friends and family members in other states or in other countries. Because of transportation technology, people can also live farther away from where they work.

Technology has helped improve medicine as well. New medicines help people live longer and better lives. Scientific research has led to new ways to fight cancer and other diseases. It has also led to the use of X rays, MRIs, and other tools to improve medical care for people.

Technology and the Environment

Technology can sometimes have negative effects on the environment. The building of businesses, homes, roads, and other structures can hurt natural habitats. A **habitat** is a place in nature where a plant or an animal grows or lives. Batteries and other electronic parts can also harm natural habitats if they are disposed of improperly.

However, technology can also help protect the environment. Many towns and cities have recycling programs. Recycling turns old materials, such as plastics and paper, into new products.

Businesses can help control pollution by inventing new kinds of technology that do not have harmful effects. Many power companies are now using more renewable energy sources.

People can also correct bad effects of technology. For example, strip mining damages the environment by removing layers of land to find minerals. People can restore the land by covering the mines with soil and planting trees or other plants. This land can then be used for parks or playgrounds.

TextWork

7 Scan the text. Underline two negative effects of technology.

8 Use the word *habitat* in a sentence about an *unintended effect* of technology.

_____

_____

_____

_____

_____

▶ **RECYCLING** Some playground equipment is built using all recycled materials.

1. **SUMMARIZE** How is technology used in the different countries of North America?

_____

_____

_____

_____

2. Use the word **habitat** in a sentence about technology and the environment.

_____

_____

_____

3. List two kinds of technology that make your life easier.

_____

_____

_____

_____

Circle the letter of the correct answer.

4. In which part of North America do most people use the least amount of technology?

   A Canada

   B the United States

   C Mexico

   D Central America

5. Which of the following is an unintended effect of technology?

   A curing diseases and illnesses

   B harming the environment

   C entertaining people

   D transporting people and goods

6. Which of the following is a negative effect of technology?

   A improved communication

   B improved medicines

   C deforestation

   D new kinds of transportation

activity

Make a Chart Make a chart that lists intended and unintended effects of technology. Give some examples of technology that you use every day. Then list their intended and unintended effects in your chart.

Review and Test Prep

**The Big Idea**

Technology has helped people live more comfortable, longer, and safer lives. Some technology has had a negative effect on the environment.

Summarize the Unit

(Focus Skill) **Draw Conclusions** Complete the graphic organizer to show that you know how to draw conclusions about technology in North America.

Evidence

Technology helps connect people around the world.

Knowledge

People have many different cultures.

Conclusion

_____

_____

Use Vocabulary

Fill in the missing term in each sentence, using the vocabulary term from the word bank.

1. Taking a cultural trait from one group and using it as your own is called _____.

2. Technology can help protect a _____ for plants or animals.

3. "Teacher" is an example of a job in the _____.

4. A government takes actions to protect a country's _____.

5. Technology helps spread cultural traits through _____.

Word Bank

service industry
  p. 308
national security
  p. 310
cultural
  borrowing p. 314
cultural diffusion
  p. 314
habitat p. 321

Think About It

6. How did improved navigation affect North America and the American Indians living there?

_____

_____

7. How do businesses decide which technologies to develop and manage? How does this benefit people?

_____

_____

8. How can technology affect culture?

_____

_____

Circle the letter of the correct answer.

9. Who often manages technology that is large, expensive, or complex?

   A the government

   B small businesses

   C individuals

   D large businesses

10. Which of these kinds of technology helps spread culture?

   A agriculture

   B electricity

   C television

   D NASA

Show What You Know

Writing Write a Report
Imagine that you are living in a time before modern technology. Describe how your life is different from your real life today.

Activity Design a Website
Make a list of the kinds of technology that you use daily. Choose one kind of technology. On a poster, design a Web page to highlight this technology and tell how you use it.

GO online To play a game that reviews the unit, join Eco in the North Carolina Adventures online or on CD.

For Your Reference

GLOSSARY

INDEX

Glossary

The Glossary contains important history and social science words and their definitions, listed in alphabetical order. Each word is respelled as it would be in a dictionary. When you see this mark ´ after a syllable, pronounce that syllable with more force. The page number at the end of each definition tells where the word is first used in this book. Guide words at the top of the pages help you quickly locate the word you need to find.

add, āce, câre, pälm; end, ēqual; it, īce; odd, ōpen, ôrder; tŏŏk, pōōl; up, bûrn; yōō as *u* in *fuse*; oil; pout; ə as *a* in *above*, *e* in *sicken*, *i* in *possible*, *o* in *melon*, *u* in *circus*; check; ring; thin; this; zh as in *vision*

GLOSSARY

A

absolute location (ab´sə•lōōt lō•kā´shən) The exact location of a place. p. 5

adapt (ə•dapt´) To adjust a way of living to land and resources. p. 28

alliance (ə•lī´ənts) A formal agreement among groups or individuals. p. 136

almanac (ôl´mə•nak) A book that is published every year and contains facts relating to countries of the world, sports, entertainment, and other areas. p. 240

amendment (ə•mend´mənt) A change. p. 191

ancestor (an´ses•tər) An early family member. p. 48

armistice (är´mə•stəs) An agreement to stop fighting. p. 135

arms race (ärmz rās) A competition between countries to add new weapons. p. 156

assassinate (ə•sa´sən•āt) To murder in a sudden or secret attack. p. 122

B

backcountry (bak´kun•trē) The land beyond, or "in back of," the area settled by Europeans. p. 82

barter (bär´tər) To exchange goods. p. 56

bilingual (bī•ling´gwəl) Able to speak two languages. p. 256

blended family (blen´did fa´mə•lē) A family that is formed when single parents from two different families marry. p. 222

blockade (blä•kād´) To use warships to prevent other ships from entering or leaving a harbor. p. 134

borderlands (bôr´dər•landz) Areas of land on or near the borders between countries, colonies, or regions. p. 66

boycott (boi´kät) To refuse to buy or use goods or services. p. 83

C

Cabinet (kab´ə•nit) A group of the President's most important advisers. p. 204

capital resource (ka´pə•təl rē´sôrs) A building, machine, technology, or tool needed to produce goods and services. p. 270

cardinal direction (kärd´nəl də•rek´shən) One of the main directions: north, south, east, or west. p. I9

cash crop (kash krop) A crop that people grow to sell. p. 68

cause (kôz) An action or event that makes something happen. p. 45

cease-fire (sēs fīr) A temporary end to a conflict. p. 157

charter (chär´tər) An official paper in which certain rights are given by a government to a person, group, or business. p. 76

civil rights (si´vəl rīts) The rights guaranteed to all citizens by the Constitution. p. 163

civil war (si´vəl wôr) A war between people in the same country. p. 118

civilization (si•və•lə•zā´shən) A group of people with ways of life, religion, and learning. p. 48

climate (klī´mət) The kind of weather a place has over a long time. p. 13

coalition (kō•ə•li´shən) An alliance or group united around a common goal. p. 169

cold war (kōld wôr) A war fought mostly with words and money rather than soldiers and weapons. p. 154

colony (kä´lə•nē) A land ruled by another country. p. 65

command economy (kə•mand´ i•kä´nə•mē) An economic system in which the government owns all resources and controls business. p. 283

communication (kə•myoo•nə•kā´shən) The exchanging of information or news. p. 240

communism (kä´myə•ni•zəm) A political and economic system in which the government owns all industries and property. p. 154

compare (kəm´pâr) To tell how two or more things are alike. p. 3

compass rose (kum´pəs rōz) A circular direction marker on a map. p. I9

compromise (käm´prə•mīz) To give up some of what you want in order to reach an agreement. p. 96

concentration camp (kon•sən•trā´shən kamp) A prison camp. p. 151

conclusion (kən•kloo´zhən) A broad statement about an idea or event. p. 301

confederation (kən•fe•də•rā´shən) A loosely united group of governments working together. p. 52

constitution (kän•stə•too´shən) A written plan of government. p. 96

consumption (kən•sump´shən) The using of a resource. p. 294

continent (kän´tə•nənt) One of Earth's seven largest land masses. p. I4

contrast (kən•trast´) To tell how two or more things are different. p. 3

cotton gin (kä´tən jin) A machine that could quickly remove the seeds from cotton. p. 105

craft (kraft) Something that is both useful and beautiful. p. 257

cultural borrowing (kul´chə•rəl bär´ə•wing) Taking culture traits from another culture and using them as one's own. p. 314

cultural diffusion (kul´chə•rəl di•fyoo´zhən) The spread of cultural traits from one society to another. p. 314

cultural diversity (kul´chə•rəl də•vûr´sə•tē) A large number of cultures in one area. p. 247

cultural region (kul´chə•rəl rē´jən) An area in which people share some ways of life. p. 243

culture (kul´chər) A way of life. p. 21

D

deforestation (dē•fôr•ə•stā´shən) The clearing of forests and trees from an area. p. 276

delegate (de´li•gət) A representative. p. 96

depression (di•pre´shən) A time when the economy does not grow and people lose jobs and have little money. p. 185

detail (dē´tāl) More information about the main idea. p. 185

developed country (di•ve´ləpt kun´trē) A country whose economy has been built. p. 25

developing country (di•ve´lə•ping kun´trē) A country whose economy is still being built. p. 25

dissent (di•sent´) Disagreement. p. 74

diverse economy (də•vûrs´ i•kä´nə•mē) An economy that is based on many industries rather than just a few. p. 292

division of labor (də•vi´zhen uv lā´bər) Work that is divided so that it is possible to produce more goods. p. 294

due process of law (doo prä´ses uv lô) The principle that guarantees that people have the right to a fair trial. p. 191

dugout (dug´out) A type of boat made by hollowing out a log and used by American Indians. p. 238

E

e-commerce (ē•kä´mərs) Business done electronically. p. 289

economic resource (e•kə•nä´•mik rē´sôrs) The people, materials, and natural resources used to make goods and provide services. p. 266

economic system (e•kə•nä´•mik sis´təm) The way people decide how to use resources to produce goods and services. p. 281

economy (i•kä´nə•mē) The way people of a state, region, or country use resources to meet their needs. p. 25

effect (ə•fekt´) What happens as a result of a cause. p. 45

elementary education (el•ə•men´tə•rē e•jə•kā´shən) The first level of schooling. p. 216

emancipate (i•man´sə•pāt) To free. p. 120

equator (ē•kwā´tər) The imaginary line that divides Earth into the Northern and Southern Hemispheres. p. I4

ethnic group (eth'nik grōōp) A group of people from the same country, of the same race, or with shared customs. pp. 228, 234

executive branch (ig•ze´kyə•tiv branch) The branch of government that has the power to enforce the laws. p. 195

expedition (ek•spə•di´shən) A trip taken with the goal of exploring. p. 60

export (ek´spôrt) To send a product to another country to be sold. p. 279

extended family (ik•sten´did fa´mə•lē) A family that includes grandparents, aunts, or uncles. p. 222

federal system (fe´də•rəl sis´təm) A system of government in which the power to govern is shared by the national and the state governments. p. 190

free enterprise (frē en´tər•prīz) An economic system in which people are able to start and run their own businesses with little control by the government. p. 284

free state (frē stāt) A state that did not allow slavery before the Civil War. p. 114

free world (frē wûrld) The United States and its allies. p. 154

freedmen (frēd´mən) Men, women, and children who had been enslaved. p. 124

fugitive (fyōō´jə•tiv) Someone who escapes from the law. p. 115

generalize (jen´ə•rəl•īz) To state how different facts in a piece of writing are related. p. 267

geography (jē•ä´•grə•fē) The study of Earth's surface and how it is used. p. 2

globalization (glō•bə•lə•zā´shən) The growth of a global economy. p. 177

grid system (grid sis´təm) An arrangement of lines that divide a map into squares. p. I10

H

habitat (ha´bə•tat) A place in nature where a plant or animal grows or lives. p. 321

hemisphere (he´mə•sfir) One half of Earth. p. I5

high-tech (hī•tek´) Based on computers and other kinds of electronic equipment. p. 288

hijack (hī´jak) To illegally take control of a vehicle. p. 174

historian (hi•stôr´ē•ən) A person who studies history. p. 47

historical map (hi•stôr´i•kəl map) A map that provides information about a place at a certain time in history. p. I8

Holocaust (hō´lə•kôst) The mass murder of Jews during World War II. p. 151

human resource (hyōō´mən rē´sôrs) A worker who brings his or her own ideas and skills to a job. p. 270

immigration (i•mi•grā´shən) The action of coming from elsewhere to live permanently in a country. p. 37

import (im´pôrt) To bring a product into a country to be sold. p. 279

indentured servant (in•den´chərd sûr´vənt) A person who agreed to work for another without pay for a certain length of time in exchange for passage to North America. p. 76

Industrial Revolution (in•dus´trē•əl re•və•lōō´shən) The period of time during the 1800s when machines took the place of hand tools to manufacture goods. p. 105

industry (in´dəs•trē) All the businesses that make one kind of product or offer one kind of service. p. 10

Information Age (in•fər•mā´shən āj) The period in history that began in the second half of the twentieth century and is marked by the growing amount of information people can get. p. 289

inlet (in´let) Any area of water extending into the land from a larger body of water. p. 8

inset map (in´set map) A smaller map within a larger one. p. I8

integration (in•tə•grā´shən) The bringing together of people of all races. p. 162

interdependence (in•tər•di•pen´dəns) The relationship between countries whose economies depend on one another for trade. p. 176

interdependent (in•tər•di•pen´dənt) Depending on one another, as many countries do, for natural resources, goods, and services. p. 275

intermediate direction (in•tər•mē´dē•it də•rek´shən) One of the in-between directions: northeast, northwest, southeast, southwest. p. I9

internment camp (in•tûrn´mənt kamp) Enclosed camps used in the United States during World War II to hold Japanese Americans. p. 148

judicial branch (jōō•di'shəl branch) The court system, which is the branch of government that decides whether laws are working fairly. p. 195

legislative branch (le'jəs•lā•tiv branch) The branch of government that makes the laws. p. 194

lines of latitude (līnz uv la'tə•tōōd) Lines on a map or globe that run east and west; also called parallels. p. I10

lines of longitude (līnz uv län'ja•tōōd) Lines on a map or globe that run north and south; also called meridians. p. I10

locator (lō'kā•tər) A small map or picture of a globe that shows where an area on the main map is found in a state, on a continent, or in the world. p. I9

locomotive (lō•kə•mō'tiv) A railroad engine. p. 104

Loyalist (loi'ə•list) A person who remained loyal to the British king. p. 90

main idea (mān ī•dē'ə) The most important idea of what you read. p. 185

majority rule (mə•jôr'ə•tē rōōl) The political idea that the majority of an organized group should have the power to make decisions for the whole group. p. 188

Manifest Destiny (ma'nə•fest des'tə•nē) The idea that the United States was meant to stretch from the Atlantic Ocean to the Pacific Ocean. p. 103

map key (map kee) A part of a map that explains what the symbols on the map stand for. p. I8

map scale (map skāl) A part of a map that compares a distance on the map to a distance in the real world. p. I9

map title (map tī'təl) Words on a map that tell the subject of the map. p. I8

market economy (mär•kət i•kä'nə•mē) An economic system in which businesses are owned and run by individuals who are free to decide what to produce. p. 284

mercenary (mûr'sə•ner•ē) A soldier who serves for pay in the military of a foreign nation. p. 92

Middle Passage (mi'dəl pa'sij) The journey millions of enslaved Africans were forced to make across the Atlantic Ocean from Africa to the West Indies. p. 75

migration (mī•grā'shən) The movement of people. p. 36

military draft (mil'ə•ter•ē draft) A way to bring people into the military. p. 137

Minuteman (mi'nət•man) A member of the Massachusetts militia who could quickly be ready to fight the British. p. 84

mission (mi'shən) A small religious settlement. p. 67

missionary (mi'shə•ner•ē) A religious teacher sent out by a church to spread its beliefs. p. 62

modify (mä'də•fī) To change. p. 30

mural (myōō'rəl) A painting or other work of art done on a wall. p. 258

national security (na'shə•nəl si•kyōōr'ə•tē) Actions taken by the government to protect a country. p. 310

natural resource (na'chə•rəl rē'sôrs) Something found in nature, such as soil, plants, water, or minerals, that people can use to meet their needs. p. 10

naturalized citizen (na'chər•əl•īzd si'tə•zən) Someone who was not born in the United States but has followed the legal steps needed to become a citizen. p. 202

naval stores (nā'vəl stôrz) Products used to build ships. p. 79

navigation (na•və•gā'shən) The science of planning and following a route. p. 60

nomad (nō'mad) A person who travels from place to place and has no permanent home. p. 238

nonviolence (nän•vī'ə•ləns) The use of peaceful ways to bring about change. p. 164

nuclear family (nōō'klē•ər fa'mə•lē) A family that is made up of a mother, father, and children. p. 222

P

parliamentary democracy (pär•lə•men'tər•ē di•mä'krə•sē) A government in which voters select members of the legislature, called a parliament, and parliament chooses the chief executive of the government. p. 208

GLOSSARY

GLOSSARY

Patriot (pā´trē•ət) A colonist who was against British rule and supported the rebel cause in the American colonies. p. 90

petroglyph (pe´trə•glif) A picture cut or carved into rock. p. 258

physical environment (fi´zi•kəl en•vī´rən•mənt) The surroundings in which people, plants, and animals live. p. 27

physical map (fi´zi•kəl map) A map that shows kinds of land and bodies of water. p. I8

pioneer (pī•ə•nir´) An early settler of an area. p. 100

plantation (plan•tā´shən) A large farm. p. 78

pluralistic (ploŏr•ə•lis´tik) Sharing parts of a culture while keeping many traditional ways of one's ancestors. p. 244

political map (pə•li´ti•kəl map) A map that shows cities, states, and countries. p. I8

political party (pə•li´ti•kəl pär´tē) A group that tries to elect officials who will support its policies. p. 204

population density (pä•´pyə•lā´shən den´sə•tē) The average number of people living in a certain area, usually one square mile or one square kilometer. p. 18

preamble (prē´am•bəl) An introduction; first part. p. 188

presidential democracy (prez•ə•den´chəl di•mä´krə•sē) A government in which an elected president heads the government. p. 210

presidio (prā•sē´dē•ō) A Spanish fort. p. 66

primary election (prī´mer•ē i•lek´shən) An election in which voters choose the candidates who will represent their political party in a later election. p. 205

prime meridian (prīm mə•ri´dē•ən) The meridian marked 0 degrees and that runs north and south through Greenwich, England. p. I5

prime minister (prīm min´ə•stər) The chief executive in countries with a parliamentary democracy. p. 208

privatize (prī´və•tīz) To move ownership of a business or industry from the government to a private business. p. 286

production (prə•duk´shən) Making a good from raw materials. p. 294

proportional representation (prə•pôr´shən•əl re•pri•zen•tā´shən) Representation that is based on the number of votes a political party gets. p. 211

protest (prō´test) To work against or object to a certain policy. p. 83

public agenda (pub´lik ə•jen´də) What the people want from the government. p. 205

R

ratify (ra´tə•fī) To approve. p. 97

rationing (rash´ən•ing) Limiting what people can buy. p. 148

raw material (rô mə•tir´ē•əl) A resource that can be used to make a product. p. 271

Reconstruction (rē•kən•struk´shən) Rebuilding of the South after the Civil War. p. 123

region (rē´jən) An area in which many features are similar. p. 21

relative location (re´lə•tiv lō•kā´shən) The position of one place compared to other places. p. 5

representation (re•pri•zen•tā´shən) The act of speaking or acting for someone else. p. 82

republic (ri•pub´lik) A form of government in which people elect representatives to run the government. p. 187

reservation (re•zər•vā´shən) Land set aside by the government for use by Native Americans. p. 127

revolution (re•və•loō´shən) A sudden, complete change, such as the overthrow of an established government. p. 85

rural (rur´əl) Relating to the country. p. 18

S

scarcity (skâr´sə•tē) The condition that exists when people want more than resources or businesses can provide. p. 273

secede (si•sēd´) To leave. p. 117

secondary education (se´kən•der•ē e•jə•kā´shən) The second level of schooling, after elementary. p. 216

segregation (se•gri•gā´shən) The practice of keeping people in separate groups based on their race or culture. p. 162

self-government (self•gu´vərn•mənt) A system of government in which people make their own laws. p. 188

separation of powers (se•pə•rā´shən əv pou´ərz) The division of powers among the three branches of government. p. 194

sequence (sē´kwens) The order in which events happen. p. 111

service industry (sûr′vəs in′dəs•trē) An industry that provides services to other people. p. 308

single-parent family (sing′gəl pâr′ənt fa′mə•lē) Families with a mother or a father but not both. p. 222

slave state (slāv stāt) A state that allowed slavery before the Civil War. p. 114

slavery (slā′və•rē) The practice of holding people against their will and making them work without pay. p. 66

society (sə•sī′ə•tē) A group of people living together in a community and who have shared customs, laws, and institutions. pp. 184, 206

specialization (spe•shə•lə•zā′shən) Becoming skilled at one kind of job. p. 287

stock market (stäk mär′kət) A place where people can buy or sell stocks or shares in companies. p. 141

subsistence farming (səb•sis′təns fär′ming) Raising only enough food for one person or family and little more. p. 282

suffrage (su′frij) The right to vote. p. 140

summarize (sum′ər•īz) To state in your own words a short version of what you read. p. 229

surplus (sûr′pləs) An extra amount. p. 273

technology (tek•nä′lə•jē) The use of scientific knowledge and tools to make or do something. pp. 288, 300

tenement (te′nə•mənt) A poorly built apartment building. p. 131

terrorism (ter′ər•i•zəm) The use of violence to promote a cause. p. 167

tradition (trə•dish′ən) A way of life or an idea handed down from the past. p. 24

traditional economy (trə•dish′ən•əl i•kä′nə•mē) An economy in which people do the same kinds of work as they always have done. p. 282

Transcontinental Railroad (trans•kän•tə•nen′təl rāl′rōd) The first railroad that crossed North America. p. 128

trench warfare (trench wôr′fâr) A type of fighting that takes place in deep trenches, dug in the ground. p. 137

triangular trade route (trī•ang′gyə•lər trād rōōt) Shipping routes that connected England, the English colonies, and Africa. p. 75

turning point (tûr′ning point) An event that causes an important change. p. 92

Underground Railroad (un′dər•ground rāl′rōd) A system of secret escape routes that led enslaved people to free land. p. 116

urban (ûr′bən) Relating to a city or a town. p. 18

urban sprawl (ûr′bən sprôl) The uncontrolled expansion of urban areas. p. 178

veto (vē′tō) To reject. p. 195

Index

The Index lets you know where information about important people, places, and events appear in the book. All key words, or entries, are listed in alphabetical order. For each entry, the page reference indicates where information about that entry can be found in the text. Page references for illustrations are set in italic type. An italic *m* indicates a map. Page references set in boldface type indicate the pages on which vocabulary terms are defined. Related entries are cross-referenced with *See* or *See also*. Guide words at the top of the pages help you identify which words appear on which page.

INDEX

INDEX

INDEX

UFW. *See* United Farm
Workers (UFW)
Underground Railroad, 116
Unemployment, *142*
Unintended effects, 319
Union, 118, 121, 122
Union Pacific Railroad, 128
United Farm Workers (UFW),
165
United States
agriculture in, 32
bodies of water, 16
borders of, 31
capital of, 203, *m203*
climate, 14
culture in, 23
division of Germany, 153
education in, 216
families, 222
highways, 39
in 1861, *m120*
land use in, 31
landforms in, 6, 15
modifying water bodies
in, 31
natural resources and, 29
official language, 255
regions of, 22, *m22*
World War II, 147–150
United States Congress, *102*
United States Postal Service,
241
**United States Supreme
Court,** 162, 174, 195
Urban, 18

Urban sprawl, 178
USS *Cole,* 171
USS *Wyoming, 133*
Utah, 49, 103, 128, 249

Vaqueros, 233
Verrazano, Giovanni da, 63
Veterans Day, 244, *244*
Veto, 195, *195,* 197
Vietcong, 158
Vietnam, 158, *158*
Vietnam War, 158
Virginia, 120, 122, 188
Virginia Colony, 68, 69, 73,
79, 88
Volcano, I7, *24,* 32, 278
Voting, 124, 140, *140*
Fifteenth Amendment
and, 161, 202
Nineteenth Amendment
and, 140, 202

W

Wagon train, *99*
Wants, 270
War
Civil War, 117–122, *122*
Cold War, 153-158, *m154,*
160
French and Indian War,
82
Gulf War, 169, *169*
Korean War, 156–157
Spanish-American War,
134

World War I, 136–137, *136*
World War II, 147–150,
m149, m150
War Department, 204
Warren, Mercy Otis, 91
Washington, *292*
Washington, George, 85, 204,
244
Water bodies, 8–9, *m9,* 10, 16,
31. *See also* specific water
bodies
Watergate scandal, 159
Weapons, *92*
Weather. *See* Climate
Weaving, *257,* 260
West Germany, 153–155
West region, 249, 254
Western Hemisphere, I5
Whale hunt, *56*
Whales, 56, 57
Whitney, Eli, 105
Wigwams, 52
Wilderness Road, 100
Williams, Roger, 74
Wilson, Woodrow, 136
Wind power, 307, *312*
Wisconsin, 23, 247
Women
equal rights and, 140
voting and, 140, 202
war and, 91
work and, 77, 137, 222–223
Wood, 271
Work
African Americans and,
137
apprentices, 77

civil rights and, *164*
immigration and, 131
natural resources and, 29
per capita income, 25
women and, 77, 137,
222–223
**Works Progress
Administration (WPA),**
143, *143*
World Trade Center, 171,
174, *174*
World War I, 136–137, *136*
World War II, 147–150, *m149,*
m150
World War II Memorial, *145*
World Wide Web, *241, 289*
Wounaan people, 260
WPA. *See* Works Progress
Administration (WPA)
Writing, 12, 20, 34, 50, 58, 64,
80, 94, 98, 106, 118, 124,
138, 144, 160, 172, 242, 250,
262, 280, 286, 290, 308,
312, 316

X

X rays, 320

Y

Yemen, 171

Z

Zapotec, 260